Walter Horn 160

Mar

Y0-DCZ-285

Thuesday - Oct 31.
chap. XIII
XIV
XVII

A CRITICAL INTRODUCTION TO THE NEW TESTAMENT

STUDIES IN THEOLOGY

Christianity and Ethics.
By Archibald B. D. Alexander, M.A., D.D.

The Environment of Early Christianity.
By S. Angus, M.A., Ph.D.

History of the Study of Theology. Vol. I.
" " " Vol. II.
By Dr. C. A. Briggs.

The Christian Hope.
By W. Adams Brown, Ph.D., D.D.

An Introduction to the Study of Some Living Religions of the East.
By Sydney Cave, D.D.

Christianity and Social Questions.
By William Cunningham, F.B.A., D.D., D.Sc.

The Justification of God.
By Rev. P. T. Forsyth.

Christian Apologetics.
By Rev. A. E. Garvie.

A Critical Introduction to the Old Testament.
By George Buchanan Gray, D.D., D.Litt.

Gospel Origins.
By William West Holdsworth, M.A.

Faith and Its Psychology.
By William R. Inge, D.D.

Christianity and Sin.
By Robert Mackintosh, D.D.

Protestant Thought Before Kant.
By A. C. McGiffert, Ph.D., D.D.

The Theology of the Gospels.
By James Moffatt, D.D., D.Litt.

History of Christian Thought Since Kant.
By Edward Caldwell Moore, D.D.

The Doctrine of the Atonement.
By J. K. Mozley, M.A.

Revelation and Inspiration.
By James Orr, D.D.

A Critical Introduction to the New Testament.
By Arthur Samuel Peake, D.D.

Philosophy and Religion.
By Hastings Rashdall, D.Litt. (Oxon.), D.C.L. (Durham), F.B.A.

The Holy Spirit.
By T. Rees, M.A. (Lond.), B.A. (Oxon.).

The Religious Ideas of the Old Testament.
By H. Wheeler Robinson, M.A.

Prophecy and the Prophets.
By Theodore H. Robinson, M.A., D.D.

The Text and Canon of the New Testament.
By Alexander Souter, D.Litt.

Christian Thought to the Reformation.
By Herbert B. Workman, D.Litt.

The Theology of the Epistles.
By H. A. A. Kennedy, D.Sc., D.D.

The Pharisees and Jesus.
By A. T. Robertson, A.M., D.D., LL.D.

The Originality of the Christian Message.
By H. R. Mackintosh, D.D., D.Phil.

A CRITICAL INTRODUCTION TO THE NEW TESTAMENT

BY

ARTHUR S. PEAKE

M.A., D.D.

PROFESSOR OF BIBLICAL EXEGESIS IN THE UNIVERSITY OF MANCHESTER

NEW YORK

CHARLES SCRIBNER'S SONS

1928

Printed in the United States of America

TO MY PUPILS

PAST AND PRESENT

I DEDICATE THIS VOLUME

IN GRATEFUL REMEMBRANCE OF

NEVER-FAILING KINDNESS

AND GENEROUS CONSIDERATION

GENERAL INTRODUCTION TO THE SERIES

MAN has no deeper or wider interest than theology; none deeper, for however much he may change, he never loses his love of the many questions it covers; and none wider, for under whatever law he may live he never escapes from its spacious shade; nor does he ever find that it speaks to him in vain or uses a voice that fails to reach him. Once the present writer was talking with a friend who has equal fame as a statesman and a man of letters, and he said, "Every day I live, Politics, which are affairs of Man and Time, interest me less, while Theology, which is an affair of God and Eternity, interests me more." As with him, so with many, though the many feel that their interest is in theology and not in dogma. Dogma, they know, is but a series of resolutions framed by a council or parliament, which they do not respect any the more because the parliament was composed of ecclesiastically-minded persons; while the theology which so interests them is a discourse touching God, though the Being so named is the God man conceived as not only related to himself and his world but also as rising ever higher with the notions of the self and the world. Wise books, not in dogma but in theology, may therefore be described as the supreme need of our day, for only such can save us from much fanaticism and secure us in the full possession of a sober and sane reason.

Theology is less a single science than an encyclopædia of sciences; indeed all the sciences which have to do with man have a better right to be called theological than anthropological, though the man it studies is not simply an individual but a race. Its way of viewing man is indeed characteristic; from this have come some of its brighter ideals and some of its darkest dreams. The ideals are all either ethical or social, and would make of earth a heaven, creating fraternity amongst men and forming all states into a goodly sisterhood; the dreams may be represented by doctrines which concern sin on the one side and the will of God on the other. But even this will cannot make sin luminous, for were it made radiant with grace, it would cease to be sin.

These books then,—which have all to be written by men who have lived in the full blaze of modern light,—though without having either their eyes burned out or their souls scorched into insensibility,—are intended to present God in relation to Man and Man in relation to God. It is intended that they begin, not in date of publication, but in order of thought, with a Theological Encyclopædia which shall show the circle of sciences co-ordinated under the term Theology. though all will be viewed as related to its central or main idea. This relation of God to human knowledge will then be looked at through mind as a communion of Deity with humanity, or God in fellowship with concrete man. On this basis the idea of Revelation will be dealt with. Then, so far as history and philology are concerned, the two Sacred Books, which are here most significant, will be viewed as the scholar, who is also a divine, views them; in other words, the Old and New Testaments, regarded as human documents, will be criticised as a literature which expresses relations to both the present and the future; that is, to the men and races who made the books, as well as to the races and men the books made. The Bible will thus be studied in the Semitic family which gave it being, and also in the Indo-European families which gave to it the quality of the life to which they have attained. But Theology has to do with more than sacred literature; it has also to do with the thoughts and life its history occasioned. Therefore the Church has to be studied and presented as an institution which God founded and man administers. But it is possible to know this Church only through the thoughts it thinks, the doctrines it holds, the characters and the persons it forms, the people who are its saints and embody its ideals of sanctity, the acts it does, which are its sacraments, and the laws it follows and enforces which are its polity, and the young it educates and the nations it directs and controls. These are the points to be presented in the volumes which follow, which are all to be occupied with theology or the knowledge of God and His ways.

A. M. F.

"O"

PREFACE

A FEW words are necessary to explain the scope and excuse the limitations of the present volume. In view of the restricted space at his disposal and the variety and complexity of the problems, the author decided to concentrate attention exclusively on the critical questions. Hence there is no account of the subject-matter of the books or outline of their contents, no biographies of the writers or histories of the communities addressed. No notice has been taken of historical problems except so far as their consideration was involved in the critical discussion. Textual criticism and the history of the canon had obviously to be excluded. But for this rigorous restriction the volume would have largely lost such value as it may possess. Even as it is, the author is well aware how inadequate the treatment must often seem. He believes, however, that there is room for a book of this size and scope, and he has tried to use the space allotted to him to the best advantage. He trusts it may serve the purpose of many who have no leisure to study a lengthier volume, and that others may find it a useful preparation for the larger works of Jülicher, Zahn, or Moffatt.

At several points questions have not been raised, or have been dismissed with a bare reference, simply because no room could be found for an adequate discussion. This was especially the case in the chapter on the Synoptic Gospels. It is true that a topic of such supreme importance as a comparison of Mark with Q in the matter of historical value, which has been forced into such prominence by Wellhausen, would in any case have been excluded by the plan of the book. But such questions as that of the stratification of Mark in the form given to it by Loisy and Bacon among others, or of the treatment of Mark by Matthew and Luke, and the principles on which their use of it proceeded, or of the reconstruction of Q, it was the author's wish to have examined at some length. This would, however, have been done at the expense of curtailing the more elementary parts of the discussion, which he was unwilling to do in the interests of the majority of his readers. A similar excuse must be offered for the neglect of the ultra-radical school of critics, whether as represented by scholars like Steck, Loman, and Van Manen, or in the modified form defended by Voelter. On the general principles which underlie the criticism of this group, the author may refer to what he said in his Inaugural Lecture at the University of Manchester. The recent work of Dr. R. Scott on the Pauline Epistles had also to be regretfully passed by. Other shortcomings may receive a partial explanation in the fact that not a little of the volume had to be dictated in such intervals as the author's state of health permitted.

The book is written from a scientific standpoint. By this it is not intended that it is written with a bias against tradition, but that it is written with a desire to be loyal to the facts. The author is conscious of no wish to be in the critical fashion or out of it. That the great questions of faith cannot ultimately be ignored hardly needs to be said, and he has not shrunk from discussing them in their proper place. But it is desirable that, so far as may be, the critical problems should be detached from them. We may look forward to the time when scholars will cease to label a criticism they dislike as 'apologetic' or 'unbelieving,' and shall also cease to deserve the affixing of such labels.

The author has finally to thank the Editor of the *London Quarterly Review* for his cordial permission to use an article on the Fourth Gospel contributed by him to that periodical.

September 8, 1909.

course that several of the topics discussed in it had not already been treated with skill and learning by earlier scholars, but they had dealt with them rather as isolated questions, whereas Baur and the brilliant band of scholars he gathered about him dealt with them as a connected whole, and also brought the literature into most intimate relation to the whole development of the primitive Church. In philosophy Baur was a Hegelian, and he reconstructed the history of primitive Christianity in accordance with the formula that thought moves through thesis and antithesis to synthesis. In other words a position is laid down which calls forth a contradiction. These are gradually drawn together and at last merged in a higher unity. Applying this formula to the history of primitive Christianity, Baur conceived the whole development to exhibit the interplay of two forces, Jewish Christianity on the one side and Paulinism on the other, which ultimately, by the drawing together of the opposing parties, were reconciled in the Catholic Church of the second century, while the representatives of the original tendencies, the Ebionites on the one hand and Marcion on the other, stood outside the compromise and were consequently branded as heretics. Naturally, however much this construction may have been suggested by philosophical principles, it was not defended simply as an intuition. Facts and divination were supposed to point in the same way, though divination guided the search for facts. The Epistles to the Galatians and to the Corinthians in particular were believed to exhibit a sharp antagonism between the original apostles and Paul, and this was found also in the Apocalypse in which the apostle John was presumed to make a violent attack upon the apostle to the Gentiles. The Clementine Homilies and Recognitions were thought to prove the bitter hostility of the primitive apostles to Paul, who was believed to be intended by Simon Magus, the opponent of Simon Peter. The neglect of Paul during the greater part of the second century was imagined to point in the same direction and be a survival of the Jewish Christian antagonism to him.

The New Testament documents had to be dated by the consideration of the place they filled in the movement from antagonism to unity. Earlier books showed the hostility of the parties at its greatest, and the more conciliatory the tendency they displayed the later it was necessary to place them. Naturally this involved a very radical criticism of the New Testament. Only five books were left by Baur to the authors whose names they bear, namely: Galatians, Corinthians and Romans i.-xiv. to Paul, and the Apocalypse to the apostle John. Even within the school this revolutionary attitude provoked dissent, and in addition to Baur's four Hilgenfeld recognised the genuineness of Rom. xv., xvi., 1 Thessalonians, Philippians and Philemon. The most serious blow was struck at the school by the publication in 1857 of the second edition of Ritschl's *Entstehung der Altkatholischen Kirche*; and although it cannot be said that New Testament criticism has returned to traditional views there has been a retreat all along the line from the positions defended by Baur. It will be instructive to linger a little on the causes which led to the collapse of the Tübingen theory. It was certainly a praiseworthy thing to recognise that the origin of the Catholic Church was a problem which had to be explained. It was also commendable to treat the New Testament literature in close connexion with the development of the Church and to overcome the isolation which had characterised earlier criticism. Moreover, there *was* a conflict in the early Church, and it was well to force the fact into prominence. But the Tübingen reconstruction was too much dominated by theory to which the facts had to bend. While reasons were assigned for the positions adopted, these were often of a flimsy character such as would have influenced no one unless he had a theory to support. It was also a radical vice of method that literary was too much controlled by historical criticism.

Apart from these general considerations, the theory has broken down in detail and that at vital points. It is not the fact that the most neutral documents were the latest. Baur was forced to regard Mark as the latest of the Synoptists, since it was the most colourless in regard to the conflict which rent the early Church. One of the surest and most generally accepted results of Synoptic criticism is that Mark is the earliest Gospel. Similarly the Gospel of Luke was regarded as a Catholicised version of the Gospel of Marcion, but it is now universally recognised that the latter was a mutilated edition of the former. The Acts of the Apostles was supposed to be a history of the Apostolic Age written from the Catholic standpoint, in which the original bitter antagonism was suppressed and a picture of almost unbroken harmony was substituted. It is now generally agreed that the elaborate and ingenious attempts to show that the writer instituted a far-reaching parallelism between Peter and Paul in order to assimilate them to each other, has broken down, and whatever the tendency of the work may have been, it was not that which Baur discovered in it. Among those who reject the apostolic authorship of the Fourth Gospel there is a very large agreement that it should be dated roughly speaking half a century earlier than the time to which Baur assigned it.

Further, it is clear from an impartial study of the Pauline Epistles which Baur recognised as genuine that they will not bear the weight which he put upon them. They testify to a much closer agreement between Paul and the 'pillar apostles' (Gal. ii. 9) than Baur admitted. The importance attached to the Clementine literature is now seen to have been wholly exaggerated and Simon Magus is usually regarded as a historical character, not as a mere literary double of Paul, though it can hardly be doubted that Paul is attacked in the guise of Simon. The character of the post-apostolic period in which Baur placed so many New Testament writings is, so far as we know it, thoroughly commonplace and destitute of originality, and it would be surprising if the creative age of the Church produced so little literature, while the period in which the initial impulse had been largely exhausted should be so rich in pseudonymous writings of the first rank. The fuller understanding of Judaism has shown that it was far more complex than was allowed for by Baur, and that the factors which went to create both the New Testament literature and the Catholic Church of the second century were much more numerous The neglect of Paul in the second century was due to no antagonism to the apostle but simply to inability on the part of Gentile Christians, who came to the Gospel with such very different presuppositions and modes of thought, to understand him. The controversy with the Jewish Christians had long ceased to have any living interest for the Church, and the declension from the evangelical position of Paul to the moralism of the Apostolic Fathers was not the triumph of Jewish legalism but only one example of the rule that a great spiritual movement quickly sinks in the second generation to the conventional level as the original enthusiasm dies down. The Tübingen school also gave greater prominence to Paul than to Jesus, as was not unnatural in view of the fact that Jesus was less easily fitted into the Tübingen formula and the Gospels were regarded rather as landmarks in the controversy than as historical sources. But no theory can be permanent which fails to see in Jesus the most powerful factor in the creation and development of the early Church.

For a time it seemed as if the new theory would secure ultimate victory. Several of the foremost New Testament scholars, however, never accepted it, and in its main lines it has been long ago abandoned. At the same time Baur's work was epoch-making in that he largely set the problems for New Testament science, and although his own solution had a far narrower range than he imagined, it possessed an element of truth, and it is not easy to overestimate the service of those who are the first to state the problems which have to be investigated. Later developments have shown a much closer approximation to traditional views of authorship, though the extent of this return to tradition is often exaggerated. It is most marked in the case of the Pauline Epistles. With the wider knowledge of the conditions it has become clear that Baur's criteria of date and authorship were altogether too narrow and the possibilities of the first century much larger than he believed.

Within the limits of our space it is not desirable to pursue the history further, since the detailed discussion of the literature will bring the later developments before us. It may be well, however, to mention here some of the criteria for the solution of the critical problems presented by the literature. We have to recognise first that the historical books of the New Testament did not owe their origin simply to a scientific interest such as animates a modern historian. It is probable that the purely historical interest of New Testament writers is underrated by some scholars to-day, but it is clear that it was no mere concern to reproduce the past which impelled them to write. The present and the future were for them the matters of most urgent concern. We thus gain no little insight into the conditions with which the authors were confronted even from the history of the life of Christ or of the primitive Church. Points which they selected for mention were often those which had the most immediate bearing on contemporary conditions. Some think that we have to do here not simply with selection but also with creation; for example, sayings were put in the mouth of Jesus which were really the outcome of the Church's later necessities. We may refuse to give anything like the scope to this principle which it at times receives and yet recognise that this motive determined the choice of many incidents and sayings. Thus the address of Jesus to the twelve or to the seventy as to the methods of their mission supplied useful directions for the Church's later propaganda. The necessity of making good the case for the Gospel both against Jews and pagans has exercised considerable influence on the selection of material. The relations of Christianity with the Roman Empire are reflected not only in the Acts of the Apostles, the Epistles, and the Apocalypse, but even in the Gospels. This apologetic motive is of great value in determining date, but certain cautions have to be borne in mind in applying it. Our information as to external conditions is still far too uncertain to supply us with a reliable series of objective tests. Thus very varied opinions are still held as to the period when Christianity was definitely recognised by the State as an illicit religion. In apocalyptic writings we have also to beware of seeking for historical allusions where the author is simply employing very ancient eschatological material.

In view of the strained expectation with which the primitive Christians looked forward to the Second Coming we cannot anticipate that a concern for narrating the Gospel history would arise till a comparatively late period. The need for preserving reminiscences of the ministry of Jesus would not be felt till a considerable time had elapsed, though in the Gentile mission the demand may well have arisen earlier than we should anticipate, since there would be very few who could give first-hand oral information. It is very difficult to believe that a collection of Christ's sayings was compiled during His lifetime, in view of the fact that His disciples did not anticipate His speedy and tragic removal. While the bridegroom was still with them they lived in joyous freedom from anxiety as to the future, and for many years after His departure from earth they looked on their life as a purely provisional and interim condition which might at any moment be brought to a splendid close. The Epistles were naturally an earlier form of literature than the Gospels, since they were elicited by the need of dealing with immediate necessities.

The best order to be pursued in the treatment of the subject is not quite easy to determine. It is probably best to begin with the Pauline Epistles, since it is desirable as far as possible to start with the earliest literature which is also contemporary with the events with which it deals. Similarly it is best to keep the Johannine literature together and reserve it for the close. The remaining Epistles naturally follow the Pauline; the Synoptists and Acts precede the Johannine writings.

CHAPTER II

THE EPISTLES TO THE THESSALONIANS

There is now a general consensus of critical opinion in favour of the genuineness of 1 Thessalonians. The external evidence is good. Irenaeus is the first to name it, and it is quoted without question as Paul's from that time onwards. It is found in the Syriac and Old Latin versions and is included among the Pauline Epistles in the Muratorian Canon. It was also placed by Marcion in his Canon of Christian writings which included a mutilated Gospel of Luke and ten Pauline Epistles (the Pastoral Epistles being excluded). The internal evidence is decisive. No one writing in Paul's name after his death would have made him anticipate that the Second Coming would take place while he was still alive, since he would know that this anticipation of survival till the Parousia had been belied by the event. The difficulty created with reference to the destiny of those members of the Church who had died before the Second Coming points to a very early stage in the history of the Thessalonian Church. The question must have been obsolete long before Paul's death. Added to this we can detect no adequate motive why the Epistle should have been written in Paul's name. It serves no special purpose for which we can naturally think of a writer as invoking his authority. The organisation is in a rudimentary stage; we meet with no technical titles for the officials. The Epistle must have been written in Paul's lifetime, and it may therefore be taken for granted that it was written by Paul himself.

There are no arguments of weight on the other side, unless we insist that the four practically unquestioned Epistles must be taken as a standard to which everything must conform. But there was no Judaising agitation in Thessalonica, so that the relation of the Gospel to the Law called for no discussion. Indeed it would have been strange had such an agitation touched the Church so early. It is not quite easy to harmonise the references in the Epistle with the story related in the Acts, but they are not contradictory, and even if they were this would be no argument against the Epistle's genuineness. Several have thought that ii. 16 implies that the destruction of Jerusalem had already taken place. If this were correct it would be simpler to consider this verse as an interpolation wholly or in part. It is not clear, however, that there is a reference to the destruction of Jerusalem even as anticipated, for Paul saw a Divine judgment in the hardening of the Jews against Christianity; and if there were, such an anticipation would not be surprising in one who was acquainted with Christ's prediction and had such experience of the Jews' obstinate antagonism to the Gospel. There is accordingly no need to detect a later hand in ii. 16, still less on this slender basis to place the whole Epistle after A.D. 70.

The date and place of writing can be fixed within very narrow limits. It is clear from a comparison of the Epistle with the Acts that it was written shortly after the apostle had left Thessalonica. He had reached Athens (iii. 1), had sent Timothy back to Thessalonica from that city (iii. 2), and had been rejoined by him (iii. 6), and this, as we learn from Acts xviii. 5, was not at Athens but at Corinth. We must assume, however, that an interval of several months had elapsed between the apostle's departure from Thessalonica and the despatch of this letter. We must allow time for Paul's journey to Athens and the subsequent arrival of Silas and Timothy, for Paul's work in Athens and later in Corinth, which had resulted in the establishment of Churches in Achaia. The rhetorical statement that the news of the Thessalonians' acceptance of the Gospel had gone into every place and the report of it had reached Paul must have some specific reference, and may point to news Paul had received from the Churches in Galatia, which may have been occasioned by a letter sent to them by Timothy. The deaths which had occurred in the numerically small congregation also point in the same direction. We can scarcely allow less than six months for the interval; perhaps it should be more.

The Second Epistle to the Thessalonians was of course rejected by the Tübingen school, but unlike the First Epistle it is still rejected by many scholars. The most obvious ground of objection is that presented by the eschatological section (ii. 1-12). It would be out of the question to rescue the authenticity of the Epistle by sacrificing this section as a later interpolation. The Epistle was written for the sake of that paragraph; remove it and we cannot understand what object could be served by the composition of the rest. If ii. 1-12 is not the work of Paul the authenticity of the whole must be surrendered. The author seems to contradict the view as to the Second Coming expressed in the First Epistle. In 1 Thessalonians Paul appears to anticipate that the Second Coming is imminent and will be sudden, and expects that some at least of his readers and himself will survive till it takes place. In the Second Epistle he tells them that they must not be led to think that it is at hand, especially mentioning that such an opinion might be derived from a letter professing to come from himself. A development of apostasy is first to take place, and the man of lawlessness is to be revealed and then slain on the appearance of Christ. The mention in ii. 2 of a letter which might be circulated in Paul's name combined with the attestation of authenticity at the close (iii. 17) has not unnaturally raised the suspicion that the author wished to substitute his own composition for 1 Thessalonians with its uncongenial eschatology. This is supported by the extraordinary similarity between the two Epistles. Moreover, the circulation of a forged letter during Paul's lifetime and while he was within easy reach is highly improbable. A further contradiction with 1 Thessalonians is found in the anticipation of suddenness in the earlier Epistle as contrasted with the account given in the Second Epistle of the events which were to lead up to it.

It is possible, however, to put the relations between the two Epistles in a reasonable light without recourse to the hypothesis of non-authenticity. While Paul in the First Epistle anticipates that the Second Coming will take place in his own lifetime, he does not intend to convey the opinion that it will take place immediately. Some of the Thessalonians, however, probably through misunderstanding of his language, imagined that the Second Advent was imminent. To correct the restlessness and disorder which ensued, Paul wrote the Second Epistle to interpret the language of the First, warning them against forgeries and explaining that the Parousia cannot be imminent inasmuch as a certain development which still lies in the future is to take place before it. Similarly he anticipates in 1 Cor. xv. the return of Christ in his lifetime, but in Romans xi. 25, 26 he says that the Gospel will fulfil its function among the Gentiles and all Israel will be saved before it takes place. And while in the eschatological discourse in the Gospels Christ emphasises the suddenness of the Second Coming, He nevertheless points out several signs of the end. It is one of our commonest experiences that a long-anticipated event happens suddenly at the last. Besides, it is easy to exaggerate here. It is upon the unwatchful that the Day of the Lord steals as a thief in the night, not on the sons of the light who are wakeful and sober (1 Thess. v. 2-6). And while it is quite improbable that a forged letter had been circulated at Thessalonica, one can easily see how Paul, conscious that his earlier letter gave no real justification for the disorder in the Church, was driven to suspect that the Thessalonians had been misled by a letter which had been circulated falsely in his name. In fact the exhortation to constant watchfulness in the First Epistle might well have been interpreted as a call to forsake the homelier duties of everyday life.

Apart from its supposed inconsistency with 1 Thessalonians, the section itself has naturally created difficulties. The ideas have no parallel in the Pauline Epistles, and to many they seem to bear the stamp of a later time. Thus Hilgenfeld explained the mystery of lawlessness as Gnosticism, but there is no trace of Gnosticism in this Epistle. Kern put forward the ingenious view that the Epistle was composed between 68 and 70, when Nero was supposed to be in hiding, restrained from entering on his career as Antichrist by the circumstances of the time and especially by Vespasian, who was at the time besieging Jerusalem. The apostasy he took to be the outbreak of wickedness on the part of the Jews during the siege. But this is open to the serious objection that a spurious Epistle should be accepted as genuine within so brief a period after Paul's death. If to escape this difficulty it be placed in the first decade of the second century, as by some scholars, then the still more formidable objection arises that the writer refers to the man of lawlessness as seated in the temple without betraying any knowledge that the temple had been long ago destroyed, to say nothing of the difficulty of suggesting a plausible reason for the composition of the Epistle at that date. As a matter of fact there is no difficulty in accounting for the anticipations expressed by Paul. Quite possibly, as Bousset and others have argued, the writer is borrowing from a very ancient Antichrist legend which would amply account for the presence of those features in the description which seem to some writers to demand a post-Pauline date. But even if this were not the case, the conditions from the time of Antiochus Epiphanes onwards would be quite adequate. The description can be readily understood from the conditions of Paul's own age. It is probably a mistake to look for the mystery of lawlessness or its personal incarnation as springing out of Judaism, the antagonism to the Gospel displayed by the Jews being quite inadequate to account for the language Paul uses in this section. From monotheists and legalists so fanatical he would expect no such blasphemous outburst of antitheism and lawlessness. It is to heathenism rather than to those who 'have a zeal for God though not according to knowledge,' that we must look. There is nothing that so closely corresponds to Paul's description as the deification of the Roman Emperors, which had gone to insane lengths with Caligula. Paul's language especially reminds us of Caligula's orders to have his statue placed in the temple at Jerusalem. The mystery of lawlessness was already at work in Paul's time, held in check for a time by Claudius the reigning Emperor, but destined on his removal to receive its final consummation in a monster of impiety who would be slain by Christ at the Second Coming. It was not unnatural that concurrently with this there should be a great apostasy within the Christian Church itself, such as is also predicted in the Gospels It is therefore quite unnecessary to descend below the reign of Claudius for the date. Nor is there anything surprising in its isolation in the Pauline Epistles. It is only by accident that we hear of it at all. Paul merely repeats what he had already told his readers, and does so simply to disabuse them of anticipations which had a disastrous moral result. Since the subject was one that touched the future of the Roman Empire, he would shrink from committing his views to writing which might get into the wrong hands. He does so here only of necessity and in veiled words.

In the judgment of some scholars a still more serious difficulty is created by the striking likeness of the Second Epistle to the First. Hausrath in fact argued that the only genuine part of the letter was the eschatological passage. It is certainly strange that after the interval which separated the two Epistles Paul should repeat himself to such a degree as he does in 2 Thessalonians. To some extent we may account for this by the similarity of the conditions, and especially by the probability that Paul, in writing to correct a false opinion on a subject he had already dealt with, would call to mind the conditions in which his former letter had been written and what he had said in it. These considerations may perhaps not entirely remove the difficulty. But the theory of spuriousness is beset with difficulties greater still, for criticism has not simply to raise objections to the traditional authorship but to suggest a reason for the composition of a spurious letter. Two such suggestions have been made. One is that it was the author's intention to replace the First Epistle, whose eschatology had been falsified, by the Second. The other is that the Epistle was not designed to replace but to explain the former in harmony with the writer's eschatological views. Against the latter theory we must urge that a much shorter letter would have been all that was necessary The former theory is not exposed to this weakness and really accounts for the repetition of so much in the First Epistle, but it is not easy to believe that a project of this kind should be contemplated. How could a writer seriously hope, at the date to which the Epistle is assigned, to foist a hitherto unheard-of composition upon the Church, especially the Church at Thessalonica ? And this difficulty shrinks into insignificance by the side of that attached to the expectation that he would get the Church to put the First Epistle in the wastepaper basket and adopt the spurious Epistle in its place. We should also have expected a later writer to draw to some extent on other Pauline Epistles and introduce some of the more distinctively Pauline expressions and ideas in order to stamp it more directly as Paul's. It seems, therefore, to be still the simplest view that the Epistle is genuine. A brief period only separated it from the First Epistle, and it also was written from Corinth.

Jülicher in "Intro to N.T." The difficulties of 2:1-12 are best explained after all by assuming the genuineness of

CHAPTER III

THE EPISTLE TO THE GALATIANS

It is clear from the Epistle itself that the Churches addressed were founded at the same time and had the same history (iv. 13-15), so that we cannot identify them with a combination of Churches founded on different occasions. The term Galatia is used both in a wider and in a narrower sense. The latter was the original sense, according to which the term indicated a district where there had been a settlement of Gauls who had invaded the country in the third century B.C. It is in this region that, according to the majority of scholars, the Churches addressed in this Epistle are to be sought. For convenience of reference this view is now commonly designated the North Galatian theory. But the term, as is now universally admitted, was also used in the wider sense of the Roman province of Galatia, which included not only Galatia proper, but also parts of Phrygia, Lycaonia, and Pisidia. In this province Pisidian Antioch, Iconium, Derbe, and Lystra were all included, so that it has been held by scholars of the first rank, such as Renan, Weizsäcker, Hausrath, Pfleiderer and Zahn, that the Epistles were addressed to these Churches, which had been founded by Paul on his so-called First Missionary Journey. This South Galatian theory has been energetically advocated by Ramsay with conspicuous ability, learning and resourcefulness, and is now accepted by a large number of scholars, though still rejected by Schürer, Chase, Wendt, Schmiedel, Jülicher, Steinmann and others. If it can be substantiated we know something of the origin of these

Churches, and against this background the Epistle stands out much more clearly. Since no Churches were founded in North Galatia on this journey we must, for the reason already given, refuse to seek the Churches both in North Galatia and South Galatia.

While the term Galatia embraced in its official sense the whole province, it does not follow that it might not also be used in the more restricted sense. The official usage is more probable for Paul, since his imperialist point of view led him in other instances to prefer the official Roman titles. Galatia bears this sense in 1 Peter i. 1. This makes room for the South Galatian theory as a possibility, though it does not decide in its favour. The proof of it is mainly rested on the contention that Paul founded no Churches in North Galatia. If he did, it was on the Second Missionary Journey. Luke tells us that on this journey Paul and his companions 'passed through the Phrygian and Galatian country' (τὴν Φρυγίαν καὶ Γαλατικὴν χώραν), and it is in this clause that we must find concealed the establishment of Christianity in North Galatia. It is so well concealed that no one would guess from it that Paul had preached the Gospel there in consequence of illness and had met with an enthusiastic reception from those who became his converts. The silence of Acts is not conclusive, for Luke's interest is concentrated on the advance towards Europe, but it raises a prejudice at the outset against the North Galatian theory, all the more that Luke gives such full details of the mission elsewhere, Cyprus, South Galatia, Macedonia, Athens, Corinth, Ephesus, though it is slightly discounted by his silence as to Paul's work in Syria and Cilicia (Gal. i. 21).

The description of the journey in Acts xvi. 6-10 is also quite unfavourable to the view that Paul preached in North Galatia. The writer's main drift is plain: he wishes to show how the plans of Paul were twice overruled by the Spirit, that he might be forced to press on into Europe, not turning aside on the one hand to Asia or on the other to Bithynia. A detour into North Galatia does not fit this general scheme. It is true that when he was forbidden to preach in Asia he might have struck across North Galatia, intending to reach the eastern side of Bithynia. But this is exposed to great difficulties. The expression to go into Bithynia meant to go to the western part of that province, but on the North Galatian theory as usually formulated a journey through North Galatia would lead to the eastern part. It is unlikely that Paul would think of going to Eastern Bithynia, for only one city in it would have been likely to attract his attention, and even if he had, he would not have been likely to go by land since the route was very difficult. Moreover, we cannot account on this view for the reference to Mysia. This route to Eastern Bithynia would not bring them anywhere near Mysia, and the author would have very carelessly omitted to say how they came into the neighbourhood of Mysia.

Again we learn that an illness of Paul was the occasion of his founding the Galatian Churches. The probability, however, that he should have preached in North Galatia in consequence of illness must be regarded as remote. For either he was taken ill when passing through it to another district, or he went there to regain his health. Against the former it must be said that the road through North Galatia led nowhere where he was likely to go, against the latter that the climate was singularly unfitted for an invalid. It is also unlikely that time can be allowed on the Second Journey for the evangelisation of the places in North Galatia, where Paul is usually supposed to have planted Churches, especially when he was enfeebled and hampered by illness.

The avoidance by Luke of the term Galatia in xvi. 6 is also difficult to understand on the North Galatian theory, since this would have been the natural as it is elsewhere the invariable term. Luke, however, says 'Galatic territory,' which suggests territory connected in some way with Galatia in the strict sense, but not to be identified with it. The whole expression 'the Phrygian and Galatian territory' Lightfoot believes to designate not two lands but one, the Phrygo-Galatic territory' as we should say. He explains that North Galatia is so called because it had been Phrygian, but on the conquest by the Gauls had become Galatic. This bit of antiquarianism, however, would be very surprising in itself, and it is exposed to the objection that North Galatia probably did not retain the name Phrygia so late as this period. Ramsay agrees that only one land is intended, and that it is called 'Galatic' because it was a district connected with or included in Galatia, but one which Luke did not choose to call Galatia, while 'Phrygian' fixes it down to the part of Galatia which included Iconium and Antioch. It must be confessed, however, that this is difficult to harmonise with the true text of Acts xvi. 6, which is most naturally interpreted to mean that they went through the district in question because they had been prohibited from preaching in Asia, and this part of their journey seems to begin after the South Galatian Churches have been left. Ramsay takes the prohibition to be subsequent to their passage through the district, which is not the more natural sense. Perhaps we should adopt the view that the term is a general one denoting the districts bordering on Galatia and Phrygia. It is also possible, and on the North Galatian theory imperative, to take Phrygia as a noun, in which case the route lies first through Phrygia and then enters Galatia. But this is not the probable meaning of the Greek; we should have expected the article to have been repeated. In xviii. 23, on the other hand, where the order of names is reversed, we should probably take Phrygia as a noun translating 'the Galatic territory and Phrygia.' The fact that on this journey Paul strengthened '*all* the disciples,' suggests that the Galatic territory included the Churches in

South Galatia. Probably the expressions in xvi. 6 and xviii. 23 are not to be treated as equivalent. It may be added that J. Weiss thinks the reference to Galatic territory in xvi. 6 to be so difficult for both views that he is tempted to regard it as a gloss introduced from xviii. 23, or preferably as due to an editorial mistake possibly resting on a confusion of Ancyra in Phrygia with the much better-known Ancyra in Galatia.

Under pressure of the difficulties urged against the older form of the North Galatian theory, several of its defenders have recently modified it, and placed the Churches to which the Epistle is addressed in the north-western part of Galatia, bordering on Phrygia. This is a great improvement on the old theory inasmuch as it brings the district in which Paul is supposed to have founded these Churches much nearer to Mysia and West Bithynia and the time required would be much shorter. There is a geographical argument against this, however, though it tells much more strongly against the older North Galatian theory. According to Acts xviii. 23 these Churches were taken by Paul on his road to Ephesus, and on either form of the North Galatian view he would have been obliged to go out of his way to visit them.

Against the South Galatian theory it is often urged as conclusive that Paul could not have addressed his readers by the term 'Galatians.' This it is said bore the ethnical significance of men who were Gauls by descent and therefore could have been addressed only to descendants of the Gauls who had settled in North Galatia. It is, however, easy to see how Paul might use the term in addressing inhabitants of South Galatia. His preference for imperial rather than native nomenclature led him naturally to choose the imperial title, which was the more honourable and also that most calculated to stimulate his readers to be worthy of all which the name implied. But he was also driven to it by the fact that no other form of address was suitable. The heterogeneous elements of which the South Galatian Churches were composed would have required an extremely cumbrous mode of address if the local designations were to be used, and what would have been even more fatal was the sinister meaning attached to the terms. To have called them Phrygians would have been an insult. The name had a suggestion of slavery and was a term of abuse. It is also urged that if we identify the visit to Jerusalem described in Galatians ii. 1-10 with that recorded in Acts xv., Paul's language in Galatians i. 21 is strange on the South Galatian theory. He says there, 'Then I came into the regions of Syria and Cilicia,' and it is argued that he could not very well have omitted to mention that he had evangelised the South Galatians themselves in that interval had he been writing to the South Galatians. It is difficult to feel the cogency of this argument. Paul is not giving an exhaustive account of his labours in the interval between his visits to Jerusalem, else Cyprus could not have been omitted, but simply saying what he proceeded to do after the former visit. Of course the difficulty falls away if the visit in Gal. ii. is identified with an earlier visit than that recorded in Acts xv. A further objection is that Paul could not have referred to the Churches founded by himself and Barnabas as if they had been founded by himself alone. This is a real difficulty. But if, as is usually supposed, the letter was written after the rupture between Paul and Barnabas and the division of their sphere of labour and Paul had taken over the South Galatian Churches, it is easy to see how he might feel the exclusive responsibility for them. On the other hand, we cannot attach such importance as some do to the support given to the South Galatian theory by the reference to Barnabas, who is also mentioned in 1 Cor. ix. 6, though there is no reason to suppose that he had visited Corinth. At the same time Paul's mode of reference in Galatians ii. 13, 'even Barnabas was carried away,' gains more force if the readers were personally acquainted with him.

The arguments which tell against the North Galatian theory are so many arguments in favour of the South Galatian, and in addition the following considerations may be urged. The narrative of Paul's Second Missionary Journey runs on quite smoothly and is free from the geographical and chronological difficulties that beset the other theory and have already been pointed out. Paul follows a route which brings him through Asia over against Mysia, near to Bithynia, in such a way that he can go through or along the border of Mysia to Troas. And the journey can be done in the time allowed for it by the exigencies of chronology. The account of Paul's preaching there in consequence of illness is explained by a conjecture of Ramsay, that he caught a malarial fever in the enervating climate of Pamphylia, which is most dangerous to strangers, and on that account struck up into the high lands of the interior, which would be most likely to restore him to health. He accounts for Mark's refusal to accompany him as due to the fact that this going into the interior was contrary to their original programme. This latter suggestion is improbable, for it would argue a peculiar baseness on the part of Mark to desert the apostle at this juncture, and the phrase used in Acts xv. 38 that Mark 'went not with them to the work' suggests that the party had left Pamphylia to prosecute a missionary campaign in the interior. Moreover, a plausible case can be made out for other forms of illness than malarial fever. The reference to the case of Titus and the charge mentioned in the Epistle to the Galatians that Paul had preached circumcision are important. Timothy had been circumcised by him in this very district, and he was a member of one of these Churches. Such a case would give a handle to his enemies, and it would appeal especially to those who had known the circumstances of it. Lastly, there is the argument derived from the reference to the collection in the Pauline Churches for the saints at Jerusalem. This is referred to in the Epistle to the Galatians (ii. 10), and in 1 Cor. xvi. 1 we learn that Paul had instructed the Galatians to participate. From the indications in the Epistles we gather that the Churches in Galatia, Macedonia and Achaia contributed, and from Acts xx. 4 we find that representatives of Asia also went up with Paul when he took the offering, according to the principle laid down in 1 Cor. xvi. 3, 4. In other words the Pauline Churches generally seem to have contributed. If, however, the Churches of Galatia were churches in North Galatia, then the churches founded on the First Missionary Journey in South Galatia would have taken no part. This in itself is very improbable, but the improbability is much heightened by the fact that, according to Acts xx. 4, representatives from Derbe and Lystra, *i.e.* from South Galatian Churches, did accompany Paul, whereas no reference is made to representatives of North Galatian Churches.

The Epistle has been assigned to the most various dates; some have made it the earliest and some one of the latest of Paul's extant letters, and within these limits almost every position has been claimed for it. The divergence reflects the scarcity and ambiguity of the data for a decision; and unless we are tempted by ingenious but unsubstantial combinations we must acquiesce in a rather large measure of uncertainty. The Epistle was written after the visit to Jerusalem recorded in the second chapter, and at the time it was written Paul seems to have visited the Churches twice (iv. 13). As to the former of these points, great uncertainty hangs over the identification of the visit. This belongs to History rather than to Criticism, but it has a bearing on the date of the Epistle and must therefore be briefly discussed. In the Epistle Paul mentions the visits he made to Jerusalem, in order that he might prove his independence of the early apostles. After his return from Arabia and his departure from Damascus he went to Jerusalem to see Peter and stayed with him fifteen days. This would be the visit recorded in Acts ix. 26-30, though it is difficult to harmonise the two accounts. The second visit mentioned in Galatians is that on which he went up by revelation to discuss with the chief apostles the relation of the Gentile converts to the Law. Modern critics almost unanimously identify this visit with that in Acts xv. But Acts mentions another visit of Paul and Barnabas (xi. 30) on which they brought relief to the Christians at Jerusalem who were suffering from the famine. It is mentioned in the briefest way, and little importance seems to be attached to it by the writer. The usual identification is thus exposed to a serious difficulty. Paul is showing that he had no such contact with the older apostles as to justify the opinion that he owed anything to them. We should expect then that he would scrupulously enumerate every visit to Jerusalem. If, however, the view is right that the second visit mentioned by Paul (Gal. ii.) corresponds to the third mentioned in Acts (Acts xv.), then we have three possibilities. Either Paul has omitted the famine visit as irrelevant to his purpose, or we must regard that visit as one on which he did not come in contact with the apostles, or there is some mistake in the narrative in Acts. The second alternative is not probable. It is true that the narrative does not say that Paul came to Jerusalem on the famine visit or saw any of the apostles. The relief was sent to the brethren in Judaea and it was sent to the elders. Still, the head-quarters of the Churches in Judaea would be Jerusalem, and that is where Paul and Barnabas would naturally go. Nor is it clear that Peter was in prison or in hiding at the time, for the persecution by Herod may not have been at this time. Even apart from this, Paul could hardly afford to neglect the visit; he would have explained that though he was in Judaea he saw none of the apostles. The third alternative is adopted by some who think that the visit is misplaced, or that Acts xi. 30 and Acts xv. really refer to the same visit, that is, the visit recorded in Gal. ii. A comparison of the account in Gal. ii. with that in Acts xv. reveals some differences which are more or less capable of reconciliation, but which must have their weight in determining the question. We need attach no importance to the fact that Acts represents him as sent by the Church of Antioch, while Paul says he went up by revelation. These statements are not in conflict. Further, Paul relates a private discussion, Luke a public debate. But the former suggests (ii. 2) a tacit contrast between the private conference in which he won the leaders over, and a meeting of the whole Church. The most serious discrepancy exists between Paul's statement that the older apostles added nothing to him except that they should remember the poor, and the statement of Luke that certain restrictions were imposed on the Gentiles. It is also strange that Paul does not mention these decrees if the Epistle went to Churches in South Galatia, since we are told in Acts xvi. 4 that he communicated them to these Churches.

There is no conflict between the account in Acts xi. 30 and that in Gal. ii. But this may be due to the fact that there is no contact between them. The account in Acts is very brief, and if a mere private discussion had been in question naturally Luke would not have mentioned it. But we can see from Gal. ii. that this was by no means all that occurred. The 'false brethren' displayed much activity, and attempts were made to force Titus to be circumcised. It is also hard to see why Paul should not have mentioned that a main object of his journey was to bring relief to the poor, especially as he would thus have made it clear that his care for the poor was not first prompted by the apostles at Jerusalem. It is questionable if the famine visit, assuming it to be distinct from that in Acts xv., can be placed so late as fourteen years (Gal. ii. 1) after Paul's conversion. The latter objection tells against the view put forward by J. V. Bartlet and others that the visit recorded in Gal. ii. was earlier even than the famine visit. This view is also exposed to the difficulty that it postulates a journey to Jerusalem otherwise unknown to us, though this is not insuperable. It escapes some of the difficulties of the previous identification, and Paul's omission of the famine visit is then quite intelligible, for he did not need to continue the story of his relations with the apostles after they had recognised his Gospel and apostleship. It is not essential perhaps for our purpose to make a definite decision between these possibilities. We may leave the ground clear for a date before the Apostolic Conference of Acts xv. if on other grounds such a date should seem desirable.

A date so early seems at first sight to be definitely excluded by the fact that Paul appears to have visited the Galatian Churches twice. On the North Galatian theory his second visit to Galatia occurred on the Third Missionary Journey, on the South Galatian theory on the Second, in both cases after the Apostolic Conference of Acts xv. It is possible, however, to evade this conclusion if we identify the second visit with that made by Paul on his return journey through the South Galatian cities on the occasion of his first mission to them. And if this be held unsatisfactory it is possible to fall back on the view that we must not interpret iv. 13 as necessarily implying two visits.

It is held, however, by many that we are shut up to a date subsequent to the Second Missionary Journey by the stage of theological development reached in the Epistle. Its affinities with the Epistle to the Romans written towards the close of the Third Journey are striking, and it is commonly thought to belong chronologically to the group of which the other members are Romans and 1 and 2 Corinthians. In the Epistle to the Thessalonians, it is said, we have a much more elementary stage of Paulinism than in the great controversial group, and Galatians must therefore be later than those Epistles. The present writer can only repeat with the utmost emphasis his conviction that the inference rests on a radical error. It would argue an incredible inability on Paul's part to grasp the logical implications of his own experience, of his work among the Gentiles, of the battle for freedom he had fought at Jerusalem and Antioch, to suppose that he had but lately emerged into a clear realisation of the relations between the Gospel and the Law. His incisive refutation of Peter at Antioch contradicts such a fallacy, and Paul's amazement at the sudden defection of the Galatians would have but little warrant if he had preached nothing but an immature Paulinism among them. Even before his conversion we may well believe that he had seen what the proclamation of a crucified Messiah implied for the religion of the Law. And in his conversion his whole Gospel was implicitly given. The idea that Paul must expound his theology in every letter he wrote, even to Churches he had himself founded and trained, under penalty of being judged not yet to have grasped it, needs only to be stated for its unreasonableness to be patent. If Romans and Galatians have such points of similarity, that arises from the kinship of the subject. But this kinship is not due to the fact that Paul had only just thought out his principles to meet the crisis in Galatia, and then with these uppermost in his mind expounded them in the Epistle to the Romans. They were his fundamental principles, and therefore naturally the main theme of a letter to the Church in the imperial city which had not learnt the Gospel from his lips. But just because they constituted his Gospel, when the blow was struck at its vitals, he reiterated it to those who had already been taught it, no doubt with fresh felicity of illustration and expression, with appropriate ingenuity of appeal, but with no variation from principles long clear to him as the sunlight. When he dealt with the same theme, on which his mind had long been made up, he inevitably treated it on the familiar lines, though an interval of many years might lie between the various expositions of it.

If we accept the North Galatian theory we should probably date the Epistle on the Third Missionary Journey. If Paul was settled in any place at the time it is most natural to think of the Epistle as written from Ephesus, though too much stress must not be laid in this connexion on 'so quickly' of i. 6. In that case we should place it before 1 Corinthians and infer from the reference in 1 Cor. xvi. 1 that Paul's letter had won back the Churches to their loyalty. It is, however, possible that it was written after 2 Corinthians in Corinth. It is equally possible that it was written while Paul was travelling, and this is favoured by the absence of definite reference to the place of writing, while the mention of all the brethren who are with him (i. 2) may mean those who have accompanied him on this tour. If, however, we adopt, as we probably should, the South Galatian theory, it is more likely that the Epistle was written before the Third Missionary Journey. But this leaves us, as we have already seen, with a wide range of possibilities. We should, however, probably set aside on several grounds the view that it is to be dated before the Second Missionary Journey. The Epistle apparently implies two visits, and this is more naturally interpreted of the visits on the First and Second journey than of the visit and return visit on the First Journey. Further, the balance of argument seems to be in favour of the identification of Paul's visit to Jerusalem described in Galatians ii. with that described in Acts xv. It is, however, difficult to acquiesce in McGiffert's view that the letter was written by Paul at Antioch on his return from Jerusalem, since he went from Antioch to Galatia, whereas the suggestion in the Epistle is that he writes to them because he cannot come. What, however, seems decisive is the complete ignoring of Barnabas' joint responsibility for the Church. This appears to point conclusively to a date after their quarrel and the division of their sphere of missionary labour. Accordingly we must date the Epistle after Paul's second visit when he had separated from Barnabas and had given a handle to his unscrupulous enemies by the circumcision of Timothy. It may of course be urged against this that if Paul had seen the Churches after the conference at Jerusalem described in the second chapter, he would have told them when he was with them. But a similar difficulty attaches to the autobiography in the first chapter. Moreover, it is hardly probable that Paul would recount the secret history of his conference with the leaders at Jerusalem; he does so in the letter only under pressure of extreme provocation. It may then have been written during the Second Missionary Journey or in the interval between this and the next journey. Ramsay's view that it was written at Antioch in this interval is exposed to a similar objection as McGiffert's that it was written during the previous stay at Antioch. To identify 'all the brethren who are with me' as the whole Church at Antioch would imply an undue egotism on Paul's part; the phrase rather suggests his companions in travel. Ramsay's view is open to the further objection that he identifies the visit in Galatians ii. with the famine visit. It is surely probable that if the letter was written after the deliberations recorded in Acts xv., Paul would have made some reference to them in this Epistle.

CHAPTER IV

THE EPISTLES TO THE CORINTHIANS

I Corinthians, which had been preceded by an earlier letter (v. 9) now entirely or largely lost to us, was written by Paul from Ephesus, apparently in the spring of the year (A.D. 55) in which his work at Ephesus came to an end. The Epistle was written partly in reply to a letter from the Church at Corinth dealing with practical problems on which the Church desired guidance, partly on the basis of information as to abuses in the Church which had reached the apostle through other channels. The genuineness of the Epistle has been almost universally admitted; it was regarded as axiomatic by the Tübingen school and is accepted by all but the hyper-critics who deny the authenticity of all the Pauline Epistles. It is definitely attested by Clement of Rome before the close of the first century A.D. It was almost certainly employed by Ignatius and Polycarp, not improbably by Hermas. It is needless to discuss the suggestions that the Epistle contains portions of more than one letter. As an example it may be mentioned that a discrepancy has been discovered between the attitude adopted by Paul in x. 1-22, and that adopted by him in viii., x. 23-33. These sections are supposed to belong to different letters, both earlier than the bulk of I Corinthians. It is true that there is a difference. But it points to no development in Paul's views; it rests on the fact that in viii. he discusses the question of meats offered to idols from the standpoint of the 'intellectuals' at Corinth. He reaches the conclusion that even if we grant that from such a nonentity as the idol no moral defilement can come, we must not suffer those who are not emancipated from the thraldom of their old associations, because they cannot really be damaged by the intrinsic mischief of the food, to be spiritually ruined by violation of their conscience in deference to our precept and example. In x. 1-22, however, he states the question in his own way. Behind the lifeless idol block there was the living demon, and those who participated in the idol sacrifices were in peril from the demoniacal virus with which they were infected.

The Second Epistle to the Corinthians is not so well attested by external evidence as 1 Corinthians. It is very strange that Clement of Rome seems to have been entirely unacquainted with it, and to have made no reference to it in the letter he wrote for the Church of Rome to the Church of Corinth. Since his silence is not accounted for by any unsuitability of content to his purpose, the probable inference is that he did not know of it. The Epistle seems to have come into general circulation less rapidly than 1 Corinthians. It was probably used by Polycarp shortly afterwards and was taken by Marcion into his canon. It is frequently quoted as Paul's by Irenaeus and later writers and is included in the Muratorian Canon.

If, however, there had been no external attestation at all in antiquity and the Epistle had been discovered in our own day, its genuineness would be amply proved by its internal characteristics. It is its own adequate attestation. The complexity of relations between Paul and the Corinthian Church, the note of reality which rings in every sentence, the mighty personality which the letter reveals, are far beyond the reach of the most skilful imitator Besides, we could not understand why so much labour should be expended to create an intricate historical situation which could serve no purpose a later writer would have had in view and be completely without interest for second century readers. Nowhere is the hypothesis of pseudonymity so grotesque as in the case of this Epistle, nowhere is it so manifest a sign of complete critical incompetence.

But while the genuineness of the letter is beyond all reasonable question, the critical problems it presents are of the most complicated and difficult character. Partly they are historical, concerned with the relations between Paul and the Corinthian Church in the interval between the two Epistles, partly they are critical. With the former we have to do only so far as they affect our decision on the latter. The circumstances which led to the writing of 2 Corinthians are indicated by Paul himself at the opening of the letter and again in the seventh chapter. He had sent a very severe letter to the Corinthian Church, written with many tears out of much affliction and anguish of heart. After he had despatched it he suffered an agony of apprehension lest the severity of his tone might produce a complete rupture between himself and the Corinthian Church. His anxiety to meet Titus and learn the effect of his letter was such that he could not avail himself of the opportunity afforded him of preaching the Gospel in Troas, but crossed into Macedonia where he met Titus and learnt to his relief that the Corinthian Church had now returned to its loyalty, at least so far as the majority was concerned. An offender round whom the controversy had gathered and whose punishment Paul had demanded, had been punished by the majority. Paul regards the punishment that had been inflicted as sufficient and now requests the Church to forgive him.

It is natural that earlier scholars should have assumed that the letter which Paul regretted to have sent was 1 Corinthians, though difficulties were felt in reconstructing on this hypothesis the history in the interval. When

Paul sent the First Epistle he anticipated that his letter would be followed by a visit from Timothy (iv. 17, xvi. 10). When he writes the Second Epistle, however, he makes no reference to Timothy's visit, although Timothy was with him when he wrote, but says how intensely anxious he was for the return of Titus. The discussion of this difficulty and the numerous solutions which have been proposed only concern us slightly here. For a good while now the opinion has been very widely held that the letter which caused Paul such anxiety cannot have been 1 Corinthians. It is perfectly true that there were severe passages in the letter, but its total impression, even if we suppose that these passages stood out in exaggerated prominence in Paul's recollection, simply does not answer to Paul's description. It is not comparable in the sharpness of its tone to the closing portion of 2 Corinthians itself, which for concentrated and passionate invective has no parallel in the Pauline Epistles. In the next place the reference to the offender does not suit the incestuous person whose punishment Paul had solemnly decreed in the First Epistle. The father of the latter was presumably dead, but the injured person of 2 Corinthians was still alive. Moreover, if we identify the offender in the two Epistles, the grossness of the offence seems to be passed over altogether too lightly in the Second. Accordingly it is now held by a large number of scholars that we must reject the identification of the severe letter with 1 Corinthians and regard it as a later letter. Whether we are to suppose that Paul paid a visit to the Corinthian Church in the interval and was deeply insulted by a ringleader of the opposition, or whether the severe letter was elicited by an unfavourable report from Timothy, or whether the history should be reconstructed in some other way is a question that lies outside our discussion. The first view, it may simply be said, seems to the present writer the most probable. It is in any case likely that the offender of 2 Corinthians had grossly insulted Paul either in person or in the person of his representative.

But if we have to surrender the identification of the severe letter with 1 Corinthians the question arises whether it has been completely lost. This view is adopted by many modern critics including Holsten, Holtzmann, Jülicher, Sanday, Bousset, and Lietzmann. It was suggested by Hausrath, however, and the suggestion has been very widely adopted, that we are to find a large part of this letter in the last four chapters of 2 Corinthians. A hypothesis of this kind no doubt has strong *prima facie* evidence against it. These chapters have come down to us as part of the Epistle to which they are attached, and there is no external evidence nor yet any indication in the history of the text that they ever had any independent existence. Moreover, it is said that these chapters do not answer to the description of the letter which Paul himself gives. We have no reference in these chapters to Paul's demand that the offender should be punished, though this must have been contained in the severe letter. It is also urged that 2 Corinthians xii. 16-18 is decisive against the hypothesis. In that passage we have a reference to a visit of Titus and work in the Church at Corinth accomplished previously to the sending of the letter. Since Titus seems to have been sent either with that letter or shortly before or after, we cannot suppose that the severe letter could contain the reference in xii. 16-18, and therefore must infer that these chapters cannot be identified with the severe letter. It is not easily conceivable, however, that Titus should have been burdened with the duty of attending to the collection at the very time when the Church was in open mutiny. We must therefore suppose that this is a different visit. The objection that there is no demand for the punishment of the offender in 2 Cor. x.-xiii. is relevant only if we suppose that no part of the severe letter has been lost. It is very probable that if the two letters were accidentally united the end of one and the beginning of the other must have been lost, otherwise it would have been obvious that they were distinct. The difference in tone between the first nine chapters and the concluding chapters, which makes it psychologically inconceivable to many that they should belong to the same letter, is accounted for either by the view that here Paul addresses only the rebellious minority —but this is contradicted by various passages in these chapters and Paul must have made the transition plain— or by the view that meanwhile unfavourable news had come from Corinth, which is negatived not simply by the misjudgment of the situation on the part of Titus which this would involve, but by the absolute failure of any indication of such news, or lastly by the supposition that Paul himself ceased to dictate and began to write and was carried away by the strength of his feelings, a supposition which presumably does not arise from any experience of dictated correspondence.

The present writer sees no escape from the conclusion that the closing chapters of 2 Corinthians formed part of the severe letter. It is significant that two lines of evidence should converge upon it. On the one side we have the description of a letter in the early chapters of 2 Corinthians which it seems impossible to identify with our First Epistle; and then as corroborating this we have the surprising character of the last four chapters of 2 Corinthians as part of the same letter which we find in the first nine chapters. It is difficult to believe that the two sections of the Epistles hold together. If 2 Corinthians is a unity, we have the following state of things: Paul sends a very stern letter to Corinth, and is filled with regret for the writing of it, and apprehension as to its reception. In the joyful reaction caused by the good news of Titus, he writes a letter overflowing with affection at the beginning, and concluding with a sharpness of invective to be paralleled nowhere else in his Epistles.

If we identify these chapters with the letter which caused him such pain to write and such anxiety when written, we escape from the serious difficulty of supposing that Paul concluded the letter, begun in the strain of forgive and forget, with so vehement a defence against his antagonists. Was Paul the man, after the Church had returned to its loyalty, and he had thanked God devoutly for it, to open the old wound and pour forth on the heads of his enemies vials of unrestrained indignation? If, when the Church was in arms against him, he doubted whether he had made a mistake in sending one letter, would he be likely, after the reconciliation, to send another of the same character? Indeed one may well ask what must the letter have been which filled him with such tormenting anxiety if, after the fright he had given himself, he could calmly send the last portion of 2 Corinthians in the serene confidence that this would seal anew the compact of peace between them? It is in itself conceivable if the composition of the letter was spread over several days, or even if an anxious sleepless night intervened between the two parts of the letter, that Paul's sense of relief may have been replaced by indignation as he brooded on the unhappy past. Not only, however, is this highly improbable, but it would be rather difficult to understand why he should have allowed the first part of the letter to stand and not substituted something more consonant with his altered mood. We need not join with Paul's Corinthian critics in conceiving him to be so flighty and mercurial as that.

It is not improbable that we have another fragment from Paul's correspondence with Corinth included in the Second Epistle. It was long ago observed that vi. 14 - vii. 1 interrupted the progress of thought and that vii. 2 connected admirably with vi. 13. Since Paul refers in 1 Cor. v. 9 to an earlier letter which he had written to Corinth, and the subject matter of this intrusive paragraph in 2 Corinthians suits very well what we may infer the lost letter to have been, it is not an unnatural hypothesis that it originally formed part of it. We can hardly suppose that any one would have deliberately inserted it at this point, so that if this theory is correct we must assume that it owes its present position to some accident, such as has occasioned the combination of 2 Cor. x.-xiii. with 2 Cor. i.-ix. If however, as many scholars think, the passage may be accounted for in its present position, we must reconcile ourselves to the view that the letter which preceded 1 Corinthians has been lost. In any case there is no valid ground for the supposition that 2 Cor. vi. 14 - vii. 1 is spurious, though it is quite possible that the closing words are not preserved for us in precisely the form in which they left the hands of Paul. That some things in the section cannot be matched elsewhere in the Pauline Epistles is of course true, but of how many other passages might not the same thing be said?

CHAPTER V

THE EPISTLE TO THE ROMANS

This Epistle is attested not simply by patristic, but by New Testament evidence. It was certainly used by the author of 1 Peter and probably by the authors of James and the Epistle to the Hebrews. Clement of Rome, Ignatius and Polycarp draw freely upon it; it was included in the Canon of Marcion. Later evidence which is abundant need not be quoted. Its genuineness is assured by internal evidence, and by its intimate connexion with the other Pauline literature. It was written apparently at Corinth, a few months after 2 Cor. i.-ix., and its tone testifies to the apostle's success in winning back the allegiance of that community. One of the most important of the seriously debated questions relates to the composition of the Roman Church. The more usual view is that the Church was in the main a Gentile Church with Jewish elements. The other view held by Baur and many more is that it was in the main Jewish Christian with Gentile elements. In favour of the latter view it is said that Paul refers to Abraham as 'our forefather,' and in the present chapter speaks of his readers as 'men that know the law,' and as having been 'made dead to the law through the body of Christ.' He also says 'we have been discharged from the law, having died to that wherein we were holden.' It is also thought that only in this way is it possible to find a valid reason for the inclusion of the chapters on Election, since the Gentiles would not feel so keenly as Jewish Christians the difficulty caused by the Jewish rejection of the Gospel. But these arguments are none of them strong and are amply met by the admission that there was a Jewish Christian element in the Church, and the probability that some of the Gentile Christians had been proselytes before they became Christians. Further, parallels for some of the passages supposed to prove Jewish origin may be quoted from Epistles which were certainly not written to Jews. Thus in 1 Cor. x. 1 Paul speaks of the Israelites in the wilderness as 'our fathers.' And the reference to the Roman Christians as men who knew the law finds a parallel in the Epistle to the Galatians where Paul presupposes a knowledge of the law in the Galatian Christians who were Gentiles. The same Epistle also furnishes a parallel to the statement that his readers have died to the Law: cf. Gal. iv. 1-9 (esp. *vv.* 5 and 7), Col. ii. 14. And the problem discussed in Rom. ix.-xi. was not handled because it was one of special interest to Jewish Christians. It was forced on the attention of all who tried to construct a philosophy of history on Paul's lines.

The positive proof of the predominantly Gentile composition of the Church is very strong. There is first the intrinsic improbability that Paul with his delicacy about his apostleship as exclusively to Gentiles should have sent an elaborate theological discussion to a Church mainly composed of Jewish Christians at least without an explicit defence of his action. Further, it is difficult to explain away the definite language which seems to point to Gentiles as his readers. He includes the recipients of the letter among the Gentiles (i. 5, 6), wishes to have fruit in them as in the rest of the Gentiles (i. 13), and gives as a reason for his readiness to preach the Gospel at Rome that he is a debtor to Greeks and barbarians. The life of his readers before conversion had been one of lawlessness. In xi. 13, 14 he calls his readers 'Gentiles' and contrasts the Jews with them. In xi. 25, addressing them by the general term 'brethren,' he proceeds in a way applicable only to Gentiles. In xv. 15 also, if this is part of the Epistle, he gives explicitly as his reason for writing that he is an apostle of the Gentiles. We can hardly be wrong, then, in the conclusion that the Church, while including Jewish Christians, was in the main a Gentile Church. That Paul should write a letter announcing his intended visit is quite natural. Numerous attempts have been made to explain why, in view of his intended visit, he addressed to the Church this elaborate treatment of great theological themes, this exposition of his Gospel. A discussion of these is unfortunately precluded by the necessary limits of this book.

The integrity of the Epistle has been much debated. Leaving aside other questions as to its composition which need not be discussed, the problem of the concluding chapters has called forth several solutions. The consideration of the phenomena belongs partly to textual criticism, but they must be briefly mentioned. (a) The benediction is no doubt rightly placed in xvi. 20b, but some manuscripts place it between *v.* 23 and *v.* 25, while some place it at the end of *v.* 27. (b) In some manuscripts the doxology *vv.* 25-27 is placed at the end of chapter xiv. (c) Marcion's copy of the Epistle apparently lacked chapters xv. and xvi. Baur on grounds mainly of internal criticism considered that these chapters were a spurious addition. This view no longer finds acceptance and need not be discussed. Renan made the ingenious suggestion that the main part of the Epistle was sent to several Churches, but with different endings in each case, i.-xi. with xv. to the Romans, i.-xiv. with xvi. 1-20 to the Ephesians, i.-xiv. with xvi. 21-24 to the Thessalonians, and i.-xiv. with xvi. 25-27 to an unknown Church. The Epistle came to its present form through a combination of these separate endings. Lightfoot thought that the Epistle was originally written

codex G. western

to the Romans as we have it, but ended at xvi. 23, *vv.* 21-23, however, being a postscript added by Paul's companions. Later Paul prepared the Epistle for wider circulation by striking out the mention of Rom. i. 7 and xv. and xvi., but added the doxology xvi. 25-27 at the end of xiv. Later the doxology was transferred to the close of the Epistle. It may be urged in favour of this view that the MS. G omits 'in Rome' both in i. 7 and in i. 15. It is difficult to think that the omission can be accidental in both cases, and this favours the view, not of course as has been suggested that the Epistle was not sent to Rome at all, but that copies had been prepared from which the local designation had been eliminated. Renan's theory accounts for the textual facts but is unnecessarily complicated. Moreover, it is difficult to understand why chapters xii. and xiii. should be regarded as not sent to Rome, for which the latter in particular was exceptionally well suited. Moreover, xv. cannot be separated from xiv. Lightfoot's theory is less arbitrary, but it is difficult to accept the view that any edition of the Epistle which contained chapter xiv. did not also contain xv. 1-13, which continues the discussion of the same subject. At the same time the textual facts favour the view that abbreviated copies of the Epistle were in circulation.

In holding that xvi. 1-20 went to Ephesus Renan was only taking a view which, since it was first expressed by Schulz in 1829, has met with very wide acceptance, especially in recent times. How much of chapter xvi. belongs to the letter to Ephesus is disputed, whether it included xvi. 1, 2 or began with xvi. 3, whether it stopped with *v.* 16 or *v.* 21. It is considered very improbable that Paul should have known so many persons in a Church which he had not visited, whereas in a Church in which he had for a long time laboured these greetings would be quite natural. The reference to Prisca and Aquila points to Ephesus. It is true that they had been connected with a Church in Rome at an earlier date, but they were in Ephesus a little while before this Epistle was written (Acts xviii. 18, 26, 1 Cor. xvi. 19) and later (2 Tim. iv. 19). It is improbable that they should have been in Rome again in the interval. The list itself is thought in some respects to suit Asia better than Rome, especially the reference to Epaenetus. Further, the warning in 17-20 is surprising in a letter written to a Church which was not personally known to Paul and in which he had no authority.

It is difficult to evade these arguments, and yet there are weighty considerations on the other side. It is probable enough that many of Paul's friends would be in Rome, the capital of the Empire to which all roads led, especially as the early Christians belonged to the social stratum in which a wandering life would be very common. In the next place it may fairly be argued that this long list of names is less surprising in a letter to the Roman Church than in a letter to such a Church as Ephesus. Paul's method elsewhere is very instructive. There are no salutations of individuals in either of the letters to Corinth, in that to the Galatians, the Philippians or the Thessalonians. Where a salutation is given it is of a collective character. Prisca and Aquila and the house of Onesiphorus are saluted in 2 Timothy, Philemon himself in the letter addressed to him. In Colossians, however, we have a considerable number of salutations, though in this case they are sent simply by individuals to the collective community. It is therefore very significant that in the letters addressed by Paul to Churches where he had laboured no individual salutations are included, whereas a whole series of individuals either sends or receives greetings in the two Epistles sent to Churches where Paul had not laboured. If then we are to judge by Paul's habit, the number of names saluted points to Rome more strongly than to Ephesus. Paul naturally made the most of every personal link with the Church he was about to visit, and on which for its high importance he desired to bring all his influence to bear. The combination of names, so far as the inscriptional evidence goes, favours Rome rather than anywhere else. In particular, the reference to those of the household of Aristobulus and the household of Narcissus points very strongly to Rome, both Narcissus and Aristobulus being friends of the Emperor Claudius. In spite of the very large acceptance which the hypothesis that the greetings were sent to Ephesus has received, it is still rejected by several of the most eminent scholars, including Harnack, Zahn, Sanday and Headlam, Denney, Ramsay and Lietzmann. If the textual difficulties connected with the last two chapters were relieved by the theory it would be an additional argument in its favour, but that is not the case. The only argument which causes the present writer to hesitate is the difficulty of supposing Prisca and Aquila to have been in Rome when the letter was sent. But this is outweighed by the difficulty of accounting for the presence of this letter or fragment of a letter addressed to Ephesus in an Epistle to the Romans. The burden of proof lies on those who would dislodge it from its present position, and the attempt to do so can hardly be said to have succeeded.

O.K.

CHAPTER VI

THE EPISTLES OF THE IMPRISONMENT

THIS group of Epistles includes those to the Ephesians, Colossians and Philemon, and that to the Philippians. The first question to be considered is the place of Philippians in the group. It is usually considered to be the latest, though Bleek in Germany, and Lightfoot followed by several scholars in England, have regarded it as the earliest. The main argument is the doctrinal similarity of Philippians and Romans, while it is said the other Epistles of this group present no such marked resemblance to Romans. From this it is inferred that Philippians stands next to Romans in point of time. The argument has been turned by others against the genuineness of Colossians and Ephesians. Thus Pfleiderer, arguing on the hypothesis that if all are genuine Philippians is the latest, urges that the absence from Philippians of the features specially characteristic of Colossians and Ephesians simply proves that the latter cannot be authentic. This objection is conclusively met if the order advocated by Lightfoot is the true one. But neither Lightfoot's nor Pfleiderer's conclusion is necessary. Within the Pauline literature itself analogies can be found to support the common view. It is probable that Galatians is earlier than Corinthians and Romans, though here again, on the ground of doctrinal and phraseological similarity, Lightfoot placed Galatians between Corinthians and Romans. If in spite of this similarity, the Epistles to the Corinthians are interpolated between Galatians and Romans, there is no reason why Ephesians, Colossians and Philemon should not be placed between Romans and Philippians. So, too, we have the best of reasons for believing that Paul's theological system was formed before any of our Epistles were written, yet those to the Thessalonians do not exhibit the peculiarly Pauline stamp. We cannot therefore defend the priority of Philippians on this ground.

It is also argued that if Philippians had been written later than Colossians, we should have expected to find traces of the polemic against the Colossian heresy and of that side of truth by which Paul had met it. But this does not follow. Ephesians, written at the same time, and presenting many points of contact with Colossians, does not refer to the heresy, or expound the cosmic significance of the Person of Christ. Nor would Paul feel it necessary in a letter to the Philippians to deal with a heresy which had not touched their Church. In fact the letter as originally planned, would probably have been without the polemic against the Judaizers in chapter iii. This is Lightfoot's opinion, and if correct we should have had an Epistle written after the worst of the struggle with the Judaizers was over, but with little or no reference to it. Again it is urged that we must put Colossians and Ephesians as late as possible, because the Church seems to be in a more advanced state. The false doctrine in Colossians and the emphasis on the Church in Ephesians bring these Epistles close to the Pastorals, with their references to heresies and developed ecclesiastical organisation. But against this we must set the fact that matters do not move at the same rate everywhere, and in the time of Ignatius and Polycarp they seem to have advanced more rapidly in Ephesus and that district than in Philippi. Besides a year at most can lie between the letters, an utterly negligible interval in this connexion. Further, Philippians was intended mainly as a letter of thanks for the kindness of the Church, and warning against dissension and ambition. In such an Epistle indications of the stage of development will not be present to anything like the same extent. Against the parallels between Romans and Philippians we may set striking parallels between Romans and Colossians. In favour of the later date of Philippians it may be said that Paul's anticipations of a speedy decision on his case are rather more definite in Philippians and less optimistic. The Philippians had had time to have heard of the illness of Epaphroditus, and to have sent to Paul the expression of their anxiety. Not much stress, however, can be laid on this, as no very long time was needed for the journey between Rome and Philippi. The order generally adopted seems to be most probable, and Philippians should be dated last of this group.

The Epistles to Philemon, the Colossians and the Ephesians

It is not necessary to discuss the authenticity of the Epistle to Philemon, for although this has been disputed it is now amply recognised on all hands. It was included in the Canon of Marcion and the Muratorian Canon, and the absence of reference to it by many early Christian writers is fully accounted for by its untheological character. The internal evidence is decisive. No one could have imitated Paul in so inimitable a way, nor could any plausible reason be assigned for its composition in Paul's name. It can hardly be doubted that its genuineness would not have been disputed had it not been for its connexion with the Epistle to the Colossians. Instead, however, of using the spuriousness of Colossians to discredit Philemon, we should regard the unquestionable genuineness of Philemon as a guarantee for the authenticity of Colossians. The two letters were written at the same time and sent by the same messenger. Usually it is thought that the letters were sent from Rome. Since Paul was a prisoner at the time, the only reasonable alternatives are Rome or Caesarea. It is practically certain that Philippians was written at Rome. This is suggested by the reference to the praetorian guard and the Christians in Caesar's household, and also by the fact that Paul anticipates that his case will soon be settled. This he could not have done at Caesarea since he appealed to Caesar and therefore knew that he must be sent to Rome. Now if we could make Philippians the earliest of the imprisonment Epistles, this would carry with it the inference that Philemon and Colossians must have been written at Rome rather than Caesarea. Since, however, we have accepted the reverse order, we cannot use the place of Philippians to determine that of the other Epistles. Nevertheless they were probably written from Rome. We cannot infer from the difference between these Epistles and Philippians that they must be more widely separated in time than the hypothesis of Roman origin for all of them will permit.

Nor does the argument that Paul speaks in Philippians of going to Macedonia on his release, but in Philemon of visiting Colossae, prove that the letters cannot have been written from the same place. Paul's plans altered with the circumstances, as his correspondence with Corinth illustrates, and why should he not have visited one Church on his way to the other ? Caesarea was a most unlikely place for a runaway slave from Colossae to visit. It is far more probable that Onesimus should have tried to lose himself in Rome, which though farther away, was more easily reached. Moreover, Philemon could as little as Philippians have been written in the later part of Paul's captivity at Caesarea, since the expectation of release expressed in both is incompatible with his appeal to Caesar. But neither does it suit the early part of his captivity there, for that he should delay his long-projected visit to Rome in order to visit the Churches on the Lycus is highly improbable, especially in view of the foreboding expressed in Acts xx. 25. And how are we to understand Paul's silence about Philip, who had shortly before entertained him, and his failure to enumerate him among the few Jewish Christians who were his fellow-workers? We may then confidently suppose that none of the Epistles of this group was sent from Caesarea.

Although the authenticity of Colossians[1] has been doubted not simply by the Tübingen school but by several other critics, it is now accepted by the majority even of radical critics, though still rejected by some, for example Schmiedel. It was included in the Canon of Marcion, and it is mentioned by name in the Muratorian Canon and by Irenaeus. It is not improbable that it was employed by Justin Martyr and Theophilus, possibly also by some of the Apostolic Fathers. It is no deficiency in external evidence but the internal characteristics of the Epistle which have caused its genuineness to be assailed. The absence of the more conspicuous phrases of Paulinism and the retirement into the background of the chief Pauline ideas has been alleged as an objection, though it is clear that when the controversy which gave them prominence had passed away, they would be likely to lose such prominence, nor is it reasonable to insist that Paul must have written all his letters on the same model as those of the second group. It has also been objected that the conception of the Person of Christ is not Pauline, for while Paul viewed Christ as the Redeemer, Colossians places Him in a transcendental relation to the universe, of which He is represented not simply as the Creator but the goal. But this doctrine is to be found in 1 Cor. viii. 6, xv. 24-28 in an undeveloped though essentially identical form, nor can the high doctrine of the Person

[1] For a fuller discussion of the critical problems of Colossians the writer may refer to his commentary in the *Expositor's Greek Testament*, vol iii.

of Christ constitute an objection for any who accept the Epistle to the Philippians. The emphasis placed on the cosmical significance of the Person of Christ is accounted for by the fact that this was the best defence against the false doctrine which Paul was attacking. Nor can there be any valid objection drawn from the mention of the hierarchies of angels, since if such were recognised by the false teachers it would have been unwise for Paul to have omitted to speak of them. Moreover, there are references in the undoubted Epistles, which harmonise well with what is said of angels in Colossians.

It is, however, the very fact that this heresy is attacked which has been urged with greatest force against the Pauline authorship. It is asserted that this heresy belongs to the post-apostolic period. But it may be said in reply that the type of heresy is rudimentary, such as may well have originated at Colossae by a fusion of Christianity with some one or more of the prevalent speculative systems. And no weight can be attached to the mere argument that this heresy existed in the post-apostolic period. Even if this could be proved, more would be required to invalidate the authenticity of the Epistle. It would have to be shown that the heresy really originated later than the time of Paul. But we have no evidence for this, and there are strong probabilities, quite apart from this Epistle, that the contrary is really the case. It is not second-century Gnosticism which is attacked, probably it is not Gnosticism at all. The differences of style between this Epistle and those of the preceding group have also been urged against its genuineness. There are such differences. The style of Colossians is slow and laboured, without the swift and rushing movement of the earlier polemical Epistles, differing from them also in its form of argument and its choice of logical particles. Synonyms are accumulated and clauses built up by curious combinations of words.

There is a fondness for long compound words, many of which occur nowhere else in Paul, many but seldom. A large proportion is to be found in the second chapter, where the peculiarity of the subject matter largely accounts for the peculiarity of the diction. Here again it is legitimate to fall back on the difference in the circumstances both of Paul and his readers, and the difference in Paul's own state of mind. The four great Epistles are scarcely normal, they are written rapidly while the controversy is at its height, and Paul feels that he is fighting for the very existence of the Gospel. This letter is written in the calm of enforced retirement, and if it is controversial, the kind of controversy required is different.

The points of contact with the Epistle to the Ephesians have also been regarded as suspicious. But this would not, in the ordinary course of things, condemn both Epistles as spurious, but only the one which displayed the secondary form, since the fact that the original was imitated in a letter put forward as Paul's would go to prove that this original was really his. But the relation between the two Epistles is more peculiar. It is not the case that one exhibits throughout the more primitive form. Sometimes Colossians seems to do so, sometimes Ephesians. Holtzmann was led to this result through a very detailed and elaborate investigation. To account for this he put forward the following theory. A letter was written by Paul to the Colossians, and this letter is embedded in our Epistle. On the basis of this letter a later writer composed our Epistle to the Ephesians. He was unwilling that Paul's original letter should lose the benefit of this, so he interpolated into it passages from the Epistle to the Ephesians and also passages directed against Gnosticism, and thus produced our Epistle to the Colossians.

By this hypothesis Holtzmann accounted for the phenomenon referred to that now one and now the other Epistle presented the original form. The complexity of the hypothesis tells fatally against it. It is almost incredible that any writer should set to work on this method. Assuming that he had a much shorter Colossians before him, we could understand his attempt to construct a new Epistle on the basis of it, though it would not be easy to explain why he did not draw also on the other Pauline Epistles. But that he should return to give the original epistle the benefit of his own contributions to Ephesians is hardly to be credited. What practical purpose could be served by this expansion? He had already secured by the composition of Ephesians the publication of these thoughts. And what a hazardous enterprise to substitute the new Colossians for the epistle which was well known to the Church at Colossae! And why not have said all he wanted to say in one letter, our Ephesians expanded by attacks on the false teachers? Moreover, there is no trace in the textual history of the process through which Holtzmann imagines that the literature has gone. His theory was very carefully examined by Von Soden, who showed that many of the passages condemned by Holtzmann as interpolations were not at all inconsistent with a Pauline authorship. He also showed that Holtzmann's reconstruction of the original Epistle was open to serious objections. He himself rejected the following only: i. 15-20, ii. 10, 15, 18b. But at a later time he accepted the genuineness of the Epistle almost as it stands, though he has recently returned to his rejection of i. 15-20. The genuineness of Colossians has important consequences for Ephesians, since if Holtzmann is right in asserting that several parallel passages do not depend on Colossians, we are shut up to the view that both Epistles came from the same hand, and that the hand of Paul. In such a case we can hardly speak of secondary or derived passages, as we should if two authors were concerned. But in any case we may feel some confidence that the authenticity of

Colossians will come to be accepted in the near future by general consent.

The authenticity of the Epistle to the Ephesians has been much more widely denied than that of the sister Epistle, and is still rejected by many eminent critics. The external evidence is good. It was probably used by Ignatius and Polycarp and the author of the Shepherd of Hermas, though this of course would be consistent with a date at the beginning of the second century. It was included by Marcion in his collection, and is mentioned in the Muratorian Canon. It is quoted as Paul's by Irenaeus and later writers. Moreover, it is likely that it was employed by the author of 1 Peter, which is probably the genuine work of that writer. In that case our Epistle must be genuine. If 1 Peter belongs to the reign of Domitian or Trajan, or if the literary relation between the two Epistles should be reversed, we cannot argue so confidently from their connexion to the genuineness of the Epistle.

If genuine, it can hardly be doubted that the Epistle was not sent to Ephesus, at any rate exclusively. It would be incredible that in a letter to a Church where he had laboured so long and to which he was bound by such ties of affection, Paul should abstain from personal greeting or reminiscences of his work in Ephesus and should give no sign of intimate personal relations with his readers. It would be still more strange that he should speak as in iii. 2-4 as if their knowledge of his ministry was only by hearsay, and his own knowledge of their faith was of a similar character (i. 15). In fact if we had to believe that the letter if Pauline must have been sent to Ephesus, this would strongly reinforce the already serious arguments against its authenticity. This, however, is not the case. It is true that the title 'to the Ephesians' was given to the Epistle quite early, and that tradition regarded it as addressed to that Church. But Marcion spoke of it as the Epistle to the Laodiceans, which may of course have been a critical deduction from the reference in Col. iv. 16 to the Epistle from Laodicea, but may point to acquaintance with a copy of the Epistle bearing that title. If the words 'in Ephesus' in i. 1 are original, we should be obliged to accept the traditional theory of the destination. They are omitted, however, by our two best manuscripts ℵ and B, and struck out by the corrector of 67, who has preserved many old readings. They were not read by Origen, and Basil says that all the old copies did not contain them. Tertullian charges Marcion with falsifying the title; it is therefore clear that he did not himself read 'in Ephesus' in the text or he would have appealed to this. On the other hand, it may be urged that it is in all other MSS. and Versions and supported by the majority of the Fathers.

The omission of the words also creates a serious difficulty. On the usual theory that the letter was addressed to several Churches which harmonises well with its general character and the double title, it is frequently assumed that a blank was left in the copies to be filled with the name of the Church to which any copy was delivered. It is in that case remarkable that the oldest authorities mention no place at all. We should have expected various readings but not complete omission. It is nevertheless not easy to believe that the original text was identical with the usual text save for the omission of 'in Ephesus.' The best translation of such a text would be 'to the saints who are also believing (or faithful) in Christ Jesus.' But this implies that there might be saints who were not believers. P. Ewald suggests that there may be an error in the text, due to wearing of the papyrus at the corner. He reads τοῖς ἀγαπητοῖς for τοῖς ἁγίοις τοῖς, 'to those who are beloved and believing.' The hypothesis of a circular letter best accounts for its general character, for the absence of personal salutations and the discussion of local problems. If so, it may be identical with the letter from

Laodicea (Col. iv. 16), though this is uncertain. It is on the whole probable that Ephesus was included among the Churches to which it was addressed. This would best account for the fact that it passed into circulation as an Epistle to the Ephesians.

But while the hypothesis of a circular letter escapes some of the objections to the authenticity, several still remain. The most serious is that based on the style. The sentences are long, cumbrous and involved to a degree unparalleled elsewhere in Paul. The collocation of words and clauses creates innumerable ambiguities, which involve the exegesis of the Epistle in constant uncertainty. The ideas are also thought to be in some instances un-Pauline. Redemption is assigned to Christ rather than to God; reconciliation is explained as uniting Jew and Gentile, not God and man. The Second Coming is no longer expected in the near future; on the contrary, Paul speaks of the ages which are to come. The conception of the Church has advanced in a Catholic direction. Montanist tendencies were at one time discovered in it, and though these can no longer be taken seriously, several consider that there are references to Gnosticism. Difficulty is occasioned by the association of the other apostles with Paul in the revelation of the calling of the Gentiles and particularly in the objective reference to 'the holy apostles and prophets' (iii. 5 and 6). Finally, the relations with Colossians have much more frequently been urged against the genuineness of this than of the companion Epistle from the time when De Wette stigmatised it as a diffuse expansion of Colossians which had lost its unity through the omission of the polemic against the false teachers.

The weightiest objection is the un-Pauline character of the style. It is true that the force of this argument is broken for all who accept the genuineness of Colossians by the similar phenomena which constitute a link between this and the other letters. We must also allow for the influence of enforced inactivity, but though these considerations mitigate the difficulty, they cannot be said entirely to remove it. There is no necessary antagonism between the ascription of redemption to Christ and its ascription to God. Similar statements in other connexions may be quoted from the undoubted Epistles. Thus in Rom. xi. 36 all things are through God, in 1 Cor. viii. 6 all are through Christ. Reconciliation between Jew and Gentile does not exclude reconciliation to God, which in fact is expressed in ii. 16. The ages to come may very well be considered as following the Parousia rather than as preceding it. We have no ground for the assumption that the conception of the Catholic Church must have been later than Paul, indeed it is quite in a line both with his thought and action. His attempt to keep the Churches together expressed in the collection for the saints at Jerusalem, his feeling that local idiosyncrasies must be curbed by the general practice of the Church (1 Cor. xiv. 33, 36), his imperialist instincts which had controlled his missionary activity and which were nowhere so likely to find expression as in Rome, all urged him in this direction. Nor was the idea wholly a new one. Gal. i. 13, 1 Cor. x. 32, xii. 28 speak of the Church apparently in the universal and not in the local sense. Paul was strongly impressed with the importance of unity, and would check a spirit of exclusiveness whether it came from Gentile or from Jew.

As to traces of Gnosticism it may be said, that if they are not present in the Epistle to the Colossians, we need not look for them here, but if they are to be found in this Epistle, this no more proves its spuriousness than it does that of Colossians. It is certainly remarkable that Paul should associate the other apostles with himself as recipients of the revelation that the Gentiles were fellow-heirs with the Jews. Yet he certainly associated them with himself in the general Gospel that he preached (1 Cor. xv. 11). He had won them to his side in his conflict for the Gentiles; the case of Cornelius might seem to warrant the strict accuracy of the statement. It is no doubt difficult to believe that Paul could have spoken of 'the holy apostles,' which sounds like the reverential designation of a later writer, especially as he included himself among them. We must remember, however, that the term does not carry with it the associations of our English word, it is not a claim to saintliness so much as a recognition of dedication. We might of course regard the adjective as a later addition, though we should have expected it to have been inserted in other places as well. The relationship to Colossians, as already pointed out, when considered in the light of Holtzmann's investigation, tells rather in favour of than against the authenticity of the Epistle. The explicit and repeated claims to Pauline authorship must be seriously respected, and cannot be set aside except for grave reasons. It is true that a measure of doubt hangs over the Epistle, yet there is much to be said on the other side. It is more probable that so great an Epistle expressing in many respects Paul's mind so well should be attributed to him rather than to another. The case for its spuriousness has not been made out, and till that is done it is safer to accept its genuineness.

The Epistle to the Philippians

This Epistle is so generally recognised as authentic, even by radical critics, that little need be said about it. It was, of course, rejected by Baur and the earlier members of the Tübingen school with the exception of Hilgenfeld, who has been followed by most recent critics, apart from Holsten and one or two others. Baur objected to it on various grounds, all of which were frivolous. The mention of bishops and deacons pointed to a post-Pauline stage of ecclesiastical organisation, there was no originality in the letter, it showed traces of something like Gnosticism, and the doctine of justification was not that of Paul. Clement is identified with the Roman Clement, the disciple of Peter, and thus the Epistle shows the union of the Pauline and Petrine parties which were supposed to be typified by the two women whom Paul exhorts to be of the same mind in the Lord. That the Epistle, however, did not suit the conciliatory function thus ascribed to it by Baur, is shown clearly enough by the strong attack on the Judaizers in ch. iii. Nor could the numerous personal notices be readily accommodated to the idea of a tendency writing.

Holsten thinks the Epistle was written soon after Paul's death. His argument against the genuineness rests largely on the divergence between its doctrine and that of Paul, which he thinks he has discovered. But there is no discrepancy between the claim to have been blameless in (outward) fulfilment of the Law's command (iii. 6) and the confession of failure to attain inward conformity to the Law which we find in Rom. vii. Nor does Paul acquiesce in preaching (i. 15-18) which had in Galatians drawn down his solemn anathema. It is no doubt true that the Christology is more developed than in the four great Epistles, yet it is not in conflict with them, and does not go beyond what they imply. It may be gravely doubted whether Paul would have recognised the doctrine of Christ as the heavenly man, which is constantly imputed to him, but if he had, he might still have spoken of the Incarnation as in ii. 5-8. Nor is there any disagreement between the doctrine of justification as exhibited here and as shown in the four great Epistles. As for the style, that again has little weight, unless the Epistles of the second group are made a standard to which all Epistles of the apostle in order to be counted genuine must conform. And with what hope of success could the writer attempt to palm off a spurious letter on the Philippian Church, soon after Paul's death? The external evidence is good. It was apparently used by Ignatius and is referred to by Polycarp. It was in Marcion's Canon, and is mentioned in the Muratorian Canon. It is quoted in the letter of the Churches of Lyons and Vienne, and from Irenaeus onwards it is regularly quoted as Paul's. Few things in modern criticism are better assured than the authenticity of this Epistle, and it may be accepted without any misgiving.

CHAPTER VII

THE PASTORAL EPISTLES

UNDER this title are included the two Epistles to Timothy and the Epistle to Titus. These Epistles are rejected by critics more universally than any other of the Pauline Epistles, and many would regard their spuriousness as placed beyond question. This decision is not reached on the external evidence, which is perhaps as early in attestation as can be reasonably expected. They are included in the Muratorian Canon, and quoted by Irenaeus and later writers as Paul's. Their existence in some form early in the second century is attested by quotations in Polycarp. On the other hand, Marcion did not admit them to his Canon. This has been attributed to dislike of their contents, and it can hardly be denied that he could not have accepted the condemnation of asceticism and docetism which they contain or the estimate placed on the Jewish Scriptures. But similar contradictions of Marcion's doctrine are to be found in Epistles which he accepted, and it is not easy to see why he should have hesitated in this case any more than in others to assume that the original writing had been falsified by interpolations and include them in an expurgated form in his Canon. We are therefore not at liberty to brush aside his dissent as based on dogmatic rather than historical grounds; one to whom Paul's lightest genuine word was so precious must, if he knew the letters, even though letters to individuals not to Churches, have weighed their genuineness and found it wanting, not wholly one may believe on subjective grounds. But the internal evidence is regarded as decisive. And this has been felt so strongly that they have been condemned as spurious, not simply by the Tübingen school and practically all advanced critics, but by critics who may be commonly reckoned on the conservative side. Schleiermacher and even Neander rejected 1 Timothy. Meyer, Beyschlag and Sabatier rejected all three. Even those scholars who accept their authenticity as Godet, Hort, Sanday, admit that the objections are real.

The first objection which may be taken is that the Epistles cannot be assigned to any period of the apostle's life otherwise known to us. It is now generally agreed, though a few scholars still maintain the contrary, that the attempts to place them in the period covered by the Acts of the Apostles have not succeeded, and that if they are genuine, they must be dated after Paul had been released from the imprisonment recorded in Acts. This resolves itself into the question whether Paul was released. If he was not released the Epistles as they stand cannot be genuine; if he was they need not be. A famous passage in Clement of Rome (chap. v.) has been interpreted as favouring the view that Paul visited Spain. This would involve his release from imprisonment, as he certainly had not been to Spain before it. But it is questionable if Clement's language means this. For while the phrase 'having come to the bound of the West' strongly suggests Spain rather than Rome when taken by itself, this is neutralised by the words which follow, 'and having witnessed before the rulers, he departed thus from the world,' which evidently refer to the Roman imprisonment, and therefore fix 'the bound of the West' as Rome rather than Spain. Further, Clement seems to date Paul's death before the Neronian persecution, for he says that a great multitude was gathered to Peter and Paul, referring to the martyrs who suffered under Nero.

It has also been urged that if Paul was not released the Book of Acts ends very strangely. But to this it may be replied that if he was released, it ends more strangely still. A leading feature in the Acts is the way in which the author constantly brings out the favour shown by the Roman governors and officials towards Christianity. If he had been able to end his work with the statement that Paul's trial before the Roman Emperor had issued in his triumphant acquittal, the apology for Christianity to the Roman Empire would have received a splendid climax. Nor is this met by the argument that in any case Paul was finally condemned by the Emperor. For the answer to this was that in Nero's better days he had been acquitted, and condemned only in the later period of misgovernment. The fact that this climax is not found is in itself almost decisive against the hypothesis of release. This is confirmed by the prediction of Paul in his address to the elders at Miletus, that they should see his face no more. For, while Paul may have uttered a foreboding which was falsified by the events, and was in fact later contradicted by him in his expectation of release from imprisonment, we have to remember that Luke not only includes it in his account of the speech, but pointedly calls attention to it, with no hint that they did see him again after all. Nor is it probable that we can account for Luke's stopping where he does on the hypothesis that he intended to add a third book to his history, giving a narrative of Paul's trial and release and subsequent career. He can hardly have broken off in the middle of the story of the imprisonment. On the other hand, assuming that Paul was not released, the author has closed the story in the most skilful manner, emphasising that for two full years Paul was in his own hired lodging, receiving all who came to him, preaching the Kingdom of God and teaching the things concerning the Lord Jesus Christ with all freedom without any hindrance. This conclusion leaves the reader with the impression that while a prisoner in Rome, under the eye of the Imperial government itself, Paul was allowed the utmost possible liberty in preaching the Gospel, and had to submit to no interference from the authorities. A plea for toleration could scarcely be more happily conceived. It has been argued that according to Roman Law at the time Paul must have been released. But Paul was probably not put to death as a Christian, but as a disturber of the peace. However innocent he might be, the fact that his presence had caused numerous disturbances in various parts of the Empire, would at any time have been held sufficient reason for his execution. Perhaps we might adduce the Pastoral Epistles themselves as evidence for his release. If they are genuine Paul must have been released, if spurious the author or authors by placing them outside the period covered by the Acts testified to a belief that Paul's life did not end with the imprisonment then recorded. But stress cannot be laid on this, for writers of spurious literature did not as a rule trouble themselves too minutely about considerations of this kind.

Difficulties are also alleged as to the personal and other details mentioned in the Epistles. That Timothy is still spoken of as young is not unnatural in the mouth of Paul, considering the relations which had subsisted between them. What is strange, however, is that Paul after leaving Timothy and Titus should have felt it necessary to write these elaborate instructions to them, which might just as well have been given while he was with them. It may be said that the letters would be valuable for purposes of reference, and that Paul knowing the failings of Timothy would feel that a letter such as 1 Timothy would be useful to him in enforcing discipline, since he could, if necessary, show it to any who might be disposed to question his action. This may pass as an explanation, though it can hardly be called satisfactory, and this objection must be left to weigh against the genuineness. It also seems strange that in a letter to Timothy, his chosen helper, who had been with him so long, Paul should need to assure him in such strong language as is used, that he was a preacher and an apostle, and a teacher of the Gentiles (1 Tim. ii. 7; cf. 2 Tim. i. 11). It is urged on the other hand that Paul was writing to the Churches indirectly, and that this might be meant for them. This possibly mitigates the difficulty, it certainly does not remove it, and it also must stand as a real objection. We need attach no importance to the mention of 'kings' in the plural (1 Tim. ii. 2) as if the author must have had the system of joint emperorship in view. The precept to pray for them is quite general, therefore there is no need to relegate the Epistle to a date later than 137.

Nor is it necessary to accept Baur's assertion that in the phrase 'antitheses of knowledge falsely so called' (1 vi. 20) the term 'antitheses' is taken from the title of Marcion's treatise, and 'knowledge falsely so called' from Hegesippus. It is probable that the latter phrase was not used by Hegesippus at all, but is simply due to Eusebius himself (cf. Eus., *H.E.* iii. 32 with iv. 22). Even if it were, this proves nothing, for it is mere assumption to say that a Jewish Christian like Hegesippus would not have quoted a work attributed to Paul. If, as several scholars still think, the former phrase really refers to Marcion's *Antitheses*, the lateness of the Epistle would not be proved. The Pastoral Epistles as a whole seem to have been known to Polycarp, they must therefore have been composed early in the second century at the latest. The reference to Marcion's work would therefore have to be treated as a later interpolation, along with several other passages, which in Harnack's judgment, as in that of some other scholars, reflect the condition of things in the middle of the second century. But the reference to Marcion is by no means certain. More suspicious is the apparent quotation of a saying of Jesus as Scripture (1 Tim. v. 18). But this may be explained by the fact that a quotation from Deuteronomy immediately follows the reference to Scripture, so that this reference may not be intended to cover the saying of Jesus. The objection that the injunction to make no new converts bishops implies that a considerable interval had elapsed since the foundation of the Churches referred to, while true in itself is not serious, for these Churches had been founded long enough to warrant this.

One of the most serious difficulties is that caused by the stage of ecclesiastical organisation which seems to have been reached. It is not clear that in the case of Paul a belief in the speedy Second Coming of Christ would be incompatible with attention to details of organisation. There are, in fact, indications to the contrary in his undisputed letters. Paul united in himself the fervent anticipations of the early Christians generally with a cool practical common sense which made him act as if the Second Coming might be for a long time delayed. As to the actual details of organisation, it is important to observe that presbyters and bishops are not distinguished from each other, as in the congregational episcopacy so fervently championed by Ignatius. We have only two orders and not, as in the second century, three. The position of Timothy and Titus does not correspond to that of the bishop of a later time. They are rather Paul's representatives, legates entrusted with temporary missions. What does strike us as strange is that so much stress is laid on the organisation and on the ecclesiastical appointment, so little on the gifts which members of the Church could exercise independently of official position. This is explained partly by the hypothesis that the spiritual gifts were dying out, partly by the fact that Paul wished to prepare the Church to meet the loss caused by his own death and that of the other leaders. It is questionable, however, whether these explanations are satisfactory. It is not certain that the gifts were dying out, nor is it easy to understand why Paul should not have felt it necessary to give these instructions at a somewhat earlier period when his life was imperilled, yet we do not find them in earlier Epistles. The strength of the argument against the genuineness lies here, as in some other cases, not in the details, where the edge of criticism may be turned, but in the general improbability that Paul should have had such a situation to deal with as is presupposed, and have dealt with it in this way. It is not quite like him to be so preoccupied with the details of organisation. On the other hand it is not at all impossible. Granted that the gifts were dying out, his practical instinct would lead him to provide an organisation to take their place.

Another difficulty is raised by the references to the false teachers. It is generally assumed by those who deny the authenticity that the heresy attacked was some form of second century Gnosticism. This requires the proof of two propositions, that the false teaching is Gnostic in its character and that, if so, it could not have been in existence so early as the lifetime of Paul. It must be remembered that similar allegations have been made with reference to the Colossian heresy, but probably erroneously. In determining the character of the heresy we must distinguish between the descriptions given of false teaching already present and of that which is predicted, only the former being strictly relevant to the question of date, though the germs of future developments will no doubt be present (1 Tim. iv. 1-3, 2 Tim. iii. 1-5). Further, when individuals are singled out it cannot be assumed that they represent the general direction which the false teaching took (2 Tim. ii. 17 *sq.*). And we must not identify non-Christian teachers with heretical Christians (Titus i. 15, 16).

The heresy was clearly Judaic in type, but not Pharisaic. It reminds us rather of that attacked in the Epistle to the Colossians. This of course does not exclude the possibility that Jewish were associated with heathen or Gnostic elements. Hort has examined the nature of the heresy in his *Judaistic Christianity*, and reached the conclusion that 'there is a total want of evidence for anything pointing to even rudimentary Gnosticism or Essenism.' The 'genealogies' he explains not as the strings of emanations, such as we find in Gnostic writers, but as the legendary histories of the patriarchs, especially such as we find in the Book of Jubilees. The term was used in this sense. The phrase 'antitheses of knowledge falsely so called' he says cannot refer to Marcion's work *Antitheses*. 'Knowledge' he explains as the technical term for the body of law based on the decisions of the rabbis, and the 'antitheses' as 'the endless contrasts of decisions founded on endless distinctions which played so large a part in the casuistry of the scribes as interpreters of the Law.' If he is right in this there is no need on the ground of the heresy attacked to bring the Epistles below the date of Paul. At the same time there is the difficulty that Paul should have felt it necessary to warn trusted disciples and representatives such as Timothy and Titus against embracing these opinions.

Another series of objections is drawn from the theological character of the Epistles which is said to be at variance with the theology of Paul, or to have lost its distinctive features, to be moralistic in tone rather than evangelical. Perhaps the most significant and characteristic peculiarity is the use of the word 'faith.' In these Epistles the term is almost used in the sense of orthodoxy, or even of the actual contents of the wholesome doctrine, whereas with Paul faith has a very different sense. It is true that in Rom. xii. 6 the objective sense of the word 'faith' is supposed to be present, but even if so it is questionable whether a single instance matches at all the very definite sense the term has in the Pastorals. It is a watchword of the author, and we have no parallel for this in the earlier Epistles. And this insistence on the importance of sound doctrine is also far more prominent than in any other Epistle of Paul. More significance attaches to these general characteristics than to specific differences that have been pointed out. These are inconclusive, and it is needless to linger upon them.

Still weightier is the objection derived from the style and language of these Epistles. No doubt undue stress has been laid on the number of words peculiar to this group. Those that are really significant are not exceptionally numerous. As in Colossians the false teaching attacked determines to some extent the character of the phraseology, and it is quite conceivable that Paul's vocabulary may have been enriched in the interval. It is not here, however, that the real difficulty lies. The old energy of thought and expression has gone, and the greater smoothness and continuity in the grammar is a poor compensation for the lack of grip and of continuity in the thought. We may appeal to the change in circumstances, to the exhausting character of his labours and the weariness of old age, and to the fact that senility often overtakes men of such strenuous thought and action at a rapid rate. Yet it is questionable if the interval which separates the latest of the imprisonment Epistles from 1 Timothy would not be incredibly short to account for such striking change. In that Epistle and in a less degree in Titus it is difficult to hear the true Pauline ring. This does not well admit of detailed proof, it is a matter of impression, but to those who are impressed by it, it is of all arguments among the most cogent. There is a peculiar phraseology which belongs only to these Epistles and is found more or less in all of them but not in the other writings of Paul, and it is not clear that it is accounted for by changed circumstances or the increasing infirmity of the apostle.

The arguments against the genuineness may be summarised as follows, neglecting those which seem to be without force. It is strange that Paul should have written letters of this kind to such companions and disciples as Timothy and Titus, and that he should have felt it necessary to assert to them his apostleship and warn them to keep clear of heretical teaching. If the letters fall outside the period covered by the Acts they are probably not genuine, since Paul's imprisonment, there recorded, seems to have ended not in release, but in death. As to organisation we find much stress on ecclesiastical appointment, little on the spiritual gifts, and it is not quite like Paul to be occupied so much with details of this kind. The general emphasis on the importance of sound doctrine and the use of faith as almost equivalent to orthodoxy are strange in Paul. So too the tone of the letters is moralistic rather than evangelical, though the latter element is not absent. And finally the style is quite unique and unlike that of the other Epistles, and the ring of the letters does not remind us of Paul.

In favour of the genuineness, apart from the good external evidence, the following arguments may be urged. It is very improbable that any one writing in Paul's name with a distinct purpose in view should have inserted some of the trivial details or injunctions which are quite natural in a letter of Paul, but by no means natural in a letter that is not genuine. Such is the reference to the cloke left at Troas with the books and the parchments. There are also numerous personal references which give a strong impression of authenticity, and are unlikely to have been written by any one else. These details and personal references, however, occur almost entirely in two passages in the Second Epistle to Timothy, i. 15-18 and iv. 9-21. Pfleiderer and Hausrath think that these sections are genuine Pauline fragments, though it is not quite clear to what circumstances the latter should be assigned. It is, of course, difficult to understand how these fragments were detached from their original connexion, and this tells against the theory. And it might be argued that the admission of these fragments as genuine guarantees the genuineness of the Epistle in which they are found, and that it is arbitrary to detach these sections which tell so strongly in favour of its genuineness. It may be granted that these sections are not so closely united with the Epistle as to be inseparable from it. The case then resolves itself to this: Are the arguments against the genuineness of this Epistle as a whole so strong that it must be rejected? If so there is nothing arbitrary in trying to rescue any passages that may be Pauline. On the other hand if the arguments against the genuineness are not so strong, the fact that these sections are incorporated will tell strongly in favour of the genuineness of the Epistle.

Several recent scholars who cannot accept the genuineness of the Epistles as they stand recognise a much larger Pauline element in them than these two sections. It is usual to find the largest genuine matter in 2 Timothy and the least in 1 Timothy, and this accords well with the general impression made by the reading of the Epistles. Thus Harnack thinks that very considerable sections of 2 Timothy and perhaps a bare third of Titus might be regarded as genuine in substance, though, apart from the historical sections, few Pauline verses have remained quite unaltered. In 1 Timothy not a single verse can be indicated which clearly bears the stamp of Pauline origin, still it is not improbable that even it contains some Pauline material. Harnack argues in favour of a release and a second imprisonment, but as he adopts the earlier chronology he places the release in 59 and the death in 64. Apart from late additions he dates the Pastoral Epistles 90-110.

McGiffert thinks that in 2 Timothy the whole of the first chapter except possibly *v.* 6b and certainly *vv.* 12-14, perhaps most of ii. 1, 8-13 and the whole of chapter iv. except *vv.* 3, 4, may probably be Paul's. Titus contains, he thinks, the following Pauline elements, iii. 1-7, 12, 13, and possibly parts of the first chapter. There are perhaps slight scattered elements of Paul's writings in 1 Timothy. He denies a release from the imprisonment mentioned in the Acts, and has therefore to place these genuine Pauline elements before that imprisonment came to an end. Bartlet, who agrees with McGiffert that Paul was not released, holds that the letters are, on the whole, genuine throughout. He gets over some of the difficulties caused by the denial of a second imprisonment by admitting with McGiffert that 2 Timothy combines portions of two letters written at different times and under different circumstances.

Many scholars insist that the Epistles must be taken as they stand and are either entirely genuine or entirely spurious. Hort admits that the objections are real, but says that to the best of his belief the Epistles are genuine, and that not in part since the theory of extensive interpolation does not work out well in detail. Hort's judgment on such a matter deserves the most respectful deference even from those who are compelled to adopt a different conclusion. The two points on which the present writer feels clearest are that the Epistles cannot have come from Paul's hand in their present form, yet that they contain not a little Pauline material. The impossibility of elaborating a wholly satisfactory theory and separating the genuine nucleus from later accretions, can hardly override these primary results. It would be unreasonable to demand that critical analysis should achieve its work before the composite character of the documents can be admitted.

CHAPTER VIII

THE EPISTLE TO THE HEBREWS[1]

THE Epistle to the Hebrews contains no indication either of the author's name or of the community to which it was addressed. Its existence is attested by quotations in Clement of Rome which are woven into the author's arguments without any suggestion that the words are borrowed. This use assures us that it belongs to the first century. We may first discuss the question of its destination. The title 'to the Hebrews' might in itself suggest that it was an encyclical letter addressed to Jewish Christians. But assuming the integrity of the Epistle this view is impossible, for the letter was clearly written to a definite community to which the author himself belonged. Where this community was situated is, however, a matter only of uncertain inference. The Epistle has naturally been regarded as addressed to Jerusalem. Here the temptation to abandon the Gospel for the Law would be most keenly felt, especially with the pressure of persecution, the fascinations of the cultus, the sense that their country and their race needed them in its sore distress. No objection to this can be rightly based either on vi. 10 or xii. 4. In view of the fact that many Christians in Jerusalem must have heard Christ, the language of ii. 3, which implies that the community had been converted to Christianity by those who had heard Him, certainly does not favour

[1] The conclusions adopted in this chapter rest on considerations much more fully stated in the writer's commentary in the *Century Bible*.

Jerusalem. It is not likely that Timothy would have had any influence at Jerusalem nor yet the writer himself, inasmuch as he not only writes in Greek rather than in Aramaic, but is limited in his use of the Old Testament to the Septuagint. We should certainly have expected that the religious conditions in Jerusalem would have been much more definitely reflected in the Epistle. It is probable that the author wishes his readers to break decisively with Judaism as a religious system, hence his description of that religion is almost entirely Biblical and not concerned with the temple ritual. Had he been writing to Christians in Jerusalem who were under the spell of the worship there, some explicit reference to this worship would almost certainly have been included.

It is not unnatural, in view of the Alexandrian character of the theology, that the Epistle should have been thought to have been sent to Alexandria, but the writer may have learnt his theology elsewhere than in that city, and his origin says nothing as to the Church with which he was connected when the Epistle was written. The argument that the description of the sanctuary suits the Egyptian temple at Leontopolis better than the temple at Jerusalem is irrelevant even if true, since the author's discussion is based exclusively on the tabernacle. What seems fatal to the Alexandrian destination is that in the catechetical school at Alexandria the tradition affirmed Pauline authorship.

Much the most probable suggestion is that it was sent to Rome. The only geographical indication in the Epistle is in the words 'they of Italy salute you,' and the most obvious though not the only possible interpretation is that a group of Italian Christians who are absent from Italy send greetings to their fellow-countrymen in Italy. If in Italy, it is most natural to seek the community in Rome. This is confirmed by the fact that it is in Rome that our first evidence of the existence of the Epistle is to be found, namely in Clement of Rome.

It was probably not sent, however, to the whole Church of Rome. The composition of this Church was predominantly Gentile, and in spite of the high authority which the view that the readers were Gentiles can claim, the present writer is convinced that the readers were of Jewish nationality. The allusion to the circumstances of the readers suggests a small and homogeneous group in a large city We may best think of a house-community, such as we find mentioned in Rom. xvi., or perhaps a Jewish Christian synagogue (cf. x. 25, 'not forsaking your own assembly'). It is easier to understand why the name of the author should have quickly faded into oblivion if it went to a small and rapidly disappearing group in the Roman Church.

That the readers were Jewish Christians has been held practically without exception till a comparatively recent period. It is now considered by many scholars that they were Gentiles or that the author writes without any reference to their nationality. There are of course some passages in the Epistle to which this view seems to do a fuller justice. Especially the enumeration of elementary doctrines in vi. 1, 2 would, it is said, suit those who came to Christianity from Paganism, but not those who passed into it through Judaism. They would lie behind the Jews' conversion to Christianity, but would need to be dealt with in the instruction of Gentile converts. Moreover, the faults against which the writer warns his readers are, it is urged, characteristic of a Gentile rather than a Jewish Christian community. The former argument has real weight, yet it is by no means conclusive. If it is said that these were doctrines which a Jew on becoming a Christian would not need to learn, it may be argued, on the other hand, that it was precisely the doctrines which were in a sense common to Judaism and Christianity which needed to be interpreted from the Christian point of view. The second argument depends for its force on a too optimistic view of converts from Judaism. Their moral level was unquestionably higher than that of pagan Christians, yet exhortations of the kind contained in the Epistle were certainly not superfluous when addressed to Jewish Christians.

For the positive proof that the readers were Jewish Christians we may cheerfully abandon some of the inconclusive arguments which have been adduced and lay stress on the Epistle as a whole. The author's method of handling his argument seems to be conclusive on this point. He writes no academic dissertation, but a word of exhortation to save his readers from threatened apostasy. And this was apostasy, not as is often said to paganism or complete irreligion, but to Judaism. If we concentrate our attention on details and phrases such as 'to fall away from the living God,' the other view gains a certain plausibility. But it is the Epistle as a whole which decisively negatives this view. For in a letter designed to secure his readers from a lapse or relapse into paganism we should have expected much that we do not find in the Epistle, and we find much in it that we should not have expected. We should have anticipated an attack on paganism, instead of which we have an elaborate many-sided demonstration that Judaism is inferior to Christianity. It is futile to say that the author's arguments carry no conviction to modern readers. One is at a loss to know what conviction they could have carried to any readers exposed to temptations from heathenism. It is quite a mistake to assume that it is only in a misinterpretation of xiii. 9-16 that we find a warrant for the traditional view. The whole tenor of the writer's argument is designed to prove that what the readers think they have in Judaism they have in a perfect form in Christianity.

What in the present writer's judgment definitely proves the Jewish Christian character of the readers and that their temptation was to relapse into Judaism is the use made of the Old Testament. It is quite beside the mark to say that the Old Testament was regarded as authoritative by Gentile as well as by Jewish Christians. It is more to the point to observe that the grounds of acceptance were very different. The Jew whether Christian or not accepted the Old Testament as the sacred book of his nation, his belief might be confirmed by Christianity but it was essentially independent of it. With the Gentile Christian the case was altogether different. The Old Testament meant nothing to him apart from his Christianity. It was as an integral portion of his new religion that he recognised its authority. Of what use then was it to supply a Gentile in danger of apostasy from Christianity with arguments drawn from a book in which he believed simply because he was a Christian? The author's argument has force only if his readers accepted the Old Testament independently of their acceptance of the Gospel, and this suits Jewish Christians but not Gentiles. It may be added that, even setting aside the inconclusive details, there are many phrases in the Epistle which point much more naturally to Jewish Christian than to Gentile readers, but where the main argument is so conclusive it is less necessary to lay stress on minor points.

We may now consider the question of its authorship. In view of the fact that it was employed so early in the Roman Church, the attitude adopted to it by later Western writers is very curious. Its use by Hermas and Justin Martyr is uncertain. It has left no trace on the other Apostolic Fathers or apologists. The Gnostics ignored it. Marcion's failure to include it in his Canon may be due to ignorance of it or dislike of its contents. It shows that even if he knew it he did not consider it to be Paul's. Its absence from the Muratorian Canon probably implies that the writer attributed to it no canonical authority, though if we had his list in its original form it is possible that we might find it included. One of the most striking facts is that Irenaeus does not employ it in his chief work, in which the Pauline Epistles are so extensively used. He is said to have quoted the Epistle, and Hippolytus certainly did so, though we are told that he did not accept the Pauline authorship. Caius, another Roman Christian, also refused to attribute it to Paul. This attitude characterised the Western Church till the time of Augustine and Jerome.

It was claimed for Barnabas in North Africa by Tertullian, on what grounds we do not know. He betrays no knowledge that any one had ever thought of Paul as its author. Cyprian and Novatian derived from it no arguments in favour of their own special views, though the Epistle might have been plausibly quoted to support them.

It is in Alexandria that we find the earliest evidence for the Pauline authorship. At first the main difficulty seems to have been that the Epistle made no claim to be Pauline and that the style rather resembled Luke's. Origen dealt much more thoroughly with the question. He was himself struck by the divergence in style and apparently by the different complexion of the thought from that of Paul. In spite of this feeling, which seems to shine through his expression, he acquiesces in the tradition that the thoughts are Paul's but holds that the Epistle was actually composed by one who wrote down his teaching from memory with his own annotations, possibly as tradition suggests by Clement of Rome or Luke. Naturally the restrictions laid by Origen on the full recognition of the Pauline authorship came to be disregarded in the Eastern Church, where it was recognised as Paul's by the fourth century. In the Western Church it was generally rejected. Augustine and Jerome were alike hesitant about it but yielded to Eastern opinion and accepted the Pauline authorship, and this secured its acceptance in the Western Church.

Of the names associated with the Epistle in antiquity we may at once set aside Luke and Clement of Rome, the former on the ground of his Gentile origin, the latter in virtue of his marked inferiority in grasp and insight. The external evidence for Paul and Barnabas cannot be regarded as strong. The Alexandrian evidence for Paul is late, and more than cancelled by the attitude in the rest of the Church. Had there been any ground for recognising Pauline authorship the Epistle could not have had the fate which overtook it in the Western Church. It was known in the Church of Rome before the close of the first century, but Clement's use of it without indication of author's name or even of the fact that he is quoting is not easy to reconcile with Paul's authorship and suggests that there was some reason for this reticence. Nor would the attitude of Tertullian be easy to explain, for he is obviously unaware that any claim can be made for Paul and half apologises for appealing to a work which could not rank with apostolic writings. His own view that it was the work of Barnabas is more difficult to estimate. The matter-of-fact way in which he assumes it indicates that he was conscious of having a body of opinion behind him, and it may have been derived from the Montanists of Asia Minor. On the external evidence the case is stronger for Barnabas than for Paul, but it is weak for both.

Turning now to the internal evidence, the one fixed point is that the Epistle was not written by Paul. This is conclusively proved by every line of evidence. The absence of his name at the beginning has no parallel in his Epistles. The style, as even the Alexandrians saw, is inconsistent with his authorship, the personality revealed in the writing is of an order altogether different from that of Paul, the formulae of quotation from the Old Testament are quite different, and so is the text of the Septuagint employed. The Epistle is planned on quite other lines, the exhortations being inserted in the course of the argument, not massed together at the close. The theology is constructed from a standpoint which differs radically from Paul's, a divergence which does not touch individual points of doctrine alone but goes through the entire systems. And in view of Paul's emphatic assertion that he had learnt his Gospel from no human teacher, we must conclude that he cannot have penned the confession of second-hand instruction received from the immediate hearers of Jesus.

If the view were correct that the Epistle was sent to Jerusalem, we could think of no member of the Pauline circle more acceptable to the Christians there than Barnabas. If, however, the Epistle went to Rome the authorship of Barnabas can hardly be considered probable in view of the lack of evidence connecting him with Rome. The internal evidence is not inconsistent with his authorship, and too much stress ought not to be laid on the alleged ritual inaccuracies as disproving authorship by a Levite. At the same time in a Christian who had been for a long time associated with Jerusalem we should have expected some reference to the temple. Moreover, it is not quite easy to understand why his name should have become disconnected from the Epistle. Silas answers some of the requirements inasmuch as he was a member of the Pauline circle and a friend of Timothy. The points of contact between the Epistle and 1 Peter would also receive some explanation if Silas, by whom we are told Peter wrote his Epistle, were also the author of our letter.

Luther's suggestion of Apollos has met with marked favour among modern scholars. He was an Alexandrian, eloquent, mighty in the Scriptures, powerful in confutation of Jewish arguments and establishment of the Messianic dignity of Jesus. In all these respects he perfectly fits the conditions required by the character of the letter. Still there are objections to his authorship. If Clement knew who the author was, and it is hardly likely that he could have been ignorant, his silence in his letter to the Church at Corinth is rather strange on the assumption that it was written by Apollos. It is quite possible that Apollos was at some time connected with Rome, but we have no evidence to this effect; whether he had received instruction in Christianity from those who had heard the Lord is very dubious.

Of the other members of the Pauline circle who are known to us much the most probable suggestion is that Priscilla and Aquila were responsible for the letter. In this form the suggestion was first made by Harnack, but Bleek had previously recognised the strong claims of Aquila to consideration while deciding in favour of Apollos. Harnack's suggestion was favoured by the present writer in his Commentary, by J. H. Moulton and by Schiele, and it has recently been reaffirmed with new arguments by J. Rendel Harris. There are no tangible objections to it except the use of a masculine participle where we should have expected a feminine, but this would involve merely the change of a single letter, and with the dislike of the idea that a woman could have written it the correction to the present text became very early inevitable. A lack of feminine qualities has been detected by some writers in the Epistle, but we may not unreasonably distrust their insight into the complexities and possibilities of feminine psychology. Besides, there are indications of an opposite nature. In this connexion the absence of any reference to Deborah in the eleventh chapter seems to the present writer the most serious objection.

No doubt what really underlies the somewhat contemptuous attitude towards Harnack's theory adopted by some scholars is the masculine feeling that it is a thing incredible that any woman should have been equal to the composition of such an Epistle. With absurd prejudices of this kind one cannot argue, but if the claims of Aquila deserve serious consideration the claims of Priscilla, who seems to have been the abler of the two, deserve it even more. The teacher of Apollos may be credited with the composition of such an Epistle as readily as Apollos himself. And this accounts better than anything else for the remarkable fact that the writer's name has not been preserved to us. As the earlier freedom with which the Gospel had emancipated women and set them at liberty to use their special talents for the edification of the Church, gave way to a stiffer and narrower ecclesiasticism which defrauded them of their rights, there was every temptation to suppress the unwelcome reminder that a woman had so far ventured out of her sphere as to write such an Epistle, so quickly did the Church forget that in Christ Jesus there can be neither male nor female. And of all members of the Pauline circle for whom the authorship could reasonably be claimed, Priscilla and Aquila are the only ones whose connexion with Rome and especially with a house-church in Rome, can be established (Rom. xvi. 5). It is quite true that the argument falls far short of demonstration. We have to content ourselves with probabilities, and the combination of the Roman destination of the Epistle with the suppression of the author's name favours the identification of the author with Priscilla.

An interesting suggestion has been made by Ramsay that the Epistle was written by Philip from Caesarea to the Judaising section of the Church at Jerusalem, and is the outcome of discussions of Christians at Caesarea with Paul during his imprisonment there. He takes the concluding passage to have been written by Paul. This theory is accepted by E. L. Hicks with the improvement, however, that he denies Paul's authorship of the concluding verses. The latter scholar draws out numerous parallels between Ephesians and Colossians which he assigns to the Caesarean imprisonment and our Epistle. Two reasons compel the present writer to reject this ingenious and suggestive theory. One is that he cannot believe the Epistle to have been written to Jerusalem, the other, which seems to him even more decisive, is that the type of theology which the Epistle presents is so radically different from that of Paul that he can have had nothing to do with the letter either directly or indirectly.

Wrede has put forward the theory that the work is not a letter at all but a treatise, which was fitted with its concluding verses by an editor who wished thus to turn it into a Pauline Epistle. The only tangible argument in favour of this suggestion is that the Epistle has no address. But this argument cuts also the other way, for if the writer wished to turn the letter into a Pauline Epistle we cannot understand why he did not adopt the most obvious method and place Paul's name at the beginning of the letter. Besides, it is not correct that the work is a mere abstract treatise. There are constant references to the conditions and perils of the community of such a kind that we can largely reconstruct its history and present situation. Finally, if the editor had wished in the closing verses to pass the Epistle off as Paul's he would surely have spoken with much greater definiteness and identified the writer with Paul far more clearly.

The date of the letter is very difficult to determine. Our lower limit is given by the Epistle of Clement, which was written about 95 A.D. The reference to Timothy suggests that Paul was dead. Many would place its composition between Paul's death and the destruction of Jerusalem. Most of the arguments are inconclusive. The reference to the Jewish ritual does not imply that the temple was standing, for the author leaves the temple out of sight, nor are we entitled to argue that if Jerusalem had been destroyed he could not have failed to mention so signal a condemnation of the Jewish system. Previous destruction or profanation of the temple had not implied the abolition of the religion, and why should the destruction by Titus form an exception? The present tenses which have suggested that the ritual was still going on, may be matched from Josephus or Clement who wrote after the destruction of Jerusalem. If x. 32-34 refers, as many think, to the Neronian persecution, the most probable suggestion would be that the Epistle was written when the persecution by Domitian was anticipated. It is difficult, however, to believe simply on the ground of the word 'made a gazing-stock' that the Neronian persecution can be intended, the language used being much too mild. It is perhaps best to suppose that the letter was written in the interval after the death of Paul and when the Neronian persecution was in its initial stages. But there is no warrant whatever for a dogmatic decision between this and the later date.

CHAPTER IX

THE EPISTLE OF JAMES

THE Epistle has been generally assigned to James the Lord's brother. There is much to make this plausible. He was president of the Church at Jerusalem, his piety was of a strongly ascetic type and commanded the veneration of Jews as well as Christians. He was, even as a Christian, strongly attached to Judaism, though he acted on occasion as a mediator between Paul and the extreme Jewish Christians. And the Jewish Christians generally seem to have looked up to him as a leader. Certain characteristics of the Epistle appear to confirm the traditional view of its authorship. It is very Jewish and is remarkably poor in specifically Christian elements. Much of it indeed might have been written by one who remained at the Old Testament point of view. So much, in fact, is this the case that Spitta has suggested that it is a Jewish writing, turned into a Christian by two small interpolations. This theory, in which he does not stand quite alone, is unlikely, for the supposed Christian reviser would not have rested content with so slight a dash of Christianity, and the parallels with the Sermon on the Mount cannot so plausibly be referred to a Jewish origin. Besides, we must have regard not simply to what the Epistle contains, but to what it does not contain. But that such a theory should have been possible shows how little that is definitely Christian is to be found in the Epistle. So far as Christianity is represented in it, it is on the ethical and practical, not on the speculative side. The preponderating importance attached to the Second Coming, which furnishes the sanction of warnings and the basis of encouragement, was also characteristic of the Jewish Christians, but by no means exclusively so. The attitude assumed to wealth and the wealthy faithfully represents the Ebionism of the Jewish Christians. When the writer condemns the respect of persons in some of the Christian synagogues, he is not simply blaming his readers for the preference they show the rich, but says that God has chosen the poor to be rich in faith and heirs of the kingdom, whereas the rich are their oppressors and blaspheme the name of Christ. Similarly in ch. v. he predicts the woes that are to fall on the rich for their oppression of the poor and the righteous. If he does not say that wealth is a bad thing in itself, he comes very near it. His conception of Christianity as a law is also very Jewish. The Christians meet in synagogues, the organisation is simple. Indications of Palestinian origin are discovered. There is no reference to the destruction of Jerusalem or to the Gentile mission. These characteristics have been thought by many to demonstrate not simply that James wrote the Epistle, but that it is the earliest book in the New Testament.

Both views, however, are now widely rejected. The Epistle is written in better Greek than we should have expected in a composition by James, but he may have had assistance in this. It is also thought that the situation presupposed carries us down a long way beyond his time. The vices rebuked seem to imply a rather long development. Moreover, the writer's silence about Christ, especially about His death and even His earthly life, in spite of the rather frequent references to His teaching, is strange in one who stood in the position of James. It is remarkable that he quotes the prophets and Job as examples of patience and says nothing at all about Jesus in this connexion. There is also a remarkable absence of features which were prominent in the theology of the primitive Church. There is no reference to the controversy with Judaism as to the Messiahship of Jesus. The simplicity of the theology is not necessarily a sign of early date. In general standpoint the Epistle is nearly akin to that which we find in the theologians in the first part of the second century, especially Hermas. Harnack asks with great force whether we can suppose that about 30-50 A.D. there was a Christianity like that of Hermas, Clement, Justin and 2 Clement, and that ninety years later it reappeared though in a weakened form, while Paul, Hebrews and John came between (*Chronologie*, p. 486).

The section on justification by faith raises the problem of its relation to Paul in an acute form. It is held by many that James is here taking the view that a dead orthodoxy, exemplified in the theoretical confession of monotheism, sufficed for salvation. In that case there need be no reference of any kind to Paul's doctrine, since Paul certainly did not mean by faith an intellectual orthodoxy. It is difficult, however, to believe that the passages are independent, since it is not simply a question of the formulae but the fact that the example of Abraham is chosen to prove both formulae, while the problem is further complicated by the reference to Rahab which looks as if the author had also the Epistle to the Hebrews before him. The present writer finds it difficult to believe that James is the earlier. The contradiction is not so direct as is sometimes supposed, but it may be questioned whether the attempts at reconciliation are completely successful. Probably, however, we have not in any case to do with an attack upon Paulinism but rather on those who sheltered their failure in practice behind a Pauline formula whose implications they entirely misunderstood. This fact in itself favours a fairly late date. The moral degeneracy which has affected the Churches is often regarded as a sign of late date. This criterion, human nature being what it is, is of course quite inadequate. So far as it goes, however, it seems to suit a late better than an early period, especially the pre-Pauline period. And here again the affinities to Hermas are very marked. The references to persecution can be harmonised with any date. What, however, speaks strongly against the early date is the salutation. It is extremely difficult to believe that an encyclical letter should be written by James to the Jewish Christians of the Dispersion at so early a period.

The external evidence also is not favourable to the early date. Origen is the first to mention it by name, and the form of expression which he chooses indicates his knowledge that doubt was felt as to the authorship. It is possible that it was used by Irenaeus and Tertullian, though extremely doubtful. It was included in the Syrian Version known as the Peshitta, but this is probably too late to make the fact of any significance. There seems to be nothing in the external evidence to counterbalance the evidence for late date which the internal evidence suggests. If we accept the authorship by James we should probably do better to place it as late in his lifetime as possible, though while this would have the advantage of making the phenomena which point to a somewhat advanced development more easy, it would be more difficult to evade the conclusion that the Pauline formulae are definitely attacked. More probably, however, we should abide by the post-apostolic date. The absence of any reference to Gnostic tendencies favours a date comparatively early in the second century.

Of the author we know nothing. He speaks of himself as James. It does not follow that the Epistle is pseudonymous. Such may have been the author's name. Harnack considers that the work was not originally an Epistle but rather a homily of the type of the so-called Second Epistle of Clement, which was turned into a letter of James about

Conflict with Judaizers. 50 A.D. – 60 A.D.

the end of the second century. He argues that the work was not forged in the name of James about 120-140 A.D., inasmuch as the author nowhere hints that he intends to be taken for James, which he must have done on the contrary supposition. Moreover, the address contemplates collective Christendom, but part of the work at least contemplates a definitely limited circle. Further, its discontinuity and its lack of connexion suggest that we must look upon it as a compilation. We gain no clear insight into the characteristics of the community or communities to which it is directed. This difference in the readers addressed is matched by a similar lack of homogeneousness in the contents. Part, Harnack says, is like a reproduction of sayings of Jesus, part Hebraic but in the spirit of the old prophets, part in power, correctness and elegance to be classed with good examples of Greek rhetoric (iii. 1-12), part the work of a theological controversialist. The most paradoxical thing of all is that a certain unity both of moral feeling and language gives an internal unity to the composition in spite of its lack of connexion. While no certain explanation can be given of these phenomena, they suggest that the different pieces were not originally written for their context, so that we must distinguish between the author and the redactor. The author drew from Jewish proverbial wisdom, from speeches of Jesus and from Greek wisdom. The book was probably compiled soon after his death.

The lack of unity is acutely felt by other scholars. Jülicher considers that it is due to the gradual growth of the Epistle. Von Soden also believes that certain sections are so deficient in characteristic Christian ideas (iii. 1 - 18, iv. 11 - v. 20) that we may conjecture that they are of Jewish origin. The only section in which definitely Christian ideas are discussed is ii. 14-26. At the same time it would be a mistake, he holds, to consider that we have here a Jewish work which has been taken over by Christians

Jesus: James, Jude, Simon, Joseph.
John 7:5.
In "James" 15 sayings of Jesus
" 1:12 "Crown of Life" cf. Pet. John in Rev, & Paul

And that not only because the discussion of justification would be difficult to explain, but because specifically Jewish ideas have been replaced by what is purely ethical.

An interesting suggestion has been put forward by G. Currie Martin to the effect that the work really contains a collection of sayings of Jesus which were made by the author the basis of short homilies or reflections collected in the Epistle by some of his disciples after his death. J. H. Moulton, who agrees that the Epistle contains a considerable number of otherwise unrecorded sayings of Jesus, has made a still more interesting suggestion that the Epistle was written by James of Jerusalem but was addressed not to Christians but to Jews. This has the very great advantage that it explains why a Christian writing should be so destitute of avowedly Christian elements. The writer would not damage his appeal by specific references to Christ, above all to the scandal of His cross. But he included many sayings of Jesus in the hope that their own intrinsic beauty and worth would commend them to the readers and prepare them for a truer estimate of the crucified Nazarene whom they hated and despised. This involves that, as other scholars have suggested, the references to Christ were not a part of the original composition. This theory escapes several though not all of the difficulties which have to be urged against the view that the Epistle was written by James to Christians. The passage about justification is perhaps the most difficult to reconcile with it, but the hypothesis deserves serious consideration.

nothing in it. sheer

"James" written by James the Lord's brother — I Cor 15:5 [illegible] (In May 30 A.D.) converted "Son of God" James the Just. Head man in Jer. Pillars. 62 A.D. martyred [illegible] by Jews [illegible] worked.

CHAPTER X

THE FIRST EPISTLE OF PETER

THIS Epistle claims in its salutation to be the work of Peter, and this claim is attested by very full external evidence. It was known to the author of the Second Epistle of Peter and to Polycarp and to the author of the Teaching of the Twelve Apostles. According to Eusebius it was also known to Papias. It is not mentioned in the Muratorian Canon, but Eusebius includes it among the generally accepted Epistles. It is quoted as Peter's by Irenaeus, Clement of Alexandria, Tertullian and Origen. It is probable that it was quoted by Clement of Rome before the close of the first century, though, as in most of these cases, the relationship might be reversed. If the Epistle of James belongs to the early years of the second century it is not at all impossible that the author has drawn on this Epistle.

The traditional view, however, has been attacked by many modern critics on various grounds. It has been frequently asserted that the attitude of the State to Christians depicted in the letter cannot be harmonised with a date earlier than the edict of Trajan in his letter to Pliny. This view has been rejected by the highest authority on Roman history, Mommsen, and by writers such as Neumann, Ramsay and Hardy, who have devoted special attention to the subject. Whereas, however, Ramsay thinks that the state of affairs contemplated cannot have arisen earlier than 80 A.D., Mommsen, Hardy and others, think it may have originated as early as the time of Nero. If Ramsay's date is correct, it is hardly likely that the Epistle can be by Peter, for he probably died in the Neronian persecution. Ramsay thinks that he may have lived much longer than is usually supposed and have written the Epistle, but this has found little support. In view of Mommsen's judgment it seems safe to assume that the relations of State and Church indicated in the Epistle could very well have been reached in the reign of Nero, and therefore no serious difficulty need be felt on that score in the way of accepting its Petrine authorship. It must be added, however, that while Von Soden and others reject the date in the reign of Trajan, placing the Epistle in the reign of Domitian about A.D. 92-96, Schmiedel with full knowledge of the arguments on the other side holds to the origin of the Epistle in the time of Trajan ('Christian, Name of,' in *Enc. Bibl.*).

The other serious objection to Peter's authorship is the theological standpoint. It is urged that if Peter were the author we must have had far more traces of the influence of Christ's teaching, whereas what we find is very marked influence of the teaching of Paul. B. Weiss has attempted to show that the Epistle was written before any of Paul's letters, and that so far as there is dependence it is of Paul on Peter and not of Peter on Paul. In this he is followed only by Kühl, and the theory may be safely set aside. Others, while admitting Pauline influence, have minimised its extent. But neither does this seem a legitimate way of meeting the difficulty. We may rather state the problem in this form. Granting that the dominant influence is that of Paul, is this incompatible with Petrine authorship? It should be observed that the influence of Christ's teaching is not wholly absent, and there are reminiscences which gain much of their point if they are seen to rest on the personal recollections of an eye-witness.

It is, however, true that the emphasis lies on the work of Christ rather than on His teaching. But this is not unnatural. However great the impression made on Peter by the teaching of Jesus, that made by His death and resurrection must have been far greater. At first the meaning of the death was by no means clear to the apostles. But helped by the references of Jesus to it in such sayings as 'The Son of Man came not to be ministered unto, but to minister, and to give his life a ransom for many,' and 'This is the new covenant in my blood, which is shed for many for the remission of sins,' and further by the prophecy of the Suffering Servant of Yahweh, which was early applied to Christ, they connected the death of Christ with the forgiveness of sins. And thus there naturally came a change in the centre of gravity. The death of Christ was no longer a perplexing incident, the shame of which was partially cancelled by the resurrection, and to be wholly done away when He returned in glory. It was seen to have an essential significance for salvation. And so Paul testifies to the unity between himself and the original apostles in the gospel they preached, and enumerates among its tenets that Christ died for our sins according to the Scriptures. Even then if Paul had never become a Christian, we ought not to have been surprised if in an Epistle of Peter a leading place should be given to the death and resurrection of Christ. But since Paul had developed a theory of the work of Christ as atoning for sin and doing away with it, it is not surprising that Peter should avail himself of the thoughts of his brother apostle in speaking of the same theme. He had long before reached the same general result as Paul, and the whole account we have of him gives the impression of a highly-receptive and large-hearted personality. Nor ought we to forget an added reason why such emphasis should be laid on the suffering and death of Christ. The Epistle was not called forth by the desire to give theological instruction so much as to meet an urgent practical need. A State persecution had begun, and it was necessary to encourage the readers to patient endurance, and even joy in their distress. It is natural that in dealing with this problem of suffering, Peter should lay much stress on the suffering and death of Christ.

A very interesting suggestion has been made by McGiffert to the effect that the Epistle may have been written by Barnabas. There are several features which would suit Barnabas. He may have been a witness of the sufferings of Christ. He knew Silvanus, he was a relative of Mark which would account for the reference to 'my son.' He was a missioner to some of the Churches addressed, and he was said to have written an Epistle. Two Epistles were ascribed to him in antiquity, the Epistle to the Hebrews and the so-called Epistle of Barnabas. His authorship of the former is on the whole improbable, and it is almost certain that he did not write the latter. May he not then have written our Epistle? The Pauline character of the theology might perhaps be more easily explained on this hypothesis. If we were compelled to surrender the Petrine authorship, Barnabas would certainly be a plausible suggestion. At the same time there are considerations which tell against it. At the date to which McGiffert assigns it in the reign of Domitian, probably before A.D. 90, Barnabas must have been very old. He may of course have survived to this time, but this is hardly probable. Besides, if Barnabas wrote the letter we cannot understand why it should not from the first have circulated as his. The senior companion of Paul was of sufficient weight to give his own name to the Epistle and not send it forth anonymously, leaving a later scribe or editor to attach Peter's name to it.

Von Soden's suggestion that Silvanus was the author is also not lacking in plausibility. He was a companion of Paul, and the Pauline character of the letter would be thus accounted for. Moreover, the author says 'by Silvanus our faithful brother as I account him I have written unto you briefly.' This probably implies that Silvanus was his amanuensis, and it is not unlikely that Peter, who was unskilled in literary composition, might leave a good deal of the actual wording of the letter to Silvanus. That Silvanus, however, long after the death of Peter should have written the letter in Peter's name, and put this testimony to himself in Peter's mouth, can hardly be considered probable. If the Epistle was not written by Peter, the mention of the apostle's name at the opening of the letter has to be accounted for. Several consider that the author of the Epistle deliberately issued it in Peter's name. It would be a mistake to apply our modern standards to such a proceeding; nevertheless it is better to avoid these suggestions unless we are driven to them. Harnack formerly suggested that it was originally anonymous and was in fact not a letter at all, but that it was turned into a letter and ascribed to Peter by an author in the second century, probably the author of the Second Epistle. It is, however, extremely difficult to detach the beginning and the end from the letter, and the theory of its originally non-epistolary character is hardly borne out by the composition itself. His latest utterance implies a greater readiness to accept the Petrine authorship. McGiffert agrees that the Epistle was originally anonymous, and that the addition of Peter's name was the mere guess of a scribe.

If Peter wrote the Epistle its date is determined within rather narrow limits. He seems to draw upon the Epistles to the Romans and to the Ephesians, so that if the apostle perished in the persecution of Nero we should be obliged to date it in the early sixties. The reference to the Church in Babylon, when combined with the amply attested tradition that Peter was crucified in Rome after a pastoral activity of several months, favours the view that Rome was the place of its composition. The only tenable alternative to this would be to regard Babylon as the famous city of that name. More probably, however, the mystical Babylon is meant, though it must be confessed that this designation of Rome is more natural in apocalypses than in an Epistle. The letter was addressed, as we see from i. 1, to the sojourners of the dispersion in Pontus, Galatia, Cappadocia, Asia and Bithynia. The reference to the dispersion suggests that the readers were Jewish Christians. This, however, is not favoured by the language of the Epistle. The leading thought with the writer is that the Christians are the true Israel, and it is in the light of this thought that the utterances must be interpreted. The references made by the author to the pre-Christian condition of the readers cannot reasonably be harmonised with the theory that they were Jewish Christians. He can hardly have said of them that in time past they were no people (ii. 10) or have spoken of their former manner of life in the terms of i. 14, 18, iv. 2, 3. The implied contrast between the present and the past in iii. 6 also suggests that they had first become descendants of Sarah when they became Christians.

CHAPTER XI

THE SECOND EPISTLE OF PETER AND THE EPISTLE OF JUDE

THESE writings are so closely related that it is desirable to treat them together. We may take first the relation between the two Epistles. The extent of coincidence between them is so great that one must have copied the other. In the judgment of most scholars Jude is the original from which 2 Peter borrowed. It is in the first place curious that, if 2 Peter were the earlier, Jude should have contented himself with extracting simply the section against the false teachers. But apart from this general improbability, when we come to place the two documents side by side and test them, it is generally easy to explain why the author of 2 Peter has altered Jude, but it is not easy to see why, if Jude had 2 Peter before him, he should have altered his original to the form that we find in his Epistle. Obscurities in 2 Peter can in some cases be cleared up by reference to Jude. Moreover, the task of the writer of Jude would, as Chase has pointed out, have required little short of a miracle of literary skill. He 'eliminated harsh and tortuous phrases, brought together scattered ideas, infused reminiscences of Enoch, and wrought the whole into natural compact and harmonious paragraphs.' This conclusion is confirmed by the fact that Jude not only fails to incorporate the greater part of 2 Peter, but betrays no trace of its influence in vocabulary or style. We may therefore take the priority of Jude.

in spite of the ingenious arguments to the contrary, as made good.

This has an obvious bearing on the genuineness of 2 Peter. It is quite true that there is no reason why Peter should not have borrowed from Jude. The First Epistle of Peter shows striking traces of the influence of the Pauline Epistles, especially of Romans and Ephesians, and Peter impresses one as a very receptive personality, so that in itself we need feel no insurmountable objection to the view that he should have borrowed from Jude. But as Adeney says: 'It is one thing to lean upon Paul, and even James, and another thing to absorb and utilise virtually the whole of the short Epistle of so obscure a writer as Jude. In defending the genuineness of 2 Peter we accuse the great apostle of plagiarising in a remarkable way.' And quite apart from this, there is the serious question whether we can bring back the date of Jude into the lifetime of Peter. If not, a work which has been based upon Jude cannot have been written by the apostle Peter. The inference from the relationship between this apostle and Jude is confirmed by comparison with 1 Peter. Mayor has calculated that as regards vocabulary the number of agreements with 1 Peter is a hundred as opposed to five hundred and ninety-nine disagreements. The relationship between 2 Peter and the Old Testament is much slighter than is the case with the First Epistle, and the author alludes less to the Gospel narrative. Spitta, who is one of the most vigorous and ingenious defenders of the authenticity of 2 Peter and its priority to Jude, is quite convinced that identity of authorship cannot be claimed for the Second Epistle, accordingly he rescues 2 Peter by surrendering the authenticity of 1 Peter. E. A. Abbott has also argued for dependence upon Josephus which would negative Petrine authorship. The resemblances must be admitted, but we cannot build with any confidence upon them. Mayor explains them 'as due in the main to the diffusion of commonplaces of rhetorical study, set prefatory phrases, and the like, which were employed by those who learnt Greek in later life.'

When we turn to the external evidence we find that its attestation in early Christian literature is very late, Origen in the third century being the first to mention it, and apparently with doubt as to its authenticity. Eusebius tells us that he had not received it as canonical. It is extraordinary if the Epistle is genuine that it should be first mentioned so late in Christian history, and that Eusebius should tell us that the tradition he had received was unfavourable to its canonicity. This is all the more remarkable when we remember that it was not to an obscure apostle or to a non-apostolic writer that the work was attributed, but to one who was at the time universally regarded with reverence. There were other writings besides the two Epistles attributed to him to which Peter's name was attached, notably the Apocalypse of Peter. These, however, were not ultimately included by the Church in its Canon, a fact for which we may be profoundly grateful. Yet the Apocalypse of Peter comes to us with better attestation of authenticity from the Early Church than the Second Epistle.

The suspicions created by the lateness of the external evidence and the dubiousness with which it is expressed are confirmed by the internal evidence. In the first place the Epistle brings before us a time when through long delay the hope of the Second Coming had grown faint. There were mockers asking, 'Where is the promise of his coming? For, from the day that the fathers fell asleep, all things continue as they were from the beginning of the creation.' It is extremely difficult to believe that such a sentence as this could have been written by the apostle Peter. He was himself one of the Fathers on whose age the writer looked back as to a distant past. Nor is it probable that in his time the hope in the Second Coming should have given place to scepticism. It is true that the author speaks in the future tense, but a consideration of the whole passage leads to the conclusion that he is dealing with a state of things which either actually confronts him or which he anticipates in the immediate future. In the next place the author's reference to the Epistles of Paul is very strange in the time and on the lips of Peter. They are spoken of as if a collection of them had been formed; they had already been the object of considerable misinterpretation. What is most remarkable of all is that they are spoken of as Scripture. It will not therefore seem wonderful that the doubts which were so widely entertained in the early Church revived again at the Reformation, and that a large number of scholars in the conservative as well as in the critical camp have definitely set aside the ascription of the Epistle to Peter. The date cannot be brought down below the close of the second century. Origen was acquainted with it, and probably Clement of Alexandria. It cannot be much earlier than the middle of the second century. This is suggested by the lateness of the external evidence, by the reference to the Pauline Epistles not simply as a collection of writings but as canonical Scripture which the heretics have wrested to their own destruction, and by the type of false teaching which is attacked. This date is also confirmed by the close relationship with the Apocalypse of Peter. No certain conclusion can be reached as to the place of composition, but the affinities with Philo and Clement of Alexandria point to Egypt, in which also the Apocalypse of Peter was probably written.

The Epistle of Jude was generally accepted as authoritative by the close of the second century. It is included in the Muratorian Canon and quoted by Clement of Alexandria, Tertullian and Origen. The omission of reference to it or even inclusion in lists of New Testament books may be accounted for by its brevity and by the objection felt to its use of apocryphal literature.

The Epistle claims to be by Jude the brother of James. If these words are an integral part of the Epistle the reference must be to James of Jerusalem, the brother of Jesus. If the Epistle is not the work of this Jude, we may either suppose that to secure attention to the letter it was written in Jude's name, against which we have the difficulty of accounting for the choice of so obscure an authority, or we may suppose that the author's name was Jude and the identification with the brother of James was due to a later hand. Many scholars believe that the Epistle cannot have been written before the second century, at a time when Jude the brother of James was dead. No weight can be attached to the quotation of apocryphal writings. These were much earlier than Jude's day, and there is no tangible reason for the assumption that he would have hesitated to employ them. Still less can we assume that he would not have employed the Pauline Epistles with which the writer was certainly familiar. More serious is the argument derived from the reference to the false teaching which is often taken to be some form of antinomian Gnosticism. The Gnostic character of the false teaching, however, cannot be proved, and immoral inferences from the doctrine of grace were drawn before the second century. At the same time the reference would suit very well the libertine Gnostics of the second century. The age of the apostles it is also said lies in the past (*vv.* 17, 18), and they are referred to as a collective body. This is certainly not impossible in a brother of Christ, though it would be more natural in a later writer. The balance of probability perhaps inclines against the authorship by Jude the Lord's brother, but there are no decisive reasons for rejecting the traditional view.

CHAPTER XII

THE SYNOPTIC GOSPELS

The Synoptic Problem

THE Gospels of Matthew, Mark and Luke have received the not very happy title the Synoptic Gospels from the fact that they largely present a common view of the Gospel narrative, so that they may be frequently arranged in parallel columns, as telling substantially the same story. This fact places them in a class by themselves, it being perhaps the only known example of a threefold biography which could be treated in this way. The agreement between them extends often to the minutest details. Side by side with this we constantly find remarkable divergence. It is this combination of agreement and difference that has given rise to what is known as the Synoptic Problem. The problem is to frame a theory which shall account for the relations between the first three Gospels, setting them in their chronological order, tracing the sources from which they have been compiled, and explaining both the coincidences and differences which they present. Since the phenomena are very complex, it is clear that a complicated rather than a simple solution will be required to do them justice.

When we compare the Gospels in detail, we observe that Matthew and Luke alone give any account of the life of Jesus before His ministry, and that their accounts are completely independent of each other, touching at very few points and difficult to harmonise. It is therefore most significant that when the two authors begin to tell the story of the ministry, they tell it in the same way. It is natural to conclude that the agreement between Matthew and Luke is to be connected with the introduction of Mark. And this is confirmed by the fact that as soon as Mark comes to an end Luke and Matthew begin to differ again in the incidents they relate. The original ending of Mark seems to have been lost. The last twelve verses which are absent in our best MSS. are a later addition, and Mark breaks off suddenly at xvi. 8. When Matthew and Luke reach this point their agreement ends and they go different ways. Luke and Matthew therefore agree in the main within the limits covered by the Gospel of Mark. Outside these limits, both before Mark begins and after he ends, they are completely independent. Thus Mark binds Matthew and Luke together. An interesting fact, which may be simply mentioned here, is that the order in which the incidents are narrated is generally the order of Mark. Sometimes all three agree in order, but where two agree Mark is practically always in the majority. Mark and Matthew may agree against Luke, or Luke and Mark against Matthew; rarely, if ever, Matthew and Luke against Mark.

But while it is true that outside the limits of Mark, Matthew and Luke have nothing in common, they have several sections in common within these limits which are not found in Mark. These sections consist for the most part of speeches not of narratives, and there is a closer correspondence between Matthew and Luke in these two sections than between any two of the evangelists, where all three cover the same ground.

Further, with the exception of two miracles (Mark vii. 31-37, viii. 22-26) and one parable (Mark iv. 26-29), the whole of Mark has parallels in Matthew or Luke or both. Of course, the parallels present considerable variation, and Mark has isolated verses peculiar to himself, but substantially with the exceptions mentioned, Mark has nothing which is not found in one or both of the other Synoptists. On the other hand, both Matthew and Luke have a large amount of matter to be found in neither of the other Synoptists.

So far, the correspondence between the Gospels referred to has been general, touching the selection of incidents or discourses, and not the language in which they are preserved. Even so we are driven to postulate the use of a common source or sources. It cannot be accidental that out of the large number of incidents and discourses in the ministry of Christ the few which are selected should be in the three Gospels to so great an extent the same. If the authors had gone to work independently, it is incredible that they should have hit on such large agreement in the selection of incidents. When we add to this that the order is largely the same and that gaps occur at the same points, the conclusion is strengthened that we must assign these coincidences not to accident but to employment of common sources. This is substantiated by other considerations.

When we examine the Gospels side by side we quickly discover that the parallels they present are characterised by remarkable verbal coincidences. If we take the Gospel of Mark and the sections parallel to it in the other Synoptists (the so-called Triple Tradition) we find that Mark and Matthew have in common nearly fifty per cent. of the total number of words in Mark, while Mark and Luke have nearly thirty-five per cent.[1] While this is so in the Triple Tradition, it is even more striking in the Double Tradition, that is in the matter common to Matthew and Luke which is not found in Mark. It should also be pointed out that these figures do not indicate how large the agreement often is, but only the average distributed

[1] The statistics in this chapter are derived from calculations, much more elaborate than can be here indicated, made several years ago by the writer.

over a considerable number of sections. Thus in Mark ii. 18-22 we have 129 words, in Matthew ix. 14-17 103, and in Luke v. 33-38 129. In this section 58 words are common to all three, and in addition Mark and Matthew have 23 in common, Mark and Luke 22, and Matthew and Luke 2. That is, 80 words are common to Mark and Matthew and to Mark and Luke, while 60 are common to Matthew and Luke. In the speech of John the Baptist to those who came to his baptism, Luke and Matthew give for several verses practically the same report, something like 87 words out of 90 being found in both.

It is clear that the common matter, even more than the common selection of incidents, and the common order, demands a common source, and this has been generally admitted. The questions that arise concern the number of sources and their character, whether oral or documentary. The latter point may be taken first. The theories that have been put forward in solution of the Synoptic Problem fall into two classes, the oral and the documentary. The oral theory accounts for the parallels, which our Synoptic Gospels present, by the hypothesis that the writers made independent use of an oral tradition. It is held that an official cycle of teaching was formed, probably in Jerusalem, that this became more or less fixed, and that it has been incorporated by our Synoptists without passing to them through documents. The documentary theory, on the other hand, while not denying that oral teaching may represent the ultimate source of our Gospels, accounts for the parallels as due to the literary use of a common written source or sources, which may either be lost sources or one or more of our Synoptic Gospels. Thus each of our Gospels may be completely independent of the others and dependent only on common documents which have perished, or two of our Gospels may have used a third, or one of our Gospels may have used the other two, and this may be further complicated by the use of one of these two by the other. It is also possible that one or two may have used lost sources along with two or one of our present Gospels. It is clear that the possibilities are very numerous, and probably most conceivable forms of the documentary theory have at one time or another been put forward. The oral theory does not admit of such complex variations.

Several considerations may be urged in favour of the oral theory. It is clear that the narratives of Christ's life and the reports of His teaching were first given to the world by word of mouth and not in documents. From the formation of the Church it was felt necessary that he, who was chosen to the apostolic office to be a witness of the Resurrection, should be one who had companied with the apostles from the Baptising by John to the Ascension (Acts i. 21, 22). Teaching on the ministry of Jesus must have been given from the first by the Apostles. And we have evidence that the Gospel of Mark actually rests on oral teaching. Papias informs us that Mark's Gospel embodies the preaching of Peter as it was elicited by the needs of his hearers. Again the preference of the Jews for oral teaching may also be urged in favour of this hypothesis. There was a reluctance to commit instruction to writing, it was considered to be better that it should be stored in the memory. 'Commit nothing to writing' was a Rabbinical maxim. It may be added finally that this theory gives an easy account of the differences in the Gospels. Three writers independently reproducing the same tradition would naturally introduce much variation.

These arguments, however, are far from substantiating the oral hypothesis. They make it probable that oral tradition to some extent lies behind our Gospels. But so much is generally admitted by defenders of the documentary theory. The dislike of writing really proves nothing. For if it did not prevent our three Gospels from being written, we are not warranted in assuming that it prevented earlier documents from being similarly composed, nor can there be any reason why the writer of a document such as one of our evangelists, should object to employ documents as sources. It is also to be noticed that Papias' account of the origin of Mark, while it assigns it to oral teaching, is yet inconsistent with the use of an oral tradition such as the theory postulates. For the latter is an official selection of incidents and discourses, largely fixed by repetition alike in order and language, whereas Peter's teaching was occasional and disconnected, drawn forth by the needs of his hearers, and in no sense systematic teaching as to the ministry of Christ. Nor must we press unduly the argument from variations. The standard of fidelity to which the evangelists would feel themselves bound in reproducing documents would not be so high as to exclude considerable variation.

But not only are the arguments in favour of the oral theory less strong than they seem at first sight, but there are most serious objections to it. In the first place there is the difficulty as to the formation of the oral tradition. To begin with, we have to account for two traditions. If we assume that the official oral Gospel contained only the sections common to all three Synoptists, then the question arises how are we to account for the matter common only to Matthew and Luke? Are their coincidences to be accounted for by the use of a common oral tradition? If so, where did this spring up, and had it any official character? If not, then we must have recourse to a documentary source, and if we invoke a documentary source to explain the Double Tradition, why not also to explain the Triple Tradition? If on the other hand we make the Double Tradition correspond to the original oral tradition, then the difficulties are increased, for we should have to explain why Mark completely overlooks it, and also why all three of the evangelists have a tradition in common, viz. the Triple Tradition, quite distinct from the official oral Gospel. If from these difficulties we take refuge in the assumption that the oral Gospel consisted both of the Double and the Triple Traditions, then the question arises why Mark should have cut out so much of it, excluding some of its most valuable portions from his Gospel.

In the next place it is difficult to explain on what principles the oral tradition was formed. Out of so large a number of incidents why should just those have been selected which we find preserved? In a collection made by an individual this is much more easy to account for than in a cycle officially formed, with the deliberate intention of giving information on the ministry and teaching of Christ. Papias' account of the origin of Mark's Gospel supplies some sort of an answer to the question why Mark gives us the selection of incidents we find in his work. Peter's object was not to give systematic teaching as to the ministry of Christ, but to meet the needs of his hearers as they arose. His choice was thus determined by practical necessities, and his treatment was homiletical rather than historical. There is another difficulty connected with the selection, though it does not affect those who believe that Christ did not visit Jerusalem during His ministry till the close of His life. It is generally supposed that the oral tradition was formed in Jerusalem. It is therefore remarkable that the Synoptists omit all account of the Jerusalem ministry till the Triumphal Entry. That the minds of the disciples turned with fondness to the Galilean ministry was natural, but it is very strange that the tradition should be so detached from the scenes amid which it was formed.

It is also difficult on the oral hypothesis to explain the degree of fixity which was reached by the tradition. This difficulty affects the selection of incidents, the order in which they were arranged, and the language. The first of these points has been touched upon, so far as concerns the original selection. But in the present connexion the difficulty touches not the choice of certain incidents, but the method by which this first selection became permanently fixed. It scarcely seems probable that a teacher should confine himself strictly to the same cycle of stories, and repeat these, and these only, so frequently, that the limits of his narration should come to be so fixed as in our Triple Tradition. But it is further noteworthy that not only the selection of narratives, but the order also is largely fixed. The order of Mark is usually followed by one if not both of the other Synoptists. It would not be so difficult to account for the order being fixed in oral tradition, if this were chronological. But Mark's order is probably not chronological. We have then to account for the formation of an artificial order. It is quite easy to suppose that a teacher narrated his set of incidents in any given order once; what is very difficult to believe is that he again and again repeated them in the same order, unless he was guided to it by some definite principle. But no such principle seems to be discernible in Mark's order. The difficulty is not that, once the order was fixed, it should be remembered, it lies a stage further back in the fixing itself. A similar difficulty attaches to the stereotyping of the language. Are we to imagine that in the course of repetition the language attained such fixity of form as we often find in the parallel sections of our Synoptists? The verbal coincidence as it is found there is very large, and the actual fixity of form in the oral tradition must have been much larger, when we allow for the imperfect memories of the writers. It is barely credible that an unwritten series of narratives should have been told with such little variation.

But this does not exhaust the objections to the oral theory. When the oral tradition had been formed, we have the difficulty attaching to the view that it can have been so faithfully remembered and reproduced by three writers independently, even granting that memories were exceptionally powerful. It is perhaps a further objection that the tradition must have been formed in Greek, whereas we should more naturally have expected it to be in Aramaic. The coincidences in the Greek are such that they cannot be accounted for by the theory that the writers translated independently from a common Aramaic original. The common source must have been in Greek.

It is also difficult to believe that the insignificant phrases which are often found in parallel texts could have been preserved in oral tradition. Nor is it likely that such dislocation of the true order as the story of John the Baptist's imprisonment would have been found both in Matthew and Mark and at the same point, if they had been depending simply on oral tradition. Probably the words 'Let him that readeth understand' in Matt. xxiv. 15 and Mark xiii. 14 attest the employment of a document, at least for this section. The interpretation let him that readeth Daniel understand is possible but improbable, since the reference to Daniel occurs only in Matthew and is apparently an editorial note. If so the words cannot be words of Jesus, for He would have said 'Let him that heareth understand.' The reference must accordingly be to him who read the address of Jesus. Since it is incredible that the two evangelists should have independently added this warning at this precise point, one must have copied from the other, or both have taken it from a common source. But this source cannot have been oral, for oral tradition is not read but heard. It must therefore have been written, and if so, a document is necessarily implied.

If then the documentary hypothesis is adopted, the next question concerns the documents, which have to be regarded as the sources of our Synoptic Gospels. It will be convenient to keep the Triple Tradition and the Double Tradition distinct. The former may be examined first. It has already been pointed out that a documentary theory may assume a large number of forms. It is therefore well to avoid any detailed statement of all that are possible in the abstract, still more any examination of them. The simplest course is to determine which of the Synoptists presents the Triple Tradition in its most primitive form. The answer to this will at once exclude a large number of theories possible in the abstract, and it will then remain only to discover whether or no we have to admit the existence of a lost source for the Triple Tradition more primitive still.

It has already been shown that Mark binds Matthew and Luke together in respect to the general plan of the Gospels. This supplies a very cogent argument in favour of the priority of Mark. This alone gives an adequate explanation of the fact that the other Gospels begin to tell the same story at the precise point where Mark begins and cease to do so just where he ends. If Mark had had Matthew and Luke before him this would have been unaccountable, and indeed, any theory other than that which regards Mark as preserving the most primitive type, would similarly fail to explain the facts. This is strengthened by the further fact that the order is predominantly that of Mark. If where two agree against the third, Mark is always in the majority, this can only be because his order is the most original. The deviations from it by Matthew and Luke can be explained without difficulty, so that they form no objection to its being taken as the fundamental order.

The same conclusion results from an examination of the verbal coincidences. Of the words common only to two evangelists in the Triple Tradition, Mark and Matthew have five to six times as many, Mark and Luke twice to three times as many as Matthew and Luke have in common. Mark has therefore much more in common with Matthew and with Luke than they have with each other. This also substantiates the priority of Mark. Further, if on the contrary we assumed that Mark used Matthew and Luke, we should have to admit that he has contrived to get into his narrative from four-fifths to five-sixths of the matter common to both, and has besides this borrowed more than thirty per cent. of the matter peculiar to Matthew and fifteen per cent. of that peculiar to Luke. And yet having compiled his narrative in this laborious and complicated way, it turns out to be simple, graphic, and straightforward in a very high degree. It may safely be said that it is barely credible that this should have happened, and the evidence here as elsewhere points unmistakably to the preservation of the earliest form in Mark. It must, however, be pointed out that this does not account for the words which Matthew and Luke have in common which are not found in Mark. The difficulty of accounting for them on the theory that these Gospels are based on Mark has led to the formulation of several hypotheses, which must be mentioned later. Provisionally the priority of Mark may be taken as made good. But this does not prove that Mark is the source of the Triple Tradition. It may simply represent it more faithfully than any surviving Gospel, but the actual source may be lost. The consideration of this point may, however, be deferred for the present.

We may now pass to the sections common only to Matthew and Luke. It has already been pointed out that these consist for the most part of speeches, and that the verbal coincidence between the Gospels in this Double Tradition is larger than that in the Triple Tradition. We may assume that a document, now usually called Q (*i.e. Quelle*, the German word for 'source'), lies behind these sections, from which our first and third evangelists have drawn. Since they consist for the most part of discourses, it is a probable conjecture that this document is to be identified with the Logia of Matthew, mentioned by

Papias. His words are 'Matthew composed the Logia in Hebrew, and each interpreted them as he was able.' The word Logia may, no doubt, be used for a collection of narratives and speeches such as our First Gospel, with a Hebrew original of which it has commonly been identified. But the word more naturally means 'discourses,' and it is highly improbable that Papias is referring to a Hebrew or Aramaic original of the First Gospel. For we have strong reason for believing that such a Semitic original never existed. Quite apart from the fact that the style of the First Gospel is not that of a translation, it is decisive that the Greek Gospel of Mark has been employed in its composition. Not only is it difficult to identify our First Gospel with a translation of Matthew's work, but it is most improbable that one of the twelve apostles, an eyewitness of the events, should have used the work of Mark, who was not an apostle, and neither saw nor heard a great deal of what he relates. It follows from this that the First Gospel can hardly be the work of Matthew. But, if not, the question arises why does it bear Matthew's name? It can only be because it has an intimate connexion with that apostle, embodying a tradition derived from him. It can hardly be an accidental coincidence, that criticism should postulate a collection of discourses as the source for the common sections of Matthew and Luke, and that tradition should assert that Matthew compiled a collection of discourses. The conclusion thus becomes highly probable that the Source of the Double Tradition is the collection of speeches compiled by Matthew, of which Papias speaks. We must suppose, then, that this was used independently in the composition of the First and Third Gospels. And since the coincidences are so large in Greek, it seems necessary to assume that the authors used for the most part the same translation. And we thus understand why the First Gospel bears the name of Matthew, because though it is not from his hand it incorporates the substance of his lost work. We thus gain as the main solution of the Synoptic Problem, the almost universally accepted Two-Document hypothesis namely that our First and Third Gospels have used as their two common sources, a document most faithfully preserved in the Gospel of Mark and a document largely consisting of speeches and sayings, probably a Greek translation of the Logia of Matthew.

It should be added, however, that some scholars who fully accept the two-document hypothesis refuse to believe that we should identify the Logia referred to by Papias with the common source of the Double Tradition. Some suppose that he intended the complete Gospel, but erroneously believed that this was a translation of the Semitic original, and though they recognise that the criticism of the Gospels forces us to postulate a common source for the Double Tradition, consider that we have no right to assume that this was what Papias had in mind. Another view has been put forward by Professor Burkitt. He also agrees that we must postulate a lost document as a common source employed by Matthew and Luke in addition to Mark. He thinks, however, that this is not to be identified with the Logia. He suggests that Papias had in mind rather a collection of Messianic proof texts from the Old Testament. It is of course significant that such passages have great prominence in Matthew, and it is probable that at a very early period in the history of the Church collections of these texts were drawn up for use by Christians in their controversies with Jews. At the same time these passages constitute a rather small part of the entire work, so that it is not quite easy to understand why the name Matthew should have become attached to the whole Gospel. It is easier to understand if it incorporated so large a work as the collection of discourses. It might of course be urged that we have no more reason for transferring the name of Matthew from the Logia to the First

Gospel than to the Third. But the authorship of the Third Gospel by Luke was a fixed point in tradition, guaranteed by the fact that the author of the Third Gospel was also the author of the Acts of the Apostles. It is true that no certainty in the matter is attainable, but it seems still to remain the most probable view that the work mentioned by Papias was the Semitic original of Q. It is more likely that the original language was Aramaic than Hebrew.

We may now return to the question whether the First and Third Gospels were based on Mark or on a document similar to but not identical with our Second Gospel. One of the main reasons for accepting the latter alternative is the existence of coincidences between Matthew and Luke in the Triple Tradition which are not found in Mark. Largely these may be explained as due to independent revision of the same document. In this way we may explain the identical substitution of more literary turns of speech for Mark's blunter and harsher forms of expression, and the consequential alterations which are sometimes considerable, or the modifications and suppressions which were prompted by reverence. But this does not cover all the cases of coincident variation from Mark, and various theories have been put forward to account for the unexplained residuum. The first is that Mark lay before the first and third evangelists in another form than that with which we are familiar. Usually it has been supposed by those who hold this view that they used an earlier Mark (*Urmarkus*). We need not argue for an earlier Mark on the ground which has sometimes been put forward that our Gospel does not correspond to the description of Mark's work given by Papias, and that we must therefore suppose that this description originally applied to another form of the Second Gospel than that which we possess. In all probability it applies sufficiently well. The statement that it was not in order is discounted by its polemical intention. Its order varied from that which Papias regarded as correct. But our different verdict on this point should not lead us to infer that Papias had a different work before him. Of course the further question is raised as to how far he was warranted in affirming that the preaching of Peter lay behind Mark's work. But that is a point which would probably tell against an earlier Mark almost as much as against the present Mark. In the main it is likely that the authors of the First and Third Gospels had Mark before them practically in its present form, apart of course from the spurious ending. In any case the difference between the two was probably so slight that substantially we might speak of them as the same book. It is perhaps more probable that if their edition of Mark varied from ours it was a later rather than an earlier that they used. If we assumed that Mark had been slightly revised and that it was this revised edition which was employed by the two evangelists, we should go a good way towards meeting the particular difficulty in question. Of course this conclusion does not settle the question whether Mark may not once have existed in a briefer form. Wellhausen for example argues that a fairly large section in it is secondary. But he leaves the question open whether this secondary element was introduced during the oral or the written stage of the Mark tradition. And he considers that Matthew and Luke used it in its present form.

The second theory is that held by Holtzmann, Weizsäcker, Wendt and Allen, that Luke had a certain knowledge of Matthew. The great objection to this is that he should have neglected so much that is peculiar to the First Gospel. Possibly he had only a cursory knowledge of it, and in any case he could only have made a very subsidiary use of it. Even allowing this, it seems strange that this knowledge should have left such slight traces. The third is the view of B. Weiss that Mark knew and employed Q. This accounts perhaps better than either of the other theories for the phenomena. For if all three Synoptists drew from Q and the first and third copied it faithfully but the second modified it in the cases mentioned, this would satisfactorily explain the coincidences of Matthew and Luke which are not in Mark, as well as their more primitive form. The chief objection to this view is that if Mark knew Q he should have made such sparing use of the work, omitting in fact its most valuable features. No theory is quite satisfactory, and the problem is perhaps not yet ripe for solution. Possibly no theories of the kind will ultimately be found necessary. If we allow for the influence of oral tradition, for the possibility that Matthew and Luke used a revised edition of Mark, and for the assimilation of the text of Matthew to that of Luke, or the text of Luke to that of Matthew, the phenomena may be sufficiently explained.

Since Q has been lost the question arises whether we can reconstruct it. The analogy of the companion document warns us that such an attempt can be only partially successful. If the single mutilated copy of Mark from which all our copies have apparently descended had disappeared, we could not have reconstructed it by a comparison of Matthew and Luke. We could not even argue that identical language in Matthew and Luke must have been derived from Mark. Moreover, where Matthew and Luke both abbreviate, much of Mark would have irretrievably disappeared. We have therefore to allow for the probability that the same causes may have prevented a complete preservation of Q even in sections which have been taken over by both Gospels. It is also possible that some sections in Q have been included by neither evangelist, nor can we feel any great confidence in assigning to Q non-Marcan matter found only in one of the Synoptists, though probably such sections exist. Some conclusions, however, seem to be fairly warranted.

The document consisted in the main of sayings and discourses, but not exclusively so. Short introductions giving the occasion would naturally be inserted, such as the mention of the fact that John sent his disciples from prison to Jesus. It contained one or two complete narratives such as the story of the Temptation and the healing of the centurion's servant. The most interesting question of all is whether it contained the history of the Passion and the Resurrection. Generally this has been denied, though Burkitt has recently argued that Luke's Passion story was largely derived from Q. If the usual opinion is correct, we ought not to infer that Q was written before the Crucifixion. The author probably did not intend to write a Gospel in our sense of the term, but to collect the sayings and discourses of Jesus. It would, in fact, be more reasonable to infer that he was already acquainted with a Gospel in which the story of Christ's Ministry, Passion and Resurrection was recorded, though it is by no means necessary to assume this, still less to argue that he must have been acquainted with Mark.

An important element in the reconstruction is the decision we form as to the use of Q by the Synoptists. It has been mentioned already that B. Weiss thinks that Q was used by Mark. This would naturally imply that Q contained a good deal more than is commonly assigned to it. Von Soden on the other hand argues that Mark obviously was acquainted with Q because he has included so few discourses. Both suggestions are precarious. So far as we know, the two documents were quite independent. A less intangible but rather perplexing problem is raised by the question, Is Q better preserved in Matthew or in Luke? So far as arrangement is concerned, the probabilities favour the greater originality of Luke. It has long been observed that Matthew exhibits a marked tendency to combine sayings or brief discourses into larger wholes. These are often found in detached fragments in Luke, frequently and perhaps usually in a more appropriate historical setting. The most striking example of this is that of Luke's parallels to Matthew's Sermon on the Mount. The corresponding sermon in Luke is almost one-third of the length of Matthew's. Yet the parts absent from Luke's version are almost all to be found scattered up and down in his Gospel. If Q contained the Sermon in the form in which Matthew gives it, it is very hard to believe that Luke should have broken it up and distributed the fragments here and there in his Gospel, supplying appropriate historical introductions. If, however, it existed much as in Luke, it seems quite natural that the author of the First Gospel, with his tendency to group similar sections together, should have taken these fragments and combined them with the sermon. Probably this applies to the reproduction as a whole. The order of Q is better preserved in Luke than in Matthew, though for a large part of the material the order of the two sufficiently coincides to enable its main outline to be recovered. This agreement makes it also probable that most if not all the non-Marcan matter contained both in Matthew and Luke belongs to Q. It is another question, however, which of the two evangelists has reproduced most faithfully the phraseology of Q. On this point scholars differ, some preferring Luke's version in substance if not in form, while others prefer that of Matthew. It is not possible in our space to investigate the question. The present writer can only say that he is inclined on the whole to give the preference to Luke. He considers that no general rule can safely be laid down, and that each case must be decided on its merits.

The date of Q cannot be settled with any confidence. It must be earlier than Matthew and Luke, but since the date of these Gospels is very uncertain, we cannot infer anything with confidence from its employment in them. Irenaeus tells us that Matthew wrote while Peter and Paul were preaching and founding the Church in Rome. The form of the statement hardly inspires confidence, and Irenaeus was thinking of our First Gospel. It is quite possible, however, that a date in the first half of the sixties might be assigned to Q. If the reference to Zachariah the son of Barachiah in Matt. xxiii. 25, Luke xi. 51 belonged to Q, it might be necessary to fix the date somewhat later. Assuming that the Zachariah intended is the man who was killed by the Zealots in A.D. 67 or 68 shortly before the siege of Jerusalem, Q would have to be at least as late as 67. Wellhausen has recently argued strongly for this identification, which has received the assent of Jülicher, but Harnack considers that it is impossible and that in any case it is probable that the words 'son of Barachiah' did not belong to Q. The work seems to have been written for the Christians of Palestine before the destruction of the Temple.

That in addition to Mark and Q other sources were employed by Matthew and Luke is very probable, especially in the case of Luke, who in fact hints as much in the preface to his Gospel. But here we are left for the most part to conjecture. It should be added, however, that this problem, especially as regards Luke, has recently been the subject of some extremely suggestive discussions.

The Gospel of Mark.

Papias gives an account of the origin of Mark which is so important that it must be quoted at length. The elder who is quoted as the authority for the statement is apparently the presbyter John. 'And the Elder said this also: Mark having become the interpreter of Peter, wrote down accurately everything that he remembered, without however recording in order what was either said or done by Christ. For neither did he hear the Lord, nor did he follow him; but afterwards, as I said (attended) Peter, who adapted his instructions to the needs (of his hearers) but had no design of giving a connected account of the Lord's oracles. So then Mark made no mistake, while he thus wrote down some things as he remembered them; for he made it his one care not to omit anything that he had heard, or to set down any false statement therein' (quoted from Lightfoot's translation). It has already been pointed out that too much stress must not be laid on the statement that the Gospel is not in order, since this is suggested by the elder's preference for the order of another Gospel, probably John. Papias accounts for the divergence from the true order by the statement that Peter's treatment of the life of Jesus was homiletical rather than chronological. Probably, however, we should be right in trusting his statement to the extent of recognising that reminiscences of Peter do lie behind the Second Gospel. Peter's prominence in it is not to be accounted for simply by the fact that he was the most important member of the apostolic band, for some of the incidents are too trivial to have found their way into a story of Christ's ministry had it not been for the personal interest which they had for Peter. Yet the Gospel is not a mere reproduction of Peter's preaching. Even on Papias' own showing the arrangement of the material, which is extremely important, was not due to Peter. The apostle gave only an accidental collection of incidents and sayings to meet the needs of his hearers. Mark has so arranged his material as to reproduce some of the main lines of the historical development. It is probable that in addition to the arrangement some of the material itself was not derived from Peter, and that not on account of its legendary character but for reasons of literary criticism which do not depend on a particular theory of the universe. The eschatological discourse in chapter xiii., which possibly incorporates a small independent apocalypse, has apparently been taken from a written source. Moreover, the presence of doublets suggests that a non-Petrine version of the same incident occasionally stands side by side with the Petrine.

There is no substantial reason for doubting the traditional authorship. The titles of the Gospels are not of course original, but they are very early, and they are probably intended to claim direct authorship. In the case of all the Synoptists they are corroborated by unbroken tradition, and no plausible reason can be suggested why Mark should have been chosen for the authorship of the Gospel if he had no hand in it. It is true that he was connected with Peter, but if Petrine authorship was to be claimed it would have been simpler to assign it to him outright, in spite of the references to him in the third person. It is of course possible that the Second Gospel is the work of a later writer incorporating an earlier work of Mark (so Von Soden and Schürer), but the uniformity of style makes it more probable that we have to do with the same author throughout. The work seems to have come down to us in a mutilated form. In spite of Wellhausen's opinion to the contrary, it is most improbable that it could have ended with xvi. 8. Possibly accident prevented the Gospel from being completed, but it is more likely that it was finished, though whether we are in a position to infer its conclusion from the close of Matthew or John xxi. is very problematical. Since all our copies are derived from the mutilated copy, we may conclude that the Gospel was at one time all but extinct. It is very striking that it should have been preserved at all in view of the fact that it was almost entirely incorporated in Matthew and Luke, and that its tone was much less congenial to Christian piety in the latter part of the first century. The tradition of its connexion with Peter probably saved it for the world.

Nothing certain can be affirmed with reference to the place of composition. Clement of Alexandria says that it was written in Rome, and this is not improbable if we accept the tradition of Peter's residence in Rome and connexion with the Second Gospel. Wellhausen argues that Jerusalem is the most probable on the ground that the oral tradition is likely to have been first committed to writing in the place where it was current. But this implies a very sceptical attitude towards the Petrine origin of the Gospel. According to Irenaeus the Gospel was written after the death of Peter and Paul, and this is intrinsically more probable than the later statement of Clement of Alexandria that it was written in Peter's lifetime but without his co-operation. Some scholars place its composition after the destruction of Jerusalem, but it is more likely that it was somewhat earlier. We have therefore as the probable limits A.D. 64 and A.D. 70. The consideration of the genuineness of Mark xvi. 9-20 belongs mainly to Textual Criticism. The MS. evidence is in itself almost conclusive against it, and the internal evidence is almost as clear, both as regards connexion with the preceding context and characteristics. Mr. F. C. Conybeare discovered in 1891 a late Armenian manuscript in which this section is headed Of the Presbyter Ariston. Perhaps he should be identified with the Aristion who is coupled by Papias with the presbyter John. An expanded form of the Greek text has been recently discovered in Egypt.

The Gospel of Matthew.

From the time of Irenaeus onwards the First Gospel was attributed to the apostle Matthew. It is quite possible that Papias held the same opinion if by the Logia he understood the First Gospel, and it is even conceivable, though not likely, that the same misconception was shared by the presbyter John. In any case we have already seen that the First Gospel can neither have been written in Hebrew nor in Aramaic nor by the apostle Matthew. It is probable that we must assign to him the authorship of Q, all the more that there was no substantial ground for the attribution of the Logia to so obscure an apostle if he had not actually written it. We have no knowledge of the author except such as we may infer from his book. That he was a Jewish Christian is clear both from the general characteristics of the work and from the fact that quotations from the Old Testament peculiar to the First Gospel diverge widely from the Septuagint showing the influence of the Hebrew original and are related to the interpretations in the Targums.

The date is a very difficult problem. It is intrinsically improbable that it belongs to the same decade as Mark and Q, both of which it has employed. The argument which has weighed most on the other side is that no indication is given in the eschatological discourse that Jerusalem had actually fallen. If, however, the author reproduced his source here with fidelity we could draw an inference only with regard to it, not to the Gospel. Some who think that it was written later than A.D. 70 argue that it cannot have been much later, otherwise the author would have made a clear distinction between the fall of Jerusalem and the Second Coming. As against this, however, it must be urged that the Gospel seems to reflect a somewhat later period of ecclesiastical development. Nothing forbids the view that this rather catholicised Gospel may have been written towards the close of the first century. If we are right in supposing that the first and third evangelists were unacquainted with each other's works, we cannot allow any considerable interval to lie between them, so that our decision on the date of Luke will affect that on the date of Matthew. We have no evidence as to the place of writing. The interest in Peter and the ecclesiastical character of the Gospel have suggested Rome to some scholars, while others on account of its markedly Jewish Christian characteristics prefer Palestine or Syria. Whether the author employed other documents besides Q and Mark is uncertain, but is not improbable.

The Gospel of Luke.

There is no question that the ancient Church from the time of Irenaeus onwards attributed the Third Gospel and the Acts of the Apostles to Luke. Its existence at a much earlier date is guaranteed by the fact that Marcion included it in a mutilated form in his Canon. This view as to the authorship maintained itself in the Church down to the critical period, and is still held by conservative scholars, though it has become almost an axiom among more advanced critics that the Lucan authorship cannot be maintained. Against this Harnack has recently put forward a very weighty protest, which seems at present to have made little impression on German opinion. The objections to the Lucan authorship are based rather on the Acts than the Gospel, but since it is on all hands admitted that both of these works were written by the same author the denial of Acts to Luke carries with it a similar verdict on the Gospel. It will be more convenient therefore to defer the question of authorship and also that of date till we come to the latter work.

We have already seen that for the account of Christ's ministry Luke drew mainly on Mark and Q. That he used other sources is probable. In his very important preface he tells us that he had had many predecessors, and although he was apparently dissatisfied with their work, it is likely that he used more than two of them. It is of course possible in the abstract that some of the matter peculiar to Luke was to be found in Q, but if so it is very hard to understand why Matthew should have omitted it. Even if he was governed by considerations of space, it would be surprising that he should have excluded some of the most beautiful sections now found in Luke in favour of matter greatly inferior in interest. It is therefore most likely that Luke derived his peculiar matter from one or more of these documents, though we need not exclude the possibility that he may have been indebted for not a little to oral communication.

CHAPTER XIII

THE ACTS OF THE APOSTLES

It may be assumed that this book comes from the same hand as the Third Gospel. This is guaranteed by the preface to the two writings, each addressed to Theophilus, and by the explicit reference to the Gospel in the preface of the Acts. The style leads decisively to the same conclusion. The uniform tradition from Irenaeus onwards ascribes this work as well as the Gospel to Luke. It was apparently known to Justin Martyr, and perhaps to Ignatius and Polycarp. We have also numerous apocryphal Acts which presuppose the history as told in our work.

If we turn to examine the internal evidence for authorship, the point of departure is found in what are known as the 'we-sections.' Certain parts of the book are written in the first person plural. This means on the most obvious hypothesis that the writer of the book was a companion of Paul on some of his journeys. This is the opinion ordinarily accepted. But in view of the difficulties which the phenomena present, many critics believe that the 'we-sections' were written by a companion of the apostle, but that the book itself was composed by a later writer who incorporated these sections with or without alteration. This hypothesis has assumed several forms, according as the 'we-sections' are attributed now to one, now to another writer. Timothy, Silas and Titus have been suggested, but the first two seem to be excluded by the language of the book itself (xx. 5, 6, xvi. 16 ff.), and there is no object in accepting Titus or any support for this view. The only form of the hypothesis which deserves consideration is that which attributes these sections to Luke and regards them as incorporated by a later writer. This has the support of tradition so far as it assigns a share of the work to Luke. And it has an analogy in the case of the First Gospel.

The real question, however, is whether these sections can be separated from the rest of the book. In the first place it would be an extraordinary proceeding for any writer, and especially for a writer of such literary skill, to have incorporated a document, or extracts from a document, without even changing the first person plural into a third person or naming the writer. For there can be no doubt that as the work reads now, the author gives the distinct impression that he himself was present at those incidents related in these sections. It seems highly improbable on the face of it that he should have allowed that impression to remain, if really it was not he but some one else whose name he suppresses while he borrows his words. But apart from this difficulty which meets us at the outset, there are others. The style of these sections is not to be distinguished from that of the rest of the book. This has been convincingly demonstrated by several scholars, among whom Hawkins and Harnack may be singled out for special mention. The suggestion made by some scholars that the identity of style is to be explained by the author's revision of the sections is difficult to harmonise with the fact that the first person plural is left untouched. Not only so, but there are cross-references from them to other parts of the book. Thus in xxi. 8 we have a reference to the fact that Philip was one of the seven, and who the seven were has been explained in ch. vi., where it is also mentioned that Philip was one of them. How he came to be in Caesarea has been told in viii. 40. It seems then far the most probable hypothesis that the work is a unity, and if so due to a companion of Paul, whom we need have no hesitation in believing to be Luke. This is corroborated by the fact that both the Third Gospel and the Acts seem to have been composed by a physician such as we know Luke to have been (Col. iv. 14). The fullest collection of evidence was made by Hobart in his *Medical Language of St. Luke.* Even when every reasonable deduction has been made the evidence is sufficiently cogent to render this conclusion highly probable, and it has recently secured the adhesion of Harnack.

Since Acts is an historical book, it is natural that our critical conclusions should be affected to a certain extent by the author's treatment of history. A discussion of his character as a historian lies outside our scope, but something must be said on the history so far as it affects the criticism. The author is distinguished by great accuracy in his use of political terms. In view of the frequent interchange of provinces between Emperor and Senate, it was not easy for a later writer to be strictly accurate, since different terms were employed for the two types. A critic would expect the 'we-sections' to be accurate. Philippi was a Roman colony, the local magistrates were duumvirs, but dub themselves praetors, and they have their lictors. But the same accuracy characterises the other parts of the work. It was thought even by some apologists that Luke had used terms incorrectly when he called the governor of Cyprus a proconsul. As a matter of fact when the provinces were originally divided it fell to the Emperor's share, but subsequently he gave it to the Senate, so that Luke is strictly right in speaking of the governor as proconsul. Another case is that of Thessalonica. Here the magistrates are spoken of as politarchs. The word does not occur in any Greek literature known to us, but inscriptions have been found at Thessalonica showing that this city had several politarchs. Achaia is another good example owing to the frequent change of government. From A.D. 15-44 it had been in the hands of the Emperor. In the latter year it was handed over to the Senate, to which it had formerly belonged and was retained by it till 67. Then it ceased to be a Roman province and became independent, but subsequently Vespasian made it a province again. In spite of the numerous changes the Acts correctly represents Gallio as a proconsul, and its description of him agrees admirably with information from other sources. None of these cases is taken from the 'we-sections,' so that even in the parts where the writer is not credited with having the accurate knowledge displayed by the author of those sections, it is plain that on such slippery ground as this he meets with no mishap. The knowledge of localities is also accurate and betrays first-hand knowledge, as does the description of the character of the people in particular places. But while these have considerable weight, and must be set down to the writer's credit, there is not the same evidential value as in the instances just given, since such knowledge might be obtained by travel a considerable time afterwards. But not only does the account show first-hand knowledge of the localities, it is also faithful to the state of things that obtained at the time, but became obsolete in the second century.

The writer shows a good understanding of the development of the early Church. He knows the composition of the community at Jerusalem, and points out quite naturally how the first sign of friction within it was due to difficulties between the Palestinian Jews and the Hellenists. He knows of the communistic basis of the Church, though that would presumably have passed away by his time even in the Jewish Christian Churches, while in the Pauline it probably never existed. He gives a perfectly natural account of the almost incidental way in which the Gospel was first preached to the Gentiles. He is also aware of the external relations of the Jerusalem Church. Thus he has accurately caught the attitude of the Jewish parties towards it. In the Gospels the Pharisees are for the most part the persistent enemies of Jesus, though the Sadducees became more prominent towards the end. In the Acts, however, the Pharisees sink into comparative insignificance, while the Sadducees are the chief persecutors of the Church. This is due partly to the fact that the Sadducees had been foremost in putting Jesus to death, but partly also to their dislike of the doctrine of the Resurrection, which was a prominent article of Christian preaching, since it all rested on the resurrection of Jesus. It is likely that if the writer had been relying on his inventive powers rather than actual historical information, he would have followed the Gospel and given the prominent place to the Pharisees as the persecutors of the Christians.

It has also been noticed that the speeches of Peter and Paul present marked parallels with the Epistles of these apostles respectively. This is an argument of a kind that requires to be employed with caution, but so far as it goes, it is a confirmation of the general accuracy of the book. With reference to the speeches generally, it may be said that in their main outlines they seem eminently appropriate to the situation in which they are placed. An example of this is the speech of Stephen. Lightfoot thinks that the speech as we have it is only a preamble to the real reply which Stephen had no chance of giving owing to his attack on his accusers in the last verses. But really it seems to be a most skilful reply, conducted except for these three verses, with consummate tact. While recounting the national history of which the Jews were proud, he yet tells it in such a way as to indicate the independence of true religion on the local sanctuary or the Holy Land which had been exemplified frequently in that history, and to hint that the rejection of Jesus by the Jews was all of a piece with the conduct of their fathers. He thus brings his own position into line with much in the Old Testament that could not be objected to by the Jews themselves. It is also a mark of authenticity that there is no reference in Stephen's speech to the abolition of the Law. This could scarcely have been kept out if the narrator had invented the speech. In the speeches of Paul too it is noticeable that when addressing non-Christian audiences he starts from what he has in common with those whom he is addressing. Thus in his speech to the people of Lycaonia he takes his stand on the truths of natural religion as they appear to the untrained intelligence. In his speech at Athens his treatment is philosophical, and he starts from the truth contained in pantheism and the kinship of men with God. Similarly he treats the Jews at Antioch. In each case the speech is relevant to the audience.

Another argument has been worked out by Paley in his *Horae Paulinae*. He has shown in numerous cases that the allusions in Paul's Epistles fit perfectly into the narrative of the Acts. This is important because the author does not seem to have used the Epistles in constructing his story, for it would be difficult to explain if he had done so why he should not have availed himself of much of the material to be found there. And even if he had used the Epistles, it is scarcely credible that the minute coincidences, which are just those that would be least obvious and most difficult to invent, should be just the coincidences that we find.

There are, however, certain difficulties raised as to matters of fact. The most serious is perhaps the reference to Theudas in the speech of Gamaliel. We know from Josephus of a Theudas who raised an insurrection in the proconsulship of Fadus. This cannot have been earlier than A.D. 44, the date when Fadus became procurator

Yet not only is Gamaliel's speech earlier than this date, but he places the insurrection before the time of Judas the Galilaean. This latter is dated in the time of the taxing soon after the birth of Christ. Two alternatives are possible. Either the author has made a mistake or the Theudas mentioned is to be distinguished from the Theudas mentioned by Josephus. The name is not uncommon, and insurrections of this kind were numerous.

One of the most serious difficulties is that occasioned by the story of the apostolic council in Acts xv. If the identification of this visit to Jerusalem with that recorded in Gal. ii. be accepted we have apparently a grave discrepancy. Paul asserts that the Jerusalem apostles imparted nothing to him, recognised the validity of his call and divided the sphere of service, making only the request that he should remember the poor. According to Acts they drew up a letter in which they made four stipulations, that the Gentile Christians should 'abstain from things sacrificed to idols, and from blood, and from things strangled, and from fornication.' It is argued that such an agreement cannot have been accepted by Paul, and therefore that his companion Luke cannot be responsible for this account. The question as to the historicity of the decrees does not concern us, unless we are prepared to draw the inference that inaccuracy on such a matter would be impossible to a companion of Paul writing a great many years later. It is now, however, more and more admitted that the underlying assumption is unjustified. It is not intended of course that there is any necessary discrepancy between Acts and Paul on this point, but only that if there were it would not necessarily involve the non-Lucan authorship. The difficulty would largely disappear if Harnack were right in adopting the contention of the younger Resch, that we should accept the Western text of the decrees though without the golden rule. In that case we have not food prohibitions in the decrees but 'the summary of Jewish ethical catechetics,' abstinence from idolatry, murder and fornication. This solution of the difficulty has been rejected by Schürer and by Sanday (*The Apostolic Decree* in the volume of Essays in honour of Zahn). It remains to be seen whether it will secure any wide acceptance. What has been said on this historical difficulty applies also to others. The primary element in determining authorship is the proof that the author of the 'we-sections' was the author of the Third Gospel and the Acts as a whole. The objections taken to the narrative must accommodate themselves to this conclusion rather than *vice versa*. The question how far other sources have been used by the writer cannot be discussed here. A whole series of attempts has been made to detect sources; the most recent discussion is to be found in Harnack's *The Acts of the Apostles*.

The question of the date is one of great difficulty. Some consider that the work was written soon after the conclusion of the narrative, that is two years after Paul's arrival in Rome. This view is suggested by the close of the Acts at this point. It is argued that if Luke had known more he would have told more, and not simply said that Paul dwelt for two years in his own hired house. This argument has been met in various ways. Some have supposed that Luke intended to write a third book in which he would have carried on the history from the point where he leaves it at the close of the Acts, and rounded it off by a peroration to match the elaborate preface to the Third Gospel and Acts. For this we have no evidence, certainly not in the use of 'first' instead of 'former' in Acts i. 1, nor have we any for the view that this book was left by him in an unfinished state. It has already been pointed out in the discussion of the Pastoral Epistles that as a matter of fact the work closes very skilfully. Other arguments are that Acts xx. 25, cf. 38, expresses the conviction that Paul would never see the

Ephesian elders again, whereas from 2 Timothy it appears that he did so. This, however, rests on the assumption that Paul was released from the Roman captivity which we have already seen reason to set aside. Moreover, there is no reference either in the Acts or in the Gospels to the destruction of Jerusalem and the terrible misfortunes which fell upon the Jews. But this argument from silence is too weak to bear any weight. The fact was notorious. The failure to use the Pauline Epistles is much easier to account for in Paul's lifetime than at a later period. But this implies rather too modern a demand on the historian.

There are very weighty arguments in favour of a later date. The preface to the Gospel definitely states that the author had been preceded in his enterprise by many. It is in the abstract quite possible that these numerous Gospel narratives may have been in existence by A.D. 60. It is nevertheless much more likely that the number points to a considerably later date. We have seen reason to believe that Luke based his Gospel on Mark and Q. So far as our evidence for date goes, it is unlikely that either of these was earlier than the sixties. Mark, it would seem, belongs at the earliest to the late sixties. If so we must place the Third Gospel in the seventies at the earliest. The later we go the more easily we can account for some of the phenomena. The version of the Judaistic controversy suggests that it originated in a period when the question had become one of rather remote historical interest, and the conception of the apostolic age was moving towards the catholicised picture of the second century. The apologetic character of both Gospel and Acts in relation at once to Judaism and the Roman Empire is similar to what we find in the Fourth Gospel, and also suggests a date not earlier than the reign of Domitian.

If the view that Luke used Josephus could be substantiated, we should be definitely committed to a date later than 93-94 when his *Antiquities* was written. Dependence on Josephus has been asserted by Holtzmann, Schmiedel, Wendt, Burkitt and other scholars, but especially by Krenkel, who in his work *Josephus und Lucas* (1894) sought to prove that Luke knew the whole of Josephus' writings and was greatly influenced by them. His demonstration of this, however, is not satisfactory. That Luke was in any way dependent on Josephus is denied by very many scholars, including Schürer, Harnack, and Wellhausen. The difficulty about Theudas has been already mentioned. According to Acts, Theudas is first mentioned and then Judas of Galilee. Both the anachronism and the reversal of the historical order would be explained if we assumed that Luke was acquainted with the *Antiquities* (Book xx. chap. 5), inasmuch as after the account of Theudas we read in the next paragraph that 'the sons of Judas of Galilee were now slain, I mean of that Judas who caused the people to revolt when Quirinius came to take an account of the estates of the Jews as we have showed in a former book.' It must, however, be confessed that not only would the author have read Josephus very carelessly, but that it would have been far more easy to account for if Josephus' reference to Judas had not been so very incidental. The other serious argument for acquaintance with Josephus is the reference to Lysanias, tetrarch of Abilene, in Luke iii. 1. Lysanias had been put to death in B.C. 36, so that we should have to assume that it is a later Lysanias who is mentioned by Luke. It is a little surprising that Luke should have introduced Abilene into his synchronism, and the suggestion is that this is due to his having read that Claudius in the twelfth year of his reign 'bestowed upon Agrippa the tetrarchy of Philip and Batanaea, and added thereto Trachonitis and Abila, which last had been the tetrarchy of Lysanias' (*Antiquities*, Book ii. chap. 7).

Others who agree that the mention of Lysanias is an inaccuracy, account for it by the fact that his kingdom continued after his death to bear his name, and that Luke did not know Josephus. The view that Luke may have been acquainted with Josephus' literary sources rather than with Josephus himself can hardly be considered a probable alternative since the chronological inaccuracies charged against him are due to incidental combinations in Josephus, which the latter would have been very unlikely to have derived from his source. The present writer is accordingly inclined to believe that Luke had a cursory acquaintance with this section of the *Antiquities*, and therefore that the Gospel was probably not earlier than 95, while Acts appears to have been written a few years later. It is true that this would make Luke rather an old man at the time, but if we assume that he was quite young when he began to accompany Paul, he would not be incredibly old. At the same time an early date, say from 75-80, is not at all impossible in view of the somewhat precarious inference from the coincidences with Josephus.

Rome – 63 A.D. – Mitchell.
by Luke.

CHAPTER XIV

THE JOHANNINE WRITINGS

WE have five writings in the New Testament which are attributed to John, namely the Fourth Gospel, three Epistles, and the Apocalypse. The critical opinion of the present time is very much divided as to this literature. Some still ascribe all five of these works to John the son of Zebedee, others are willing to credit him with the Gospel and the Epistles but deny to him the Apocalypse, while others accept his authorship of the Apocalypse but deny the apostolic authorship of the other writings. Others again attribute some or all of these writings to John, but consider that he is not to be identified with the apostle of that name. Some admit that the Fourth Gospel and the First Epistle are by one author, attributing the Second and Third Epistles to a different writer, but some believe that neither the Epistles nor the Apocalypse were written by the author of the Fourth Gospel. Questions are also raised as to the unity both of the Fourth Gospel and of the Apocalypse. In view of these and other problems it will be most convenient to begin by discussing some preliminary questions before we pass on to those that are more central.

The first is concerned with the identity of John of Asia known to us from Irenaeus, Clement of Alexandria, Polycrates and others. It has been usual to identify this John with the apostle. The Tübingen school naturally held firmly to tradition on this point, in face of the attacks of Lützelberger, Keim and Scholten, since it was an axiom for it that the apostle John was the author of the Apocalypse, with its supposed bitter attack on Paul, and the Apocalypse can have been written only by one who was intimately acquainted with the Seven Churches of Asia. Probably scarcely any one now believes that the Apocalypse contains an attack on Paul, or has any critical axe to grind in claiming the Apocalypse for the apostle. Accordingly the critical case gains nothing from the tradition of the Asian residence, while this tradition is really awkward for it when it comes to deal with the Fourth Gospel. Several scholars, however, consider that he was not the apostle but the presbyter John. Of the latter we hear simply from Papias who enumerates, in a list of those about whose discourses he was in the habit of making inquiries, two Johns. The former of these was clearly the apostle, the latter is called the presbyter John. The passage runs as follows: 'And again on any occasion when a person came (in my way) who had been a follower of the Elders, I would enquire about the discourses of the Elders—What was said by Andrew or by Peter, or by Philip, or by Thomas or James, or by John or Matthew or any other of the Lord's disciples, and what Aristion and the Elder John, the disciples of the Lord say.' (Quoted from the translation in Lightfoot's *Apostolic Fathers.*) It is clear that the term 'disciples of the Lord' is used in two different senses, in the former case in the narrow sense of apostle, in the latter case in a wider sense. It seems further to be clear that the John mentioned before Matthew is to be distinguished as the apostle from the presbyter John who is coupled with Aristion. And it may also be inferred that either at the time when Papias was writing, or more probably when he was collecting his material, John the apostle was dead, while John the presbyter was alive, unless with Drummond we explain the present tense 'say' to mean 'say in their books.'

The possibility must therefore be admitted that references to John as resident in Asia may in some instances have been intended to relate to the presbyter rather than the apostle.

The most important of these occurs in a letter written by Irenaeus to Florinus. He as well as Irenaeus had in his earlier days been a hearer of Polycarp, but had been later attracted by Valentinianism. In this letter Irenaeus gives a vivid account of Polycarp's teaching. In it he recalls 'how he would describe his intercourse with John and with the rest who had seen the Lord, and how he would relate their words.' He proceeds: 'And whatsoever things he had heard from them about the Lord, and about His miracles, and about His teaching, Polycarp, as having received them from eye-witnesses of the life of the Word, would relate altogether in accordance with the Scriptures.' It is clear from this that Polycarp was in the habit of relating in very considerable detail the discourses he heard from John and others who had seen and heard Jesus, and of recounting their narratives about His life, teaching and work. It is therefore highly improbable that Irenaeus can have made any mistake as to the identity of the John, whose teaching Polycarp used to relate. The frequency of his references to him and the detail into which he used to go, seem to exclude the possibility of such misunderstanding. It must have been clear in several instances, whether it was John the apostle or some other John of whom Polycarp was speaking.

It is urged on the other hand that Irenaeus was very young at the time, and that he was probably merely a hearer of Polycarp and not one of his familiar disciples. It is, however, very dubious whether he was so young as these scholars attempt to make out, and he himself lays special stress on his vivid recollections of that period. Moreover, the accuracy of his statement is guaranteed by the circumstances. However unscrupulously he might overstate his points against those who were not in a position to check his assertions, he could not very well have afforded to do so when he was appealing to recollections shared by the very man whose views he was engaged in refuting. It is alleged that Irenaeus made a similar mistake about Papias. He says: 'These things Papias, who was a hearer of John and a companion of Polycarp, an ancient worthy, witnesses in writing in the fourth of his books. For there are five books composed by him.' Eusebius, after quoting this statement, passes a criticism on it to the effect that Papias does not declare himself in his preface to have been a hearer of the apostles, but shows that he had received his information from their friends. He then gives an extract from the preface to substantiate his criticism. It is generally agreed that Eusebius is right, for he read his authorities with considerable care, and that Irenaeus was incorrect in his assertion that Papias was a hearer of John. But it does not follow from this that Irenaeus is likely to have made a similar mistake about Polycarp. We have no evidence that he had ever seen Papias, but we know that he had seen and heard Polycarp frequently, and had often listened to his reminiscences of John. Besides, his statement about Papias is a mere passing allusion, while his account of Polycarp's relations with John is vital to his argument. Moreover, we know that Irenaeus was immensely impressed by the idea of continuity with the apostolic teaching. He believed himself to stand in relation to the apostle John through Polycarp. That he should have made a mistake at this point is not easy to believe.

But Irenaeus does not stand alone. Polycrates, the bishop of Ephesus, in a letter to Victor bishop of Rome about the Paschal controversy mentions among the great lights that have fallen asleep in Asia, 'John who was both a witness [or confessor] and a teacher, and who leaned upon the bosom of the Lord.' This makes it probable that the apostle is intended. He adds, 'He fell asleep at Ephesus.' The date of this letter is about 190 A.D. Since the writer speaks of himself in it as 'having sixty-five years in the Lord' the date of his birth, if he was born a Christian, will be about 125. Of course we cannot assume, as Harnack observes, that he was born in Ephesus, or spent his early days there. Still this is not unlikely, and in any case the fact that he himself lived in Ephesus as head of the Christian Church there, lends great weight to his identification of the John who died there with the beloved disciple. At the same time there is force in the objection that he confused Philip the deacon with Philip the apostle. It is not certain that he did so, but it is at least sufficiently probable to lend plausibility to the suggestion that he similarly confused John the presbyter with John the apostle. This evidence of course does not attest the residence of the apostle in Ephesus unless we can identify the apostle with the disciple whom Jesus loved. Clement of Alexandria relates the story of the Apostle John and the Robber, and says that the incident happened while John lived at Ephesus.

Justin's evidence is, however, of more weight. He ascribes the Revelation to the apostle John. It is clear from the early chapters of the Revelation that it was written by some one closely connected with the Seven Churches of Asia. Accordingly Justin, whether he is a witness to the Johannine authorship of the Gospel or not, is at least a witness for the residence of the apostle John in or near Ephesus. This is significant when we remember that Justin was himself for a time in Ephesus. Nearly fifty years, then, before Polycrates wrote to Victor, the fact that the apostle John lived in Asia is indirectly attested by a writer who had himself been in Ephesus.

If, further, it be allowed, as it generally is, that the Fourth Gospel originated in or near Ephesus, then this may also be urged in corroboration of the belief that the beloved disciple lived there. If the work was written by him, this would follow as a matter of course. But if not, the prominence assigned to him in the narrative is most easily explained if it was the work of disciples of his who were concerned to vindicate their master's true position. And if such disciples wrote in Ephesus it is most likely that there John had taught them. We can the better understand why it was felt necessary to correct the impression that Jesus had promised the beloved disciple that he should not die, if he had lived or was at the time living in the community from which the Gospel proceeded. If then the beloved disciple is to be identified with the apostle John, it seems probable that the interest in him in the Fourth Gospel is due to the apostle's connexion with Ephesus. Unless very forcible reasons can be alleged on the other side, it must be admitted that John's residence in Asia is a well-attested fact.

The question accordingly arises if the arguments against it are sufficiently cogent to neutralise the reasons in its favour. In the first place, while Papias mentions two Johns, he says nothing as to their residence, and other early writers betray no knowledge that two famous Johns lived in Asia. They seem to know of one only. Accordingly it is inferred that there was only one highly distinguished John in Asia, viz. the presbyter, and that by a natural confusion he was identified with the apostle. In answer to this it may be said that we cannot assume that the presbyter John did live in Asia. If he did not, then the identity of Polycarp's John with the apostle would be very probable. But if the presbyter did live in Asia, nothing was more likely than that he should speedily be forgotten, eclipsed by the great apostle.

It must be admitted, however, that the argument from the silence of certain writers is really strong. We should have expected reference to the apostle's residence in Asia in the Epistles of Ignatius and Polycarp. The latter, however, was writing to the Philippians, and it was natural for him to refer to Paul, who had founded the Church and written at least one letter to it, while there was no need for him to mention John. The silence of Ignatius is more difficult to explain, especially in his letter to the Church at Ephesus, in which he refers to Paul but not to John, who if he had lived there, could have died only a short time before. The mention of Paul seems to be due partly to his relation to the Ephesian Church in its earliest period, partly to Paul's connexion with Antioch, where Ignatius was bishop, and especially to the fact that he was going to Rome to be martyred and thus, as he says, following in Paul's footsteps. The difficulty is a real one, but a negative argument, which might with fuller knowledge be readily rebutted, cannot count for much against the mass of positive evidence for John's residence in Asia.[1] Ignatius refers to the connexion of the Church in Ephesus with apostles, and the plural may imply Paul and John.

It would nevertheless be difficult to maintain the correctness of the tradition if the apostle John was really martyred in Palestine. No weight could attach to the bare statement found in a single MS. of the Chronicle of Georgios Hamartolos that in the second book of his Logia, Papias stated that John the apostle was put to death by Jews. The Chronicle belongs to the ninth century, and the statement is found only in one of the twenty-eight MSS. of the work. There is, however, a confirmation of it in an extract from a MS. of an epitome that seems to be based on the Chronicle of Philip of Side, which belongs to a date early in the fifth century. Here we read, 'Papias says in his second book that John the Divine and his brother James were slain by Jews.' And as confirming

1 In any case Pfleiderer's statement is extravagant that the silence of one who, in time as well as locality, stood so near the Ephesian John of tradition, and had such urgent reasons to appeal to him, is sufficient by itself to refute this tradition (*Urchristentum*, vol. ii. pp. 413, 414).

this, we have the argument derived from the oracle in Mark, that James and John should drink of the cup Jesus drank of and be baptized with His baptism. Without knowing of the alleged quotation from Papias, Wellhausen had inferred from this passage in Mark that both John and James had been already martyred when the Gospel was written. In his note on Mark x. 39 he says: 'The prophecy of martyrdom refers not simply to James but also to John, and if half of it remained unfulfilled it would hardly have stood in the Gospel. Accordingly a serious objection is raised against the reliability of the tradition that the apostle John died a peaceful death at an advanced age.'

Apparently Wellhausen does not regard the oracle as authentic, but as very old. E. Schwartz was stimulated by Wellhausen's note to publish a special discussion of the subject. He thinks that the oracle was very old, inasmuch as the later Gospels tone down the story, but he supposes it to have originated from the martyrdom of the two apostles. From the reference to the seats, the one at the right hand and the other at the left, he infers that they must actually have been martyred at the same time, and that this claim cannot have been made for them unless they had been the first of the twelve to be martyred, and for some time remained the only martyrs. These results are stated as if the mere statement of them made them self-evident, and the difficulties in the way are very lightly brushed aside. Schwartz is not disturbed by the mention of John in Gal. ii. 9 as alive when Paul and Barnabas were recognised by the 'pillar' apostles, but argues that the John intended is John Mark. Naturally this does not at all harmonise with the relative positions assigned to Paul and John Mark in the narrative of Acts. Schwartz has no hesitation in setting this aside, especially as the legendary character of the mission in Cyprus seems to him quite obvious, or in denying the identity of John

Mark with the Mark of the Pauline Epistles. A further difficulty is that Acts is completely silent about the death of the apostle John, and this is explained by Schwartz as due to deliberate suppression on account of the later tradition. Besides, how was it that John Mark, who was not one of the twelve nor yet a kinsman of Christ, came to possess so eminent a position in the Jerusalem Church as to rank with Peter and James the Lord's brother? The only answer that Schwartz is able to give is that he was the son of the Mary who permitted meetings of the Church in her house!

It is scarcely probable that, weighted with these numerous improbabilities, Schwartz's theory that James and John perished at the same time will make many converts. Besides, there is a very serious difficulty created by the fact, as Schwartz considers it, that Papias recognised the Fourth Gospel and the Apocalypse as the work of the apostle. Is it likely that he supposed that John was put to death by Herod Agrippa, and yet had already seen his vision in Patmos and written his letters to the Seven Churches? Schwartz replies that Papias tested his traditions not with reference to their historical truth or probability, but their orthodox or heretical character. But surely he can hardly have been unconscious of the glaring improbability which would thus be created, especially as his familiarity with the conditions of the apostolic age must have been sufficient to assure him that the residence in Patmos could not possibly be placed so early. It is therefore extremely difficult to accept Schwartz's view that John was martyred at the same time as James. Wellhausen at one time rejected the view that John died at the same time as James though he has since accepted it (*Das Ev. Johannis*, p. 100), and most of those who accept the quotation from Papias as authentic and historical will probably refuse to date the martyrdom of John so early as the reign of Herod

Agrippa. Clemen (*American Journal of Theology*, vol. ix.) believes that Papias made the statement attributed to him, but that it was a mere inference from Mark, and unhistorical. It should be added as a further piece of evidence that in the Syriac Calendar of the Church of Edessa, the MS. of which is dated A.D. 411, we have John and James coupled together as martyrs at Jerusalem and they are described as apostles, the date of their martyrdom being Dec. 27th. John is apparently the son of Zebedee, though in the entry for Dec. 26th Stephen is described as 'Stephen the apostle.' In a Carthaginian calendar we have John the Baptist in place of the apostle, but this is clearly a correction, for the Baptist is also commemorated on June 24th. But J. H. Bernard has shown that we cannot rely on this evidence to prove the martyrdom (*Irish Church Quarterly*, vol. i.), and his arguments have been accepted not only by J. A. Robinson but by Harnack, who has all along refused to credit the story, though he denies the Ephesian residence of the apostle.

In spite of these arguments and the confidence with which many critics accept them, the gravest doubts must arise as to whether Papias ever made the statement at all. For all scholars have said to the contrary, it is hard to believe that in the face of it the view that John died a peaceful death in Asia in extreme old age could ever have gained its universal currency. Irenaeus appeals to Papias as an authority, at the same time he betrays no shadow of misgiving that his opponents had at hand so awkward an argument with which to pulverise his statement. Eusebius similarly is quite unaware, so far as appears, that any such statement was made, and yet he read Papias thoroughly. That Eusebius deliberately suppressed the statement is hard to believe. He could not remove it from the pages of Papias if he wished, and his opposition to Papias' millenarianism might have made him welcome such an exhibition of Papias' capacity for blundering. We need not doubt that Papias must have said something which gave rise to the distorted statement that we at present possess, but what this statement was, whether it had originally reference to John the Baptist, as Zahn supposes, or whether, as Lightfoot and Harnack have suggested, something has dropped out of the text, will be shown only when further evidence is discovered.

Further, if the identification of the beloved disciple with the apostle John can be accepted we have another piece of evidence in the appendix to the Gospel. Its point is, that while Peter is to die a martyr's death, the beloved disciple is not. Whether the appendix was written by the author of the Gospel or not, it must have been written very early, and probably published at the same time as the Gospel, since we have no trace that the rest of the Gospel was ever in circulation without it. The chapter then gives us evidence, at least contemporary with Papias and probably earlier, that the beloved disciple did not die a martyr's death. Moreover, the prominence which the beloved disciple receives in the Fourth Gospel points in the same direction if the common view is correct that the Fourth Gospel originated in or near Ephesus. If the Gospel was the work of the beloved disciple, such prominence is readily accounted for. But if it was not his work, then the question arises why in this Gospel he is so much more prominent than in the Synoptists. Obviously because he was of special interest to the circle out of which it came. But if it originated in Asia, why should John the apostle be thus honoured there? The best explanation is given by the tradition which asserts that during the latter part of his life he lived in Ephesus, and gathered pupils about him to whom he was the object of special veneration. Harnack himself is so impressed by this that, while he denies the tradition, he thinks that John at some time paid a visit, though only a brief one, to Ephesus

It is questionable, however, whether a brief visit would make the impression that he seems to have made in Asia.

In the preceding discussion the qualification has been constantly made that this or that argument holds good only if the beloved disciple and the apostle John are to be identified. This identification has been universally made in tradition, and it is still accepted by the great majority of critics. Some, it is true, have considered him an ideal figure invented by the evangelist. This view, however, may be safely set aside. It would be hard to hold it in face of the phenomena of the Gospel. But it is really impossible, with any show of reason, to carry it through for the appendix. The author is obviously embarrassed by the necessity of clearing up a prevalent misunderstanding, to the effect that Jesus had promised that this disciple should not die till His return. People do not speculate on the future of non-existent persons, and certainly if the evangelist had created the figure he would never have represented such a misunderstanding as arising, still less have felt himself under the compulsion of correcting it. It is plain that the writer is confronted by a real difficulty touching a real person, about whom a current expectation had been or was likely to be falsified.

Assuming, then, that there was a beloved disciple, is any other identification than the usual one possible? The view put forward by Delff may first be mentioned. He eliminates from the Gospel most of the Prologue and the Galilaean sections. He thinks the author was named John, and belonged to one of the high-priestly families in Jerusalem, better educated than the apostles and therefore more capable of appreciating the deeper teaching of Jesus, a friend of Nicodemus. In the first edition of his Commentary on the Apocalypse (1896) Bousset put forward the view that there was a disciple of Jesus living in Asia to extreme old age, who bore the name of John, and is to be identified with the presbyter John of Papias.

This John was the beloved disciple, but he was not the apostle; he was an inhabitant of Jerusalem, and connected with the high-priestly family. He has since modified his position in a more negative direction (*Theologische Rundschau*, June and July 1905). He now leaves the question open whether the presbyter John had actually seen Jesus. He may have done so, but he may simply have belonged to the primitive Jerusalem Church, and have been called a 'disciple of the Lord' in that wider sense. He was not the author of the Fourth Gospel, which was written by one of his disciples some decades after his death. Apart from the date given for the day of Christ's death, we have no tradition in the Gospel superior to the Synoptic. The part assigned to the beloved disciple in the Gospel is of a fanciful character; indeed, on the general question as to the trustworthiness of the Gospel he occupies pretty much the same position as other advanced critics (see the summary in his *Was Wissen wir von Jesus?*).

The identification of the beloved disciple with John of Jerusalem seems to be growing in favour, and mediate or immediate authorship is claimed for this John rather than the apostle by Von Dobschütz, Burkitt and others. This theory has some advantages: it accounts for the prominence given to Jerusalem in the Fourth Gospel, and removes some of the difficulties that have been felt as to the authorship of such a work by the apostle John. In spite, however, of its attractiveness it is exposed to considerable difficulty. It is possible to identify the beloved disciple with one of the 'two other of his disciples' mentioned in the twenty-first chapter (cf. i. 35) rather than with one of the sons of Zebedee, though on a fishing expedition in Galilee we do not expect the High Priest's friend from Jerusalem. It is even possible that one who was not an apostle was present at the Last Supper, especially if he were the host in whose house the supper was held. But it is very improbable that the place of chief honour at the feast should be accorded to one who was not an apostle. Moreover, the close association with Peter points to the apostle John, since the two are closely associated in the Acts of the Apostles. It may be added that the difficulties which seem to many scholars to negative the supposition that the Gospel was written by an eye-witness are not much relieved by this hypothesis, inasmuch as they specially touch those very points on which a Jerusalem resident should have been exceptionally well-informed. On the whole, then, it seems best to acquiesce in the usual view which has recently been reaffirmed by Harnack, that the beloved disciple was none other than the son of Zebedee. So far then from having suffered martyrdom in Palestine, he lived to so extreme an old age that the saying was current about him that he would survive till the Second Coming.

It may be convenient to discuss here another question raised by the passages which speak of the disciple whom Jesus loved. In an extremely acute and suggestive study of the Monarchian Prologues to the Gospels published in Gebhardt and Harnack's *Texte und Untersuchungen*, Corssen found in the Leucian Acts of John the key to the Gospel. His discussion has attracted great attention, and Pfleiderer has accepted his results. In the Acts of John a Docetic view of Christ's Person is taken. During the Crucifixion, Jesus appeared to the apostle John on the Mount of Olives, and revealed to him that while for the crowd He was suffering in Jerusalem, John alone was deemed worthy of the revelation that the Crucifixion was an empty appearance. The Acts explained why John was the beloved disciple, a thing which the Gospel does not do. It was because of his celibacy. Corssen argued that the author of the Leucian Acts did not know the Fourth Gospel, and that if there was dependence they were the original. If the two works, however, were independent then the Fourth Gospel was based on an earlier form of the tradition later embodied in the Acts. In order to attack the Docetic doctrine the Fourth Evangelist wrote a Gospel vigorously asserting the fact of the Incarnation and real humanity of Christ. He took from the Docetists the John under whose name they had promulgated their doctrines and made him the guarantee for his own. But since caution was necessary, he did not openly say who the beloved disciple was, though he indicated that John was intended.

This theory suffers under several disabilities. In the first place, Corssen's theory of the relation between the Gospel and the Acts cannot be maintained; it is very improbable that the Fourth Gospel can be so late as the Leucian Acts; the date of the latter is uncertain, but it is not probable that they are as early as 130, and it is highly improbable that the Fourth Gospel is so late. Of course this does not negative Corssen's general theory, for the Acts may embody earlier stories. Still, these have to be postulated. In the next place, Corssen seems to invert the relation between Christ's special affection for John and his celibacy. The representation is not that his celibacy was the *cause* of Christ's love (*Monarchianische Prologe*, p. 131), but the *effect* of it. If so the Acts do not account any more than the Gospel for the love entertained by Jesus for him. The Gospel gives no explanation because none was needed; it was simply the statement of a fact. The extravagant importance attached to virginity, not only by the Gnostics but by others in the early Church, as we see from the story of Paul and Thecla, comes out in the emphasis on the virginity of the beloved disciple. But how, on Corssen's view, did the story of his virginity arise at all? He himself rejects the suggestion that it had anything to do with Rev. xiv. 4. Pfleiderer, however, has seen in that passage the key to the story; he argues from it that the prophet John to whom we owe the Apocalypse was not only a prophet but also an ascetic, and that the whole story which we find in the Leucian Acts and then in the Gospel of John about the beloved disciple arose in this way. The Gnostics made the virgin and prophet John of the Apocalypse into the beloved disciple on account of his virginity, and then in virtue of this close relation to Jesus made him the recipient of esoteric revelations; thus they managed to secure his sanction to their own Gnostic doctrine. The author of the Fourth Gospel wrested their weapon from them and turned it against them, using for his own representation the great prestige which the name of John had thus acquired. The prophet John may have been a celibate; that is pure assumption. But since in this very passage the Apocalypse represents the number of celibates who accompany the Lamb as 144,000, it seems not to have been such an exceptional virtue as to qualify for John's exceptional position. The usual view is not only far more obvious, but it has support from the position accorded to John by Jesus in the Synoptists, to say nothing of the prominence he enjoyed in the primitive Church, as shown both by Galatians and the Acts of the Apostles.

CHAPTER XV

THE REVELATION OF JOHN

It may initiate us more easily into the tangled problems of this book, if we remind ourselves of the various ways in which they have been handled by modern scholars. A quarter of a century ago the opinion was confidently expressed that from being the most obscure it had come to be the most easily understood portion of the New Testament. It was not unnatural that such an opinion should be expressed. The brilliant work which had been performed by such scholars as Lücke, Ewald, and Bleek seemed to have made plain the true character of the book. The points to which one would specially direct attention in their work were the following:—First of all, they rescued the Biblical apocalypses from their isolation. So long as the Book of Revelation could be illustrated only by the Book of Daniel and sporadic sections in the Old and New Testament, the material at the disposal of their interpreters was seriously limited. When, however, it was recognised that the Biblical apocalypses were only a section of a much larger literature, a new era in their interpretation began. They were studied in the light of this larger literature, and much that had been dark now became plain. And as these non-canonical writings have themselves been more closely studied, the results have been very fruitful for the understanding of the canonical apocalypses. In the next place they emphasised the fact that the Book of Revelation, like the

Book of Daniel, was to be understood through the contemporary history. The identification of the beast with the Roman Empire in general, and with Nero in particular, ruled the interpretation of the book, and it was confidently believed that the true key, after centuries of futile groping, had been discovered.

The dominant school of critics accordingly took the apocalypse to be a unity and to reflect the political conditions shortly before the destruction of Jerusalem. In 1886, however, Vischer published an investigation which placed the problem in a new light. He put forward the theory that the Apocalypse was a fundamentally Jewish writing worked over by a Christian hand. Harnack, his teacher, at first gave the new theory no cordial reception, but on studying the book afresh in the light of it was converted to it. As we look back it is perhaps less surprising than Harnack felt at the time that such a solution should have been put forward. The method of literary analysis had been applied to the Pentateuch and the Synoptic Gospels, not to mention other parts of Biblical literature, and it was therefore not to be wondered at that it should be applied to the Revelation. And once the idea had been started that more hands than one had been at work on the book, it was not a difficult step to the theory that one of the hands was Jewish and not Christian. In fact, it was rather an accident that it fell to Vischer to cause the sensation which was created by the publication of his study. For, apart from other suggestions, Spitta, a very acute and learned scholar, had already worked out an elaborate analysis of the book, which he published not so long after (in 1889) with valuable exegetical discussions which still reward patient study even on the part of those who cannot accept his main thesis. The method of analytic criticism, once started, ran riot, and much ephemeral literature was published designed to solve the riddle as to the structure of the book.

The movement received its quietus with Gunkel, who published in 1895 his epoch-making *Schöpfung und Chaos* ('Creation and Chaos'). The book was an investigation of the first chapter of Genesis and the twelfth chapter of the Apocalypse, but it was a fundamental investigation and embraced much more than would be suggested by the title. The literary analysis had been intended to do justice to the inconsistencies and incongruities within the book which seemed to point to the authorship of two or more writers. Gunkel introduced another method to explain the phenomena. The sharp criticism to which he subjected the theories of his predecessors misled some into thinking that he was on principle opposed to analytic criticism. This was a mistake, and those who were looking to him to lead a reaction against Old Testament criticism were sharply disillusioned by his very important commentary on Genesis, in which he not only accepted the customary analysis into four main documents and the Grafian theory as to their order, but analysed narratives which had previously been treated as unities. To the Apocalypse, however, he applied a different method. The phenomena, he said, which the analysts pointed out were there, but their explanation was incorrect. They could be rightly accounted for only on the view that the Apocalypse incorporated a very ancient eschatological tradition which originated in Babylonia and had a continuous history reaching back for some thousands of years. During that period it was natural that inconsistencies should arise, and these were not to be explained as due to the literary blending of works by different authors; they had arisen in the development of the tradition itself. Much in the Apocalypse and in Daniel was unintelligible to the authors themselves. They regarded the tradition, however, as sacred, and therefore preserved what was mysterious as well as what they understood. Moreover, Gunkel attacked not only the analysts, but those who explained the Apocalypse through contemporary history. He did not, it is true, deny references to current conditions entirely, but much that had been so interpreted he explained as far more ancient.

Gunkel's work naturally made an immense impression. It left its mark deep upon Bousset's commentary, which appeared the following year, and also on his special investigation into the doctrine of Antichrist. Bousset, however, was much less averse than Gunkel from admitting allusions to contemporary history, and he recognised the employment of sources by the author, though he believed that he was no mere compiler but had impressed his own stamp everywhere on the book. Wellhausen had some important pages on the subject in the sixth part of his *Skizzen und Vorarbeiten.* He was especially severe on Gunkel's attempt to refer, as he said, everything possible and impossible to a Babylonian origin. As regards the twelfth chapter, which constitutes the greatest difficulty for those who consider the book to be purely Christian, he agreed with Vischer as against Weizsäcker that it was in the main of Jewish origin.

In the important second edition of his *Urchristentum,* published in 1902, Pfleiderer revealed himself as an adherent of the *Religionsgeschichtliche Methode* which Gunkel had brought into such prominence. But he recognised to a very much fuller extent than Gunkel that the author had drawn on earlier literary sources. A much more pronounced return to the analytic method came with the publication of a special investigation from the pen of J. Weiss which appeared in 1904. The author had been much influenced by Spitta's keen-sighted investigation, and his analysis reminds us at certain points of that given by his predecessor, but it was more plausible and perhaps less mechanical. At the close of his investigation he brought the problem of the Apocalypse into connexion with the larger problem of the Johannine literature in general, but simply sketched his results, leaving the detailed establishment of them to a later period. His theory was as follows: John of Asia, whom, in common with a large number of modern scholars, he identified with the presbyter and not with the apostle, shortly before the year A.D. 70 composed an apocalypse. Subsequently, having outgrown his apocalyptic stage, he composed the letters which go by his name and wrote reminiscences of Jesus. In the reign of Domitian a disciple of John who had not kept pace with his master in his development took up his earlier apocalypse. He combined with it a Jewish apocalypse composed in the year A.D. 70, to some extent probably out of pre-existing materials, and added a good deal of his own and thus created our present Apocalypse. What had happened to John's Apocalypse happened later to his reminiscences. These also were taken and expanded into our Fourth Gospel. A judgment on the whole scheme can hardly be pronounced before the author's case for it is fully published, and it will then be seen whether he has been more successful than his predecessors in reversing the judgment of Strauss that the Fourth Gospel is like the seamless robe—we can cast lots for it, but we cannot divide it. So far as the Apocalypse is concerned, the theory has not been favourably received, Swete and Sanday in this country have pronounced against it, and this is true also of Jülicher in the latest edition of his *Introduction*, and Bousset in the valuable second edition of his Commentary, which appeared in 1908, to say nothing of other scholars. A very interesting and suggestive analysis of the Apocalypse has recently been published by Wellhausen. It is a very independent piece of work, reminding one not a little of J. Weiss. He considers that Nero Caesar is the correct solution of the number 666, but regards it as merely a gloss which has had the effect of throwing students off the right scent. It is not the key, as has been thought, to the understanding of the whole book, but simply to the misunderstanding of the figure of the beast.

The story of these attempts to solve the riddle of the book will naturally make on many readers the impression that criticism will be forced to confess itself bankrupt. We ought rather to conclude that we shall understand it only by an eclectic method, which combines the lines along which the solution has been sought. We must recognise in it a reflection of contemporary history, the stratification of documents, and the incorporation of very ancient apocalyptic tradition. The earlier critics were right, not only in the emphasis they laid on its relationship to the cognate literature, but in their conviction of relevance to the conditions of the time. The writer diverges from many apocalyptists in that he does not write history in the guise of prediction. Still less is he concerned with a distant future; the end is at hand. It is with the urgent problems of the troubled present and the still darker immediate future that he is concerned. There are not easily missed contemporary references. The whole aim of the Apocalypse in its present form is to encourage the Christians in the persecution they are suffering from the Roman Empire. The scarlet woman is drunk with the blood of the saints, the souls under the altar cry to God to avenge their blood, the martyrs of Jesus are seen after they have passed through the great tribulation. It is the worship of the Emperor which constitutes the peril to the Church and its terrible temptation to apostasy. Other illustrations of this reference to contemporary events or anticipations are to be found in the mention of the death of Nero and his expected return, the prediction of the overthrow of Rome, the city on seven hills, by the beast in alliance with the ten kings, and of the fall of Jerusalem except the Temple. Yet while we are to see in the Roman Empire the power to which the Church stands in implacable antagonism, while Nero is to return from hell as the beast's last incarnation, it would be a mistake to interpret all the details in the book as created by the contemporary situation. It is obviously likely that the acceptance of the other methods would carry with it a different attitude towards the interpretation of the details. If earlier sources lie behind the present form of the book, we should naturally assume that they depict a somewhat different situation. And since it is with a long-continued tradition that we have to deal, the key to some of the details may quite easily be altogether lost.

That Gunkel rightly refers much in the Apocalypse to very ancient tradition can hardly be doubted. The twelfth chapter, while, apart from Christian interpolations, in its present form a piece of Jewish Messianic theology, cannot be explained without reference to a Gentile origin. That we should follow Dieterich in connecting it with the story of the birth of Apollo can hardly be believed, and it would be premature to find in it with Gunkel a version of the birth of Marduk, for which we have as yet no Babylonian evidence. The parallel of the birth of Horus, adduced by Bousset, lies open to less serious objection. Probably, however, both the Apollo and the Horus myth are forms of the very widespread myth of the conflict between the chaos-demon and the sun-god. This has been transformed in Judaism into a Messianic forecast. And elsewhere we may discover clear traces of dependence on traditional apocalyptic lore. Where we find the writer introducing elements which seem to have no significance for himself and receive no development, we may infer with some probability that these have been derived from older tradition and have no reference to contemporary history. In other cases where we can be sure of direct borrowing from an older source, we cannot be sure whether the borrowed elements were intended by the author to refer to events in the history of his own time, or whether he simply took them over into his own scheme because he did not feel free to cast them aside although their meaning was not clear to himself. For example, the figure of the beast in the thirteenth chapter is directly derived from the seventh chapter of Daniel. The beast is represented as having ten horns, these horns are in Daniel identified as kings, therefore in Revelation they are represented as wearing diadems. Usually interpreters think the ten horns represent ten Roman Emperors, but this is difficult to harmonise with the interpretation given in the seventeenth chapter where the beast reappears, so that it is quite possible that the author took over the horns simply as a part of the tradition without attaching any special significance to them. At the same time two qualifications must be borne in mind. In the first place the very fact that the apocalyptist incorporated a piece of earlier tradition probably implies that he saw sufficient general resemblance to the contemporary conditions to induce him thus to incorporate it, so that even if the details in many cases are devoid of special importance the general outlines may bear significance for his own time. And secondly, we must not assume too readily that the details which are borrowed are necessarily without meaning. Gunkel's work, however, while most valuable and stimulating, was itself open to some criticisms. In the first place he probably much overrated the Babylonian origin of the material. In the next place he denied allusions to contemporary history where they probably really exist. Lastly, he believed too exclusively in the value of his own method. Some at least of the incongruities in the book cannot have thus originated, we must seek for their origin in the combination of literary sources.

In spite of the recoil from analytic criticism, the present writer believes that it is not possible to regard the Apocalypse as a unity. It is no doubt true that there is a very marked unity in the style and character which forbids us to suppose that the book is a mere compilation. It is with a real author that we have to do, not simply with an editor; with an author who has left his impress on the book. But while he has stamped it with his own individuality, he has borrowed from earlier sources. He hints this himself, not obscurely, in his description of the little book which he took and ate (x. 8-11), and in the veiled reference to the seven-thunders apocalypse (x. 4) which he was apparently inclined to incorporate. We have probably to recognise the presence in the book of non-Christian elements. In xi. 1, 2 the anticipation seems to be expressed that while Jerusalem would be captured, the Temple including the forecourt would be preserved. Is it likely that a Christian writer should thus contradict Christ's prediction that not one stone of the Temple should be left upon another? Reverting to the twelfth chapter, while its ultimate origin must be sought in Pagan mythology, it is very difficult to believe that the author of the Revelation simply drew on unwritten tradition. For a Christian the birth of the Messiah and His earthly career belonged to the realm of history, not of prediction. How could such a writer represent the Messiah as caught up to the throne of God immediately after His birth, that He might be saved from the dragon who was waiting to devour Him? We can see what prompted the writer to include the section; it was to warn the readers that, now the devil has been cast down to earth, an unprecedented persecution will begin, but to comfort them with the assurance that when the three and a half years allotted to him by destiny are past, he will be overthrown. For the Messiah is already in heaven, and will intervene when the time is ripe. And yet, while the section had this significance for the writer, the bizarre non-Christian elements in it would naturally have repelled him. This suggests the possibility not merely that it lay before the author in written form, but that it originally belonged to a larger document, and has been incorporated not so much for its own sake but as part of a fuller insertion.

The numerous incongruities in the book also suggest composite authorship. In some parts of the book, *e.g.* the letters to the seven churches, we gain the impression that the persecution was mild, and though severe measures were anticipated, these were not of an extreme character. But other parts are written under the influence of a very severe persecution, which has already claimed a large number of victims, and which is expected to become more terrible still. The seventeenth chapter, which is perhaps the most important in the book for the determination of the literary and historical problems of the Apocalypse, exhibits several marks of composite origin. There are two interpretations of the seven heads (*vv.* 9 and 10). In *v.* 14 the beast with the ten kings wars against and is overcome by the Lamb and his followers, while in *v.* 16 the beast and the kings utterly destroy the harlot, and do so as God's instruments. Again, the description with which the vision opens is that of the great harlot. The beast on which she rides is a very subordinate part of the picture, in which the scarlet woman forms the central figure. When, however, the explanation follows, the woman is much less prominent than the beast. Moreover, the judgment on the harlot seems to rest on different grounds. In *vv.* 1-5 her sin is that of luxury and uncleanness, with which she has contaminated the rest of the world. The goblet she holds is filled with the wine of her fornication. This is also true with reference to the closely connected eighteenth chapter. The judgment comes on her for the corrupting influence she has exerted over the world (xviii. 3, 7, 9-19, 22, 23), with her sorcery all the nations have been deceived, and the exhortation to God's people to leave her is that they may avoid contamination and judgment. But according to xvii. 6 the woman is drunk with the blood of the saints, in xviii. 20 God has judged on her the judgment of the saints, in xviii. 24 in her is found the blood of prophets, saints and all that have been slain on the earth. Much the greater part of ch. xviii. betrays no consciousness of Rome as a persecutor. It is also possible that there are two different accounts of the destruction of Babylon. In xvii. 16 she is destroyed by the beast and the ten kings, in ch. xviii. there is no reference to these, but God judges her with plagues in a single day. In both descriptions she is utterly burned with fire, and there is no necessary discrepancy between the two accounts. If composite authorship, however, be recognised, it is likely that the two belong to different strata.

Further, there seems to be a difference in the reckoning of the kings. There are only seven emperors of Rome, since the beast has seven heads. The author of xvii. 10 writes while the sixth emperor is on the throne, *i.e.* probably during the reign of Vespasian, and he expects the series to be closed by another emperor, the seventh, who is to continue a little while. According to *v.* 11 there are to be eight emperors, the eighth being Antichrist; he is identified with one of the seven heads, but he is also identified with the beast that was and is not. Several suppose that this must have been written under Domitian, and was intended to harmonise the fixed number of the emperors as seven with the fact that the seventh (Titus) after a brief reign (*v.* 10b) had been succeeded by an eighth. In that case the author saw in Domitian an earlier member of the series reincarnate, presumably Nero. It is an objection to this that we have no evidence of a belief that Domitian was Nero reincarnate, nor that he had risen out of the abyss. Moreover, the author of *v.* 11 says that he 'is not.' It may therefore be better to conclude that this author wrote under the seventh emperor and was driven to postulate an eighth ruler because he did not identify the reigning monarch with Antichrist, but had to make the eighth identical with one of the seven, because the number could not exceed seven.

On the exact analysis of this section opinions differ,

but the following general sketch is not unlikely. The earliest stratum predicts God's destruction of Rome for luxury, pride and immorality, and describes the grief at her downfall felt by those who had been associated with her sin. There is no reference to persecution, the author, while regarding the overthrow as deserved, yet betrays no exultation over it or hatred of Rome. Pfleiderer thinks this belonged to the little book and assigns it to the time of Caligula, but J. Weiss thinks it was written under the sixth emperor, *i.e.* Vespasian. A later writer represented the destruction of Rome as due to the alliance of the beast, *i.e.* Nero, with the Parthians. Probably he was a Jewish not a Christian writer who saw in Rome's overthrow God's judgment on the destroyers of Jerusalem. He describes the scarlet woman as drunk not with luxury and immorality but with the blood of the saints. This would suit the martyrdom of Christians in the Neronian persecution, only Nero was himself more responsible for this than Rome, and therefore could not so well appear as its avenger upon Rome. It is therefore more likely that the reference is to the Jews who had perished in the Jewish war, especially in the siege and sack of Jerusalem and the dark days that followed. This writer was accordingly not a Christian but a Jew and may have written under Titus. But since we have apparently a reference to the return of Nero from hell as Antichrist, a view which cannot be traced till towards the close of the first century, we have probably to postulate a third author who was a Christian and wrote under Domitian, out of experience of his persecution. It is he who represents the beast as making war on the Lamb and inserts the references to 'the blood of the martyrs of Jesus' (xvii. 6), to the apostles and perhaps prophets in xviii. 20-24.

In the examination of this chapter we have already anticipated to some extent the discussion not simply of structure but of date. So far as the former is concerned, the most important point is that we apparently have to recognise the incorporation of documentary material Jewish in origin. Since the eleventh chapter, which opens with a probably Jewish prophecy, immediately follows the episode of the eating of the book, it is a natural inference that a Jewish apocalypse begins at this point or perhaps with the tenth chapter. The date of this seems to be fixed as A.D. 70, when the Romans were besieging Jerusalem. It is very uncertain how much this apocalypse contained, and how far the elements of which it was composed were themselves ready to its author's hand. It must of course be remembered that the final author did not leave the Jewish sections untouched; he has worked them over and frequently inserted Christian additions. Pfleiderer thinks the little book contained chs. xi.-xiv., xvii.-xix. J. Weiss finds it in chs. x., xi. 1-13, xii. 1-6, 14-17 (xiii. 1-7), xv.-xix., xxi. 4-27. He considers that this was a literary unity, in which earlier groups of apocalyptic matter had been combined. Nothing definite can be affirmed as to the time and circumstances of some of the visions employed, but the author put them together in the year 70 A.D. in the belief that Jerusalem itself would not be saved, but only the Temple and the worshippers in its court. Von Soden thinks that the Jewish Apocalypse of A.D. 70 extends from vi. 12 to the end of the book, with of course a good deal of Christian redaction. And other attempts have been made to reconstruct it. Within our limits no discussion is possible. It may be questioned whether the Jewish element is so considerable as these scholars suppose. It is most clearly discernible in chs. xi., xii., xvii., xviii., though the two latter as already shown are almost certainly composite, and contain a Jewish section of later date than the main Jewish Apocalypse. It is also not improbable that ch. xii. is itself composite, though the analysts are by no means agreed as to its dismemberment.

But the Christian sections are themselves not homogeneous. It has already been pointed out that the references to persecution in the letters to the Seven Churches are quite different in character from those in later portions of the book. In the former the Jews are the enemy, in the latter the Roman Empire with its insistence on the worship of the Emperor, to which multitudes have been sacrificed. In the letters the condition of the Churches suggests no serious peril from the government, rather they are in peril from their own shortcomings, which are of a type we do not expect in communities harried by a great tribulation. The tone of severity in which they are addressed is also unsuitable to a time of bitter persecution. How much of the book belongs to the Apocalypse which the seven letters were intended to introduce is most uncertain. J. Weiss supposes that it consisted of i. 4-6 (7-8), 9-19, ii.-vii., xi., xii. 7-12, xiii. 11-18 (xiv. 1-5), 14-20, xx. 1-15, xxi. 1-4, xxii. 3-5, xxii. 8ff. (in part). Here again space permits of no adequate discussion of details, which alone could warrant a conclusion. It must, however, be recognised that, although earlier sources have been employed, the author has contrived to impart a real unity to the completed work and has not merely strung earlier compositions together. He has made it an artistic whole characterised by considerable uniformity of style and language.

While some elements in the book must be earlier than A.D. 70, the Apocalypse as it stands must be later. It employs the legend of the returning Nero, not simply in its older form of a return from the Parthians but in its later form of a return from hell. So far as can be made out, this legend does not appear much before the close of the first century. The enumeration of emperors carries us down at least to Titus and possibly to Domitian. The references to persecution, and indeed the whole tenor of the book in its final form, point strongly to Domitian's reign. The external evidence is also very cogent for a date in the time of Domitian. Irenaeus referring to the Apocalypse says 'it was seen no such long time ago, but almost in our own generation at the end of the reign of Domitian' (v. 3). The tradition as to Domitian is not uncontradicted, but as Hort says, if external evidence alone could decide, there would be a clear preponderance for Domitian. It is true that external evidence does not settle the question, but in this case it coincides with the indications of internal evidence. The phenomena which point to a Neronian date or a date at the beginning of Vespasian's reign are real, but they may be satisfied by the recognition that the book includes a large element dating from the period before the destruction of Jerusalem. A suggestion has been made by Reinach, that vi. 6 fixes the year 93 A.D. as the date of the Apocalypse. In 92 Domitian forbade the cultivation of the vine in the provinces, really as a protective measure for Italy, but under the pretext of encouraging grain and reducing drunkenness. In 93 he reversed this, so that the author apprehended that grain would be scarce and wine abundant. The state of things presupposed in the passage is so peculiar that some definite incident may well have suggested this vision. On the other hand, the edict does not account for the reference to oil.

As early as Justin Martyr the Apocalypse was attributed to the apostle John. Irenaeus assigns both the Apocalypse and the Fourth Gospel to John a disciple of the Lord, apparently meaning the apostle John, and Hippolytus, Tertullian and Origen affirm apostolic authorship. On the other hand, the Alogi rejected not only the Gospel but the Apocalypse, ascribing it to Cerinthus, probably in each case on doctrinal grounds. Their attitude was shared by Caius of Rome at the beginning of the third century. Probably no importance should be attached to these opinions, they were based on theological prejudices, not on critical considerations. Much more interest attaches to the suggestion made by Dionysius of Alexandria. No doubt his discussion of the question was prompted by his dislike of millenarianism and his desire to deprive it of apostolic endorsement. But his internal criticism of the book was very able, and he called attention to phenomena which make it difficult to believe that the Fourth Gospel and the Apocalypse could come from the same author. Since the apostolic origin of the Gospel was assumed without question by Dionysius, he had to suggest that the Revelation was the work of another John. This he argues cannot have been John Mark but some other John, and he corroborates his conjecture by the story that in Ephesus there were two tombs of John. Eusebius completes his criticism by a reference to the two Johns mentioned by Papias, and argues that if the apostolic authorship of the Apocalypse is to be denied the work should be attributed to the presbyter.

Leaving aside for the present the problem raised by Dionysius and looking at the Apocalypse by itself, there is probably no valid reason to doubt that the author really bore the name of John. It is true that apocalypses are usually pseudonymous writings, and the fact that the author does not give himself out as an ancient worthy is not decisive against the conclusion that our book conforms to the rule of its class, for a Jewish apocalypse can hardly be the measure of a Christian apocalypse in this respect. An apostle would be quite as naturally chosen as Enoch or Baruch. But if the book were pseudonymous, the author would probably have claimed explicitly to be an apostle, whereas he contents himself with the bare name of John. We need not doubt that the author who gives himself out as John really bore that name, lived in Asia, and received his vision at Patmos. It is important to remember that it is not with apocalypse pure and simple that we have to deal. The letters to the Seven Churches are certainly not apocalyptic fictions dealing with fictitious circumstances, and the same conclusion must be adopted with reference to the claim to authorship which is inseparably united with them. It must, however, be pointed out that if the book is composite the claim to Johannine authorship can be established only for a portion of the book, unless we can identify the author of the seven letters and the related sections with the final editor. This, however, is very improbable. But while we may confidently accept partial Johannine authorship, this gives us no warrant for identifying the prophet John with the apostle. The author speaks as a prophet telling the message of the glorified Christ, and the tone of authority must not be held to prove his apostolic position.

It is held by many that the identification with the apostle is excluded by the absence of reminiscences of the author's earlier intercourse with Jesus during His earthly career and by the objective reference to the twelve apostles of the Lamb. The Tübingen critics, we do well to remember, found no difficulty in holding the apostolic authorship of the whole book in spite of these objections and in spite of its very advanced Christology. And probably in this respect their judgment was sounder than that of their successors. The same objection apart from the references to the twelve apostles would lie, though in a mitigated form, against the identification with the presbyter if he was acquainted with Jesus, especially if he was the beloved disciple.

It was formerly thought by many scholars to be possible to identify the author of the Apocalypse with the author of the Gospel, the wide divergences between them being explained by the interval that was supposed to separate them. It is extremely questionable, however, whether any lapse of time would account for the development from one to the other, especially as the apostle cannot well have been less than fifty at the earliest date to which the Apocalypse could be assigned. And the same objection would hold if we ascribed all the works to the presbyter. If, however, we adopt the Domitian date for the Apocalypse, the difficulty of supposing that it was written by the author of the Gospel is probably insuperable, though it must be remembered that Harnack assigns all the Johannine literature to the presbyter. It is no doubt the case that there is a very close connexion both in vocabulary and in thought between the Apocalypse and the other Johannine writings. But these are more than balanced by the differences. On this it may be enough to quote the words of Hort, who asserted the unity of authorship and the early date for the Apocalypse. His conclusion is made all the more weighty by his protest against exaggerating the difficulties which immediately precedes. 'It is, however, true that without the long lapse of time and the change made by the Fall of Jerusalem the transition cannot be accounted for. Thus date and authorship do hang together. It would be easier to believe that the Apocalypse was written by an unknown John than that both books belong alike to St. John's extreme old age.' We cannot carry the discussion further without reference to the other Johannine literature. Without deferring it till the critical problems of the Fourth Gospel and the Epistles have been considered, it may be said that, accepting the apostolic authorship of the Gospel, we should probably assign the Apocalypse to the presbyter unless we are willing to assume the existence of a third John otherwise unknown to us.

93-94 A.D.

CHAPTER XVI

THE EPISTLES OF JOHN

THE First Epistle is anonymous, but from the time of Irenaeus, who is the first to mention it by name, it was regarded in the ancient Church as the work of John. It is quoted as such not only by Irenaeus but by Tertullian, Clement of Alexandria, and Origen. It is also assigned to him in the Muratorian Canon. Polycarp probably quotes it though this is disputed, and we learn from Eusebius that Papias employed it. Polycarp and Papias are of course authorities simply for the early date, not for the authorship. The prevailing view even among modern critics has been that the Epistle is from the same hand as the Fourth Gospel. This has been denied by some eminent scholars, for example Holtzmann, Pfleiderer, Schmiedel and Martineau. Wellhausen put forward the suggestion in his first work on the Fourth Gospel that the interpolator of John xv.-xvii. might not improbably be identical with the author of the Epistle. The discussion of the question would involve too much detail, but in spite of differences between the Epistle and the Gospel, which so far as they are not fanciful are accounted for by difference of subject-matter and aim, and possibly by an interval of time, the links of connexion are so numerous and unstudied, the peculiar Johannine style so inimitable, that it is hypercriticism to deny the identity of authorship. The question of authorship therefore need not be independently discussed; it is sufficient to remind ourselves that the author appears to claim that he had known the incarnate Christ during His earthly life.

The date of the work cannot be determined with any precision. The external testimony hardly permits us to descend below 125 A.D., but it is far more probable that we should take 110 A.D. as the lower limit. It is often said that a second century date must be adopted on account of the false teaching which it attacks. This is alleged to be second-century Gnosticism. The condition of things reflected in the Epistle is as follows. The false teaching is not a novelty. Antichrist is not one but many, and already at work in the world while the author writes. Many false prophets have gone out into the world. The representatives of the tendencies attacked had belonged to the Christian communities. They have left them, however, because they were not in spiritual sympathy with the members of those communities. The members are themselves untouched by the contamination. In virtue of the anointing spirit they know all things and do not need to be taught the truth. But there are those who would lead them astray, and much of the writer's letter is a warning and appeal intended to guard them against these dangers. Even in the Christian congregation there was a danger lest the spirit of Antichrist should manifest itself in the meetings, hence it was necessary to subject the spirits to a test. Heresy in doctrine was combined with immorality in conduct. The heresy touched especially the Person of Christ. It denied the Son, denied that Jesus was the Christ. It confessed not [or dissolved] Jesus. It denied that Jesus Christ had come in the flesh. Against it the author strongly affirms the real humanity of the Logos as attested by the evidence of the physical senses, i. 1-3. The heresy was accordingly a form of Docetism similar to that attacked in the Ignatian Epistles. But some of the expressions suggest another form of Christology, the denial that Jesus was the Christ. This has of course no reference to Judaism, but suggests the distinction made by some Gnostics between the man Jesus and the aeon Christ. In that case the reading 'dissolveth Jesus' would, whether textually correct or not, give the right sense.

On the moral side they professed sinlessness, but were antinomians who walked in darkness while they professed to be in the light, claimed the knowledge of God while they failed to keep His commandments. Hatred of one's brother is especially singled out for condemnation. They seem to have made similar claims as the libertine Gnostics. They knew God, had a special spiritual illumination, which rendered sin something out of the question for them, so that conduct became a matter of complete moral indifference. We find the combination of this with a false Christology among the Gnostics. There is no necessity to descend into the second century for this teaching, though it has a close parallel in Ignatius. Gnosticism was originally independent of Christianity and came into existence before it. It probably touched the Christian Church long before the close of the second century, even though we may justifiably refuse to recognise it in the heresy attacked in the Epistle to the Colossians. If the Epistle of Jude belongs to the first century, we have a parallel in it to some features which recur in our Epistle. The tendencies attacked in the apocalyptic letters to the Seven Churches present much that is similar, though we have no indication of false teaching as to the Person of Christ. But we read of teachers who teach immorality and to eat things sacrificed to idols; they profess to know the deep things of Satan. This is a kind of libertine Gnosticism, which is in some cases at work in the Churches themselves. If the seven letters belong to the final stratum of the Revelation, they are evidence simply for the reign of Domitian. But more probably they are a good deal earlier, in which case the development reflected in the First Epistle may easily have been reached well before the close of the first century. Naturally this does not demand but only permit a first-century date. It is at any rate noteworthy that no reference is made to the great Gnostic systems. The letter was probably written from Ephesus, perhaps to accompany the Fourth Gospel, though it is more likely that the two works were not written at the same time, especially as they do not seem to be addressed to the same conditions or designed to correct the same errors.

The Second Epistle of John seems at first sight to be a private letter. According to the English version it is addressed 'to the elect lady,' and this is probably the correct translation, though either of the two Greek words might be taken and have been taken as a proper name, and we might translate 'to the elect Kyria' or 'to the lady Eklekte.' In the latter case it is also possible to take the term 'lady' as a term of endearment rather than of dignity. It is nevertheless improbable that either of the words is a proper name. If we take Eklekte as a proper name, we are confronted by the difficulty that in *v.* 13 it is also applied to her sister, and to have two sisters with the same name is out of the question. Kyria is used as a proper name. but we should have expected rather different Greek if this had been intended. The tendency of recent writers is to regard the letter as addressed to a Church, though several, for example Salmond, J. Rendel Harris, and Harnack take it to be a private letter. The parallelism with the third letter, which is unquestionably addressed to an individual, favours a similar interpretation here, which is also the more natural meaning of the expression. The contents of the letter, however, support the alternative view. The doctrinal tenor of the Epistle is more appropriate in a letter addressed to a Church. The references to the lady's children also favour this view. That the lady and her children are loved by all who know the truth would be hyperbolical if an individual were intended. The greeting from 'the children of thine elect sister' would be very strange, if the meaning was that the children sent a greeting to their aunt. We should have expected 'thine elect sister and her children salute thee.' It is much more natural if the elect sister and the children are the Church and its members. In that case there is no material distinction between the mother and the children. The omission of the mother from the greeting would on the other interpretation be hard to account for.

Accepting this interpretation, we may ask what Church is intended. If we suppose that the Epistle is a free composition without an actual situation for its background, we might suppose that it was a Catholic Epistle addressed to the Church generally. If, however, we reject this conception of the letter, we are obliged by *v.* 13 to accept the view that an individual Church is intended. The statement that the elect lady is greeted by her elect sister is incompatible with a Catholic destination of the Epistle; it could only mean that one Church greets another. In that case the elect sister may possibly be identified with the Church in Ephesus, where the author presumably was writing. It is accordingly probable that the elect lady should be identified with one of the Churches of Asia, perhaps with Pergamum, as Findlay has suggested.

The Third Epistle is addressed not to a Church but to an individual, Gaius. The affinities with the Second Epistle are so close that we may assume that it was written by the same author and in all probability at the same time. In that case it is possible that the letters were sent to the same destination. It is a plausible suggestion that the letter referred to in *v.* 9 is the Second Epistle, and that the writer sends this letter to Gaius to guard against the suppression of his letter to the Church by Diotrephes

On the other hand, the happy relations with the Church which seem to be reflected in the Second Epistle are not quite what we should gather to have prevailed where Diotrephes was so powerful.

It has been generally held that the two letters are by the author of the First Epistle and the Gospel. The Johannine phraseology and point of view are very marked especially in the Second Epistle, though it must be admitted that there are differences on which, however, in the case of such brief and informal letters it would be unreasonable to lay too much stress. In a very important and thorough study of the Third Epistle, Harnack, who accepts the unity of authorship of all five Johannine writings, has suggested that in Diotrephes we are to see the first monarchical bishop. He objects to the supervision exercised by the elder over the local Churches, which belongs to the old system of patriarchal control of a whole province, and especially to the way in which the author interferes by his agents with the autonomy of the Churches. It is clear that Diotrephes not only refused to receive the presbyter's emissaries himself, but was in a position to expel from the Church those who gave them hospitality. That his motive was to assert local independence as against centralised administration, is of course possible, as the author asserts that personal ambition was the mainspring of his action. But it is also possible that the root of the difference may have been doctrinal rather than ecclesiastical. This would gain in probability if we could suppose that the Second Epistle was written to the Church in which Diotrephes was an officer. In that case, however, we should have expected the writer to stigmatise Diotrephes as a heretic and an antichrist, whereas he hints nothing of the kind against him. If the dispute was purely ecclesiastical, Harnack's suggestion may be correct, though it would be possible to reverse the relation and suppose that Diotrephes was fighting for the old independence of the local Churches against the presbyter's attempt to bring them under his personal control. There is no reason to suppose with Schwartz that the original letters were written by a presbyter who gave his name, and that the name was subsequently struck out in order to suggest that they were written by the famous presbyter John. It would be more reasonable to suppose with Jülicher that the letters were originally pseudonymous and designed to secure apostolic authority for the author's own ideas. There is no ground, however, for suspecting the author of sailing under a false flag. Besides, for two such insignificant compositions such an explanation is altogether too artificial. The self-designation of the author favours the view that they were written by the presbyter John.

CHAPTER XVII

THE GOSPEL ACCORDING TO JOHN

The External Evidence.

IT is needless to seek for evidence of the existence of the Gospel and its ascription to the apostle John after the time of Irenaeus. It is not disputed that he knew and used all of our Gospels and regarded them as authoritative. In fact he asserts that in the nature of the case there cannot be either more or fewer Gospels than four. The fantastic arguments by which he proves this view speak rather for than against the strength of his independent conviction that our four Gospels and those Gospels alone were canonical. It might be fairly inferred that these Gospels stood out so conspicuously in a class by themselves, that Irenaeus found it hard to imagine the Church without them. C. Taylor thinks that for his view that the four Gospels are the four pillars on which the Church rests, Irenaeus is indebted to Hermas, who represents the Church as sitting on a seat with four feet. If this were so, it would carry back not only the existence but the unique authority of the four Gospels to 155 at the latest. But not much weight can be laid on this theory. The testimony of Irenaeus is important in several ways. He had lived as a youth in Asia Minor, where he was acquainted with Polycarp, and later he lived in Rome and Gaul. He was therefore in a position to know the view of the Churches in these widely separated districts. He appeals to the

Notice Especially John

Fourth Gospel as John's with a triumphant certainty, betraying no consciousness that on this point he could be successfully challenged. His contemporary Theophilus of Antioch and his somewhat junior contemporaries, Clement of Alexandria in Egypt, Tertullian in Carthage, and Hippolytus in Rome, occupy a similar position. This testifies to a full recognition of the Gospel throughout the Church before the close of the second century. And it is important to remember that this involves a fairly long previous history. Had the Gospel been written only a short time before, it could hardly have been widely accepted as the work of the apostle John, for the question would naturally have been pressed in very large circles, How is it that we only hear of this book now, when John has been dead so many years?

But testimony to the Johannine authorship goes back to a date earlier than Irenaeus. The Muratorian Canon, which is possibly as early as about 170 A.D., not only asserts that John, whom it describes as one of the disciples, wrote the Gospel but gives a detailed tradition as to its origin. The recent discovery of Tatian's Diatessaron has proved what had been contested, though generally admitted by impartial critics, that Tatian used our four Gospels in its composition. This means, not merely that these Gospels were in existence, but that they were marked off from all other Gospels and set in a class by themselves. The date of the work is uncertain; it may be fixed with some probability about 170 A.D. It has even been argued that this was not the earliest Harmony of the Gospels, since some early writings exhibit what seems to be a blending from different Gospels in their quotations. But this theory is uncertain in itself, and obviously nothing can be built on it. Probably a little later than Tatian, Theophilus of Antioch published a Harmony of the Gospels.

Tatian was a disciple of Justin Martyr. Few questions in New Testament criticism have been more hotly and keenly debated than the question whether Justin used the Fourth Gospel. The affirmative view has been very strongly maintained not only by Lightfoot, Westcott and Sanday, but especially by Ezra Abbot and James Drummond, and has been admitted by Hilgenfeld, Keim, Wernle and others who reject the Johannine authorship of the Gospel. Loisy says his dependence on the Fourth Gospel cannot be denied, but he never cites it formally. He thinks with several other scholars that he used the Gospel of Peter (but on this see Drummond, pp. 151-155). On the other hand E. A. Abbott has recently in the article 'Gospels' in the *Encyclopaedia Biblica*, after an elaborate examination of the evidence, reaffirmed his negative conclusion. He argues that where Justin seems to be alluding to John, he is really alluding to the Old Testament or to Barnabas, or to some Christian tradition distinct from and often earlier than John; further, that when he teaches what is the doctrine of the Fourth Gospel, he supports it not by what can easily be found in that Gospel, but by what can hardly, with any show of reason, be found in the Three, and lastly that his Logos doctrine differs from that of the Fourth Gospel. He concludes either that Justin did not know the Gospel, or that more probably he knew it but regarded it with suspicion, partly because it seemed to him to contradict his favourite Gospel, Luke, partly because the Valentinians were beginning to use it. Schmiedel in the article 'John the Son of Zebedee,' after pointing out that while Justin has more than one hundred quotations from the Synoptists, he has only three which offer points of contact with the Fourth Gospel, and even these may possibly have come from another source, which the evangelist also may have used, proceeds: 'Yet, even apart from this, we cannot fail to recognise that the Fourth Gospel was by no means on the same plane with the synoptics in Justin's eyes, and that his employment of it is not only more sparing but also more circumspect.

This is all the more remarkable since Justin certainly champions one of its leading conceptions (the Logos idea), lays great weight upon the "Memorabilia of the Apostles," and expressly designates the Apocalypse as a work of the Apostle.' It must, however, be remembered that we have only apologetic treatises from Justin, and the Fourth Gospel may have seemed less suitable to this purpose. (On the argument from silence see especially Drummond, pp. 157, 158.)

The description of the style of Jesus given by Justin is sometimes said (*e.g.* by Pfleiderer) to look like a direct repudiation of the long dialectical speeches of the Fourth Gospel. When correctly translated the passage runs, 'Brief and concise sayings have proceeded from Him; for He was not a sophist, but His word was a power of God.' This does not mean that His sayings were exclusively brief utterances, but rather that this was a characteristic form of utterance. As Drummond points out, the Johannine discourses are largely made up of such sayings, while if we were to press the description as covering all Christ's teaching it would exclude the longer parables in the Synoptists.

Papias the bishop of Hierapolis in Phrygia is said by Eusebius to have 'used testimonies from the former Epistle of John.' Usually this has been regarded as practically equivalent to a recognition of the Fourth Gospel. Thus E. A. Abbott admits that he quoted from 1 John, which was written by the author of the Fourth Gospel. But since some scholars deny that the Epistle is from the hand of the author of the Gospel, we cannot appeal to this statement of Eusebius as evidence for Papias' knowledge of the Fourth Gospel so confidently as if the composition by the same author were undisputed. It has, however, been argued that Papias cannot have mentioned either Luke or John, since otherwise Eusebius, who quotes his account of the origin of Matthew's Logia and the Gospel of Mark, would have referred to his account of Luke and John. But, as Lightfoot convincingly proved, this argument from the silence of Eusebius is not valid. He promises that if any writer has anything of interest to relate as to the origin of undisputed books he will tell it, while he will mention the mere use of disputed books. Since the Fourth Gospel was an undisputed book, we are not to expect Eusebius to mention quotations from it, or use of it, but only interesting circumstances connected with it. We may infer then that Papias told nothing which seemed to Eusebius of interest as to the origin of this Gospel, but not that he did not quote it or refer to it. This double inference is justified by the general practice of Eusebius. He often fails to mention the use by early writers of New Testament books undisputed in his day, though we have actual references to them, often very numerous, in their own writings.

It is in fact now freely admitted by some scholars, who entirely reject the Johannine authorship, that Papias knew the Fourth Gospel. E. Schwartz considers that the statements made by Papias as to the origin of Mark and Matthew were intended to emphasise their inferiority to John. Mark embodies Peter's preaching, but he gives it at second hand and not in order, while Matthew's Gospel was written in Hebrew and was now accessible only in poor translations. This depreciatory estimate Schwartz says must have been in contrast to some more satisfactory work, since Papias would not accept the Gnostic principle of the insufficiency of the written tradition. This more satisfactory work cannot have been Luke; probably Eusebius preferred not to reproduce Papias' judgment on it. Accordingly it must have been John. In harmony with this we have another statement attributed to Papias and often set aside as absurd, that the Gospel of John was manifested and given to the Churches by John while he was still in the body. The point of this would be that while Mark wrote after Peter's death, and Matthew's Gospel was accessible not in the original but only in poor translations made by others, the Gospel of John was communicated by the apostle himself in his lifetime to the Churches for official use. But it is very unlikely that Schwartz is right in thinking that Papias called John 'the theologian' as the author of the Fourth Gospel. Even if the extract referring to his death at the hands of the Jews were genuine in the main, it is unlikely that this description of him is due to Papias.

The date at which Papias composed his work is uncertain. Krüger places it as early as the first decade of the second century. E. A. Abbott gives the date 115-130. On the basis of a fragment recently published according to which his work referred to people who had been raised by Christ and survived till the reign of Hadrian, Harnack, followed by Schmiedel, argues that his book cannot have been written earlier than between 140 and 160, since Hadrian's reign was 117-138. If it is so late as that the use of the Fourth Gospel, if it could be established, would not prove very much, unless we could show that Papias was in an exceptional position for knowing the facts. This would be so if, as Irenaeus states, he was a hearer of John. But scholars generally are agreed that Eusebius was correct in the inference he drew from Papias' own language that he was not personally acquainted with John. It is very uncertain, however, if the fragment comes from Papias. Schwartz thinks it does not, and Bousset agrees with him; so also J. V. Bartlet and Sanday.

Critics are also divided as to the use of the Gospel by Polycarp and Ignatius. The evidence as to the former is inconclusive, but from so brief a composition as his letter negative conclusions such as those of Pfleiderer cannot safely be drawn. It is generally allowed that the Epistle of Polycarp shows a knowledge of 1 John iv. 2, 3. But this is denied by Schmiedel, and several scholars think that the Epistle of Polycarp is wholly or in part spurious, and even if genuine need not have been written so early as the reign of Trajan (98-117) to which it is usually assigned. It is beyond question that Irenaeus confidently attributed the Fourth Gospel to John the Apostle. In view of his own definite statements it becomes very difficult to believe that in so doing he was not resting on Polycarp's statement. It is to be noticed that he asserts that Polycarp's relation of Christ's life and teaching was altogether in accordance with the Scriptures. This perhaps attests the presence in his reminiscences of a Johannine as well as a Synoptic tradition. On the other hand, it might be urged that Irenaeus makes no reference to any account given by Polycarp touching the origin of the Fourth Gospel. As to Ignatius, Pfleiderer asserts that in the whole of his genuine Epistles there is not a single sentence which points to dependence on the Gospel or Epistles of John. Had Ignatius known them, he must have used them in his conflict with Docetism. On the other hand, Wernle, while he agrees with Pfleiderer as to the bearing of the Ignatian letters on the problem of the apostle's residence in Asia, asserts that Ignatius had read the Johannine writings. So, too, Loisy says that Ignatius must have known the Fourth Gospel a long time to be penetrated with its spirit to the degree we see. This is all the more significant since, while Pfleiderer adopts the later date for the Ignatian Epistles formerly assigned to them by Harnack (about A.D. 130), Wernle places them quite early in the second century, and Loisy towards A.D. 115. 113 AD

The Gospel was also employed in some of the Gnostic schools. Heracleon, a disciple of Valentinus, wrote a commentary on the Gospel possibly as late as about 175 A.D. but more probably not long after 160 A.D. The very fact that a commentary was written shows that the Gospel was regarded as an authoritative work. This implies a fairly long previous history, and this inference is confirmed by the fact that false readings had crept into the text on which Heracleon commented. Nevertheless the date at which he wrote, and the affinity which a Gnostic would feel for a Gospel that lent itself so readily to the discovery in it of Gnostic doctrine, must be taken into account on the other side. It is more important that Basilides, according to a quotation in Hippolytus (vii. 22), used the Gospel. Attempts have been made to turn the edge of this argument by the assertion that Hippolytus did not carefully distinguish between what Basilides and what his followers had said. This is not borne out by examination of his usage in this respect. If the view first suggested by Salmon and elaborated by Staehelin, and subsequently accepted by others were correct, that Hippolytus was deceived into receiving as genuine forgeries palmed off upon him by an unscrupulous author, the quotation from the Fourth Gospel which he represents Basilides as giving could, of course, count for nothing, if among the forgeries thus accepted by him the account of Basilides' system is to be included. This theory, however, is very improbable, at any rate as far as concerns Basilides. It must, of course, be admitted that several scholars who reject the hypothesis of forgery still believe that the account of Hippolytus refers to a later development in the school and not to the views of Basilides himself. The most weighty argument in favour of this view is that it is difficult to harmonise the quotation given in the *Acts of Archelaus* by Hegemonius, in which Basilides expounds Persian dualism, with the monistic system attributed to him by Hippolytus. In spite of this real difficulty, the present writer continues to regard the exposition of his views given by Hippolytus as the more trustworthy and must refer for his reasons to his article 'Basilides' in Hastings' *Dictionary of Religion and Ethics.*

At the same time, in view of the distrust of his account which is widely entertained, it is not advisable to lay overmuch stress upon it. It is a passage out of the Prologue which is quoted, and therefore one which originated with the author of the Gospel. 'This,' says he, 'is that which is said in the Gospels "that was the true light which lighteth every man that cometh into the world."'

Against this very widespread acceptance of the Fourth Gospel as the work of the apostle John there is very little to be set on the other side. There were some people in Asia Minor, about 160-170, to whom Epiphanius, perhaps following Hippolytus, gave the name Alogi. This name had the advantage in the eyes of its inventor that it expressed his belief in their imbecility and at the same time their disbelief in the doctrine of the Logos. They were of a somewhat rationalistic turn of mind, and strongly opposed to Montanism and millenarianism. Since they disliked also the doctrine of the Logos, it was natural that they should be hostile to the Gospel which so emphatically taught it. Their rejection of it was accordingly based not on critical but doctrinal grounds, and therefore is of less importance than it would otherwise have been. They had obviously no tradition to warrant their verdict, for they attributed the Gospel to Cerinthus, which is clearly impossible. And the very fact that they thus made it the work of a contemporary of John testifies to a belief that it was as old as his time. It has also been recently argued with plausibility that Caius of Rome early in the third century attacked the Fourth Gospel (see *Ency. Bib.*, col. 1824, n. 4).

The external evidence, then, favours the view that the Gospel was written by the apostle John. It is true that it cannot be called conclusive. The possibility, though not the probability, must be left open that Irenaeus confused the apostle with the presbyter John. It even more distinctly leaves the possibility open that the Gospel incorporates a work of John. In that case we should have a similar phenomenon in the First Gospel, which is not in its present form from the hand of Matthew, but probably incorporates his collection of Logia. Whether such theories can be successfully vindicated in the case of the Fourth Gospel is a matter rather for internal criticism, which alone can detect separate strata in the work if such separate strata exist. It would, however, also be possible that the relation between the apostle and the Gospel might be similar to that asserted by Papias to exist between Peter and the Gospel of Mark. In other words John might have written nothing, but the story which he told of the ministry of Jesus might have been the basis on which the Gospel rested. Harnack, for example, considers that the Gospel was the work of the presbyter John incorporating the tradition for which the apostle was responsible.

Internal Evidence.

There are certain passages in the Gospel which have been thought to affirm that the author was an eye-witness of the events he describes, and one standing in a relation of peculiar intimacy to Jesus. The first of these to be considered is xxi. 24 : 'This is the disciple who witnesseth concerning these things and he who wrote these things, and we know that his witness is true.' The disciple referred to is identified by *v.* 20 with the disciple whom Jesus loved, who also leaned on His breast at the supper. The chapter from which this passage is taken is an appendix to the Gospel, which obviously reached its proper close with xx. 31. It is not of special importance for our present purpose to decide whether xxi. 1-23 was written by the author of i.-xx. or not. But it seems clear that xxi. 24 is not from the hand of the author of the Gospel. It is, so to speak, a certificate stating the authorship of the Gospel and affirming the truthfulness of the narrative. It has been commonly supposed that it was added by the Ephesian elders, when the Gospel was first put into circulation. Some have inferred from the present tense 'who witnesseth' that the author of the Gospel was still alive. This is uncertain, for the reference may be to the witness which the author bears in his Gospel after his death. We have no evidence that the Gospel was ever in circulation without these verses, and this favours the view that they were attached before the Gospel was published. If so, they contain a highly important piece of contemporary evidence for the authorship of the Gospel by an eye-witness. Yet the possibility must be allowed that the words 'he that wrote these things' ought not to be pressed to mean the actual composition of the Gospel. They might mean simply that the author of the Gospel based it on written material left by the disciple whom Jesus loved. On the other hand, it is quite possible that the verse in question is a late addition, resting on an inference from the contents of the Gospel, which may or may not have been mistaken. There is force in Schmiedel's remark that the fact that the testimony of the author is confirmed suggests that he is not a very authoritative person, and also that doubt has been thrown on his testimony. Nevertheless the verse is a very early piece of evidence that the Gospel was written by the beloved disciple, and as such is entitled to great weight.

The second passage is xix. 35, which has striking points of contact with xxi. 24, and has given rise to much discussion. The passage is as follows: 'And he that hath seen hath borne witness and his (αὐτοῦ) witness is true, and he (ἐκεῖνος) knoweth that he saith true, that ye may believe.' The reference is to the coming out of blood and water from the pierced side of Jesus. The question is whether the author is intending to identify himself with the eye-witness, whose testimony he reports, or to distinguish himself from him and refer to him as his authority for the statement. The question has been vainly argued on grammatical grounds. It has been said that by the use of ἐκεῖνος the author shows that he does not mean himself. It is true that a man writing of himself in the third person would not ordinarily refer to himself by this pronoun. But that is little to the purpose here. For one thing, ἐκεῖνος is a favourite word with the author, and, apart from this, it is possible, as ix. 37 shows, for a person thus to allude to himself, though the parallel is not very close. It may now be taken for granted that no decision can be reached either way on grammatical grounds. On this point it will be enough to quote the words of Schmiedel, since he holds very high rank as a grammarian, and at the same time entirely rejects the Johannine authorship of the Gospel, and does not favour the view that the author meant to refer to himself as an eye-witness: 'The elaborate investigations that have been made on the question whether any one can designate himself by ἐκεῖνος ('that') are not only indecisive as regards any secure grammatical results; they do not touch the kernel of the question at all' (*Ency. Bib.* 2543).

If then we look at the passage as a whole, it is not easy to reach a decision. The real question, as both Westcott and Schmiedel insist, is—who is meant by the phrase 'he that hath seen'? On the one hand, there is the presumption that a reference to some one in the third person more naturally suggests that the person so referred to is not identical with the speaker. And this is confirmed by the use of the first person in i. 14, and perhaps the first person in the Revelation. On the other hand, the view that the writer is here referring to another than himself, who was his authority for the statement in virtue of the fact that he had been an eye-witness of the event, labours under difficulties. It is rather strange that the writer who did not see the event should affirm the truth of the statement made by one who did. It is stranger still that he should say that his informant knows that he is speaking the truth, for it may be urged that no human being save the informant himself can know whether he knows or not. If the writer had said, 'I know that he speaks the truth,' that statement, while in the strictest sense incorrect, would have been a natural and substantially accurate way of expressing himself. At the same time, the reference to the eye-witness's consciousness that he is telling the truth seems rather pointless after the explicit statement 'his witness is true.' Why add that he knows that he tells the truth, especially with the purpose of arousing confidence in the accuracy of his statement? If they could not believe his statement, were they any more likely to believe it when he told them that he knew that his statement was true? The question will therefore have to be raised later whether a third way of taking ἐκεῖνος may not be possible.

If then, leaving aside for the present the clause 'he knoweth that he saith true,' we confine ourselves to the first two clauses, the probabilities may seem equally divided. This is practically Schmiedel's conclusion, not simply from these two clauses but from the whole verse. Accordingly he solves the problem in another way. He urges that since we cannot admit the historicity of the fact attested, for while blood may have flowed from the pierced side of Jesus, water cannot have flowed with it, we must assert that no eye-witness can have seen it. It therefore relieves the character of the author if we do not identify him with the eye-witness, for thus we avoid the charge that he gave himself out solemnly as having seen what he had really not seen at all. At the same time, he thinks that owing to the crucial importance which the water and blood had for him, we cannot be sure that he did not represent himself as an eye-witness.

The difficulties attaching to the narrative relate partly to the possibility of the incident taking place at all, partly to the likelihood of the disciple being able to observe it. The latter needs no serious consideration; we do not know enough of the circumstances to estimate his facilities for observation. As to the incident itself, it was argued by Dr. Stroud in his *Physical Cause of the Death of Christ* (published 1847 A.D.) that Jesus died of a broken heart. This was based on the statement in this verse that blood and water flowed from His pierced side, and was confirmed by other arguments such as the surprising quickness of His death, and the loud cry at the moment when it occurred. Dr. Creighton, however (*Ency. Bib.* col. 960), asserts that Dr. Stroud was wrong in his facts, and that the phenomenon does not occur, blood and water from an internal source being a mystery. He thinks that possibly the soldier's thrust may have been directed at something on the surface of the body, left by the scourging or the pressure of a cord, and adds, 'Water not unmixed with blood from such superficial source is conceivable.'

The difficulty of the narrative is enhanced by the fact that blood and water play an important part in the theology of the First Epistle of John. The writer strenuously insists that Jesus came not by water only but by water and blood. It is not surprising that some consider that the mystical significance of water and blood has coloured the narrative in the Gospel, or that this narrative is to be spiritually interpreted (so E. A Abbott). In itself then we can hardly appeal to the passage as attesting the reality of the fact, though Dr. Creighton leaves room for its possibility, and this saves us from the necessity of treating it as miraculous or of denying it, and along with it the authentic character of the testimony borne to it. Really we are still in the same position with reference to the verse; it may or may not be meant to identify the author with the eye-witness, and the ultimate decision must rest on other considerations

The eye-witness in the verse is generally supposed to be the same as the beloved disciple. Some, including Schmiedel, think that this conclusively negatives the view that he is to be identified with the author, since such a claim to have been the especial object of the love of Jesus would be intolerable on a man's own lips, but natural on the lips of one who wished to assert that disciple's proper place. Nothing certain can be based on this argument, for the expression will seem offensive or not to the reader according to his taste. Many see in it a beautiful expression of gratitude for the love with which the writer knew that Jesus had distinguished him.

Returning now to the meaning of ἐκεῖνος in xix. 35, we are confronted by the view that it refers to the exalted Christ. This occurred independently to Dechent and Zahn, and is advocated by E. A. Abbott, perhaps also independently, and by Jannaris, while it is favoured by Sanday. Wendt says it is impossible, for no one could have understood by the pronoun any one but the eye-witness. This criticism is perhaps less convincing than appears at first sight. Neither of the two alternatives already discussed is quite satisfactory, and they agree in identifying ἐκεῖνος with the eye-witness. Further, in the first Epistle ἐκεῖνος always refers to the ascended Christ, and had thus passed almost into a technical expression. And the choice of so emphatic a pronoun is best explained on this view. If the author had meant by it simply the eye-witness it would have been more natural to use αὐτός, but by the emphatic pronoun he calls the ascended Lord to witness that he speaks the truth. We thus get a worthy sense for the passage. From his own human testimony to the wonder of the blood and water the writer adds a reference to Christ's consciousness of its truth, thus satisfying the canon of double testimony and rising in his effort to produce conviction from the witness of fallible man to the knowledge of the infallible Christ. Accordingly this passage cannot be quoted either as a claim of the author for himself or a distinction between the author and the eye-witness, since either sense may be imposed upon it. It does, however, definitely contain the claim that the authority on which the statement rests was that of an eye-witness, whether identical with the author of the Gospel or not.

The third passage in which it is thought that the author claims to be an eye-witness is i. 14: 'And the Word became flesh and dwelt among us, and we beheld his glory.' Those who repudiate this interpretation argue that the passage is to be interpreted of spiritual vision. It is the language of a mystic, and not to be explained of perception by the physical senses. It is quite true that the words may be so interpreted, though the verb seems always to be used of physical vision in the New Testament. Still the passage makes the impression that perception with the bodily eye is here intended. Following the assertion that the Word became flesh, a reference to spiritual vision is not so natural. For the incarnation was a manifestation of the spiritual in the realm of the physical, and had to make its appeal to physical organs of perception. It is true that the writer says 'we beheld his glory,' and thus may seem to mean that the appeal was to a spiritual faculty, since faith alone could penetrate behind the lowly appearance to the glorious reality. But the reference might be to the Transfiguration, and if not so, the glory of Christ according to the Gospel itself was shown in miraculous acts, apprehended by the physical senses. In ii. 11 we read with reference to the miracle of turning water into wine: 'This beginning of signs did Jesus in Cana of Galilee and manifested his glory, and his disciples believed on him.' The presumption is accordingly rather strong that in this passage the writer is not simply claiming for himself such a spiritual vision of the glory of the Word as all Christians may be said to enjoy, but to have actually seen the incarnate Word as He dwelt on earth.

This presumption becomes little short of certainty if we admit, as we should do, that the author wrote the First Epistle of John. The opening words of the Epistle are so explicit, that it would be hard to say how the writer could have more definitely claimed to have submitted the real humanity of the Word to physical tests of sight, hearing, and touch. 'That which was from the beginning, which we have heard, which we have seen with our eyes, which we beheld and our hands handled, concerning the Word of life (and the life was manifested, and we have seen and bear witness, and announce to you the eternal life which was with the Father and was manifested to us) that which we have seen and heard we announce also to you.' This passage is all the more clear in its reference to physical perception, that the false doctrine attacked by the author affirmed that Christ had not come in the flesh. The reality of the flesh could be tested only by physical senses. Appeal to spiritual vision would be irrelevant. When scholars who accept the unity of authorship of the Gospel and Epistle are driven to the desperate expedient of explaining such language as implying spiritual perception in order to avoid attributing the two works to an eye-witness, it becomes clear that their testimony to authorship by an eye-witness can be suppressed only by violent methods. Wendt fully admits that both passages claim, and rightly claim, to proceed from an eye-witness. But he considers the Gospel to be a composite work, its author being a later writer who incorporated an earlier work by the apostle John. He also attributes the First Epistle to the apostle. Unless this theory of composite authorship be correct, it seems to be very hard to evade the conclusion that the author of the Fourth Gospel claims to have been an eye-witness.

Good

From the direct testimony of the Gospel to its authorship,

we turn to the indirect evidence that it supplies. The proof of the Johannine authorship of the Gospel has often been exhibited by its defenders in circles gradually narrowing down to a point. The writer is shown to be (1) a Jew, (2) a native of Palestine, (3) an eye-witness, (4) an apostle, (5) the apostle John. This method has the advantage of bringing the greater part of the evidence under review, and gradually concentrating that in favour of the Johannine authorship.

(1) The writer was a Jew. This is now more and more admitted by opponents of the authenticity. The Tübingen school denied both that he was a native of Palestine, and that he was a Jew. But the later criticism has not supported it in the latter view, and even Schmiedel thinks that he was probably a Jew, since a born Gentile would not easily have attached so great value to the prophetic significance of the Old Testament. Quite apart from this, however, there is a large mass of evidence which proves familiarity with Jewish ideas, customs, etc. This is conspicuously the case with reference to the Jewish Messianic ideas. The author has an accurate knowledge of details and shades of opinion, which would have possessed no interest for a Gentile. He takes us back into the controversies of the time of Jesus, moving among them easily, as one who had himself been familiar with them. Thus in i. 19-28 we have references to three personages expected by the Jews—the Messiah, Elijah, and the prophet. Again in i. 45 the Messiah is described as 'him, of whom Moses in the law, and the prophets, did write.' Incidentally it may be noticed that Philip calls Jesus 'the son of Joseph,' a designation which Christian writers at a very early period began to avoid. In i. 49 Nathanael hails Jesus as Son of God, and King of Israel. The latter term very soon became meaningless in the Church, the expectation of a national Messiah having no significance for Gentile Christians. But it is true to the Jewish expectation. So

in the sixth chapter the miracle of the loaves convinces the people that Jesus is the prophet that cometh into the world, and has its natural issue in the attempt to make Him the Messianic King, a point missed by the Synoptists. In vii. 25-36 we have an account of the disputes among the people concerning the Messianic character of Jesus. Some urge that the secrecy of the Messiah's origin is fatal to the view that Jesus can be the Messiah, since His origin is known. Others point to His miracles and argue that even the Messiah will not do more. So in vv. 40-43 we have a further account of the various views taken of Jesus by the multitude. Some thought He was the prophet, others regarded him as the Messiah, while others asserted that the Messiah must be of the seed of David, and of David's village Bethlehem, and therefore that Jesus could not be the Messiah since He came from Galilee. The Messianic title King of Israel is used again in xii. 13 (cf. also xix. 14, 15, 21), while in xii. 34 we have mention of a current doctrine that the Messiah abideth for ever. All this points very strongly to the author's Jewish nationality, though it cannot be pressed to prove his early date. For in itself it is quite compatible with the view that it reflects the later controversies of the Christians and the Jews, and that the writer antedates these discussions and puts the Christian argument for the Messiahship and Divinity of Jesus into His own mouth.

Other points of Jewish opinion with which he is familiar are the contempt of the Pharisees for those untrained in the law (vii. 47), the relation of punishment to sin, and the possibility that the sin of the parents might be punished in the child, and especially the possibility of sin before birth (ix. 1, 2). He is acquainted with the Jewish feasts, not merely with the Passover and Feast of Tabernacles, but also the Feast of Dedication, which is not mentioned in the other Gospels nor in the Old Testament. He knows that the last day of the Feast of

Tabernacles is the great day of the feast, and that the Sabbath mentioned (xix. 31) is a high day. He is aware of the fact that Jews have no dealings with the Samaritans, and that the command to circumcise on the eighth day overrides even the law of the Sabbath. A precise description is given of the Jewish method of embalming (xix. 39, 40). The author is aware that by entering the palace of the Roman governor the Jews would incur ceremonial defilement which would disqualify them for eating the Passover (xviii. 28), and similarly that the bodies of the crucified should not remain on the cross till the Sabbath (xix. 31). We have a reference also to the Jews' manner of purifying (ii. 6). Moreover, the style of the writer is strongly Hebraistic. His Greek is correct, but it is the Greek of one who has been accustomed to form his sentences on a Semitic not a Greek model.

Against this impressive evidence for the author's Jewish nationality there is little to be set on the other side. It has been urged that a Jew would not have spoken of 'the Jews' as the writer often speaks. Parallels may, it is true, be quoted, as Mark's reference to 'the Pharisees and all the Jews' (vii. 8), perhaps Matt. xxviii. 15, 'this saying was spread abroad among the Jews,' and Paul's statement 'to the Jews I became as a Jew' (1 Cor. ix. 20). At the same time the usage in the Fourth Gospel is much more peculiar. The term is used nearly seventy times, whereas its use in the Synoptic Gospels is rather infrequent. It occurs sixteen times in them, and in all but four of these in the phrase 'the king of the Jews.' In John we have such expressions as 'the feast of tabernacles, a feast of the Jews' (vii. 2), or 'the passover a feast of the Jews' (vi. 4), or even 'the Jews' passover' (ii. 13, xi. 55), or 'the Jews' Preparation' (xix. 42), which certainly sound strange on the lips of one who was himself a Jew. It should be observed, however, that since the feasts could be observed outside of Palestine, this usage tells not simply against Palestinian residence, but against Jewish nationality. Yet it is urged against the former by some who admit the latter. But this does not apply to the great majority of instances, which would be much more natural on the part of a foreign than a Palestinian Jew. In these the term indicates not those of Jewish nationality in general, but a special section of the Jewish people. From vii. 1 it would seem that they were for the most part living in Judaea, since it is said that Jesus was walking in Galilee, for He was not willing to walk in Judaea because the Jews were seeking to slay Him. It is true that we find 'the Jews' present at the discourse on the bread of life (vi. 40, 52). This is said to have been delivered at the synagogue at Capernaum, though Wendt argues that really it was at Jerusalem. If it was a Galilaean discourse, then we must conclude either that the reference is to Jews who were present from Jerusalem, which the context does not favour, or that the author used the term in a wider sense than was usual with him.

The most characteristic employment of the term is that for the party of hostility to Christ. We have about twenty-five instances of this (cf. vi. 13; ix. 22; xviii. 12, 14). The term is also used in some cases in which disputes or discourses about Jesus are chronicled, either because the sayings of Jesus were obscure giving rise to various interpretations (vi. 52; vii. 35, 36; viii. 22), or because some asserted while others denied the genuineness of His claims (x. 19). The term is also used in a neutral sense with no suggestion of any specific attitude towards Jesus (xi. 19, 31, 33, 36; xviii. 20); and we have references to believing Jews (viii. 31; xi. 45), and Jesus Himself says to the woman of Samaria that salvation is of the Jews (iv. 22). It may be suggested that these phenomena are not incompatible with authorship by a Palestinian Jew, in one who was a Galilaean, who wrote after the destruction of Jerusalem had annihilated the nation but embittered and intensified the racial and sectarian feelings of the Jews; when, further, the Jews and Christians were sharply distinguished from each other and the former were notoriously hostile to the latter, and when the author himself had been long absent from Palestine and separated from his own race. It was not unnatural that he should use a term, with which at the end of the first century a definite attitude of hostility to Christianity had become associated, to indicate those who adopted a similar attitude towards Christ.

The statement about Caiaphas that he was high-priest in that year (xi. 49, 51; xviii. 13) has been urged by some against the Jewish nationality of the writer, though others who admit that he was a Jew by race think that he was not a native of Palestine. It is said that the author was so ignorant of Jewish affairs that he regarded the High Priesthood as a yearly office, a mistake which Holtzmann and his namesake Oscar Holtzmann suppose to have arisen from the fact that the Asian high-priesthood did change hands every year. It is by no means unanimously accepted among those who deny the Johannine authorship that the writer really made this mistake. Schmiedel, it is true, speaks as if it needed no proof, and asserts that against this serious mistake the evidence of accurate acquaintance with geographical and historical detail has but little weight. But Keim, who rejected the Johannine authorship, expressed a different view. He says: 'The high-priest of the Death-Year is significant and does not at all betray the opinion of a yearly change in the office.' This seems to be the correct view to take. The author meant to lay stress on the fact that Caiaphas was the high-priest in the year in which Christ died. He appears to have in mind the yearly sacrifice which the high-priest had to offer on the Day of Atonement, and it thus becomes significant that Caiaphas as high-priest had a part in putting to death the antitype of that yearly sacrifice. The author repeats the phrase three times (xi. 49, 51; xviii. 13), and evidently attaches much importance to it. For he uses ἐκεῖνος, which is a favourite word with him when he wishes to make an emphatic statement. The expression has been happily paraphrased 'high-priest that fateful year.' It has all the more point when it is remembered that under the Roman rule the office so frequently changed hands, and while Caiaphas himself held it for at least ten years, his three immediate predecessors held it for only three years between them. And it is difficult to admit that one so well acquainted with Jewish life, thought, and customs as the author clearly was, could have blundered on a matter of such common knowledge. It may therefore be granted as a result of the preceding inquiry that the author was a Jew.

(2) The author was a Palestinian Jew. This proposition is still strongly contested by opponents of the Johannine authorship, though many of the definite arguments on which stress has been laid are now largely abandoned. It used to be urged that a whole series of geographical blunders had been committed by the author. To-day the best representatives of the opposition to the traditional view have withdrawn from this position. Schürer thinks that in each case the author may very well have been correct (*Contemporary Review*, Sept. 1891, p. 408). Schmiedel says that if the places in question have not been satisfactorily identified, 'the fact ought not to be urged as necessarily proving defective knowledge on the part of the author' (*Ency. Bib.*, col. 2542). He mentions other points in which the evangelist's accuracy may be vindicated, such as the forty-six years during which the Temple was in process of building, and the name of the ravine mentioned in xviii. 1 (on the text see article 'Kidron,' *Ency. Bib.*, col. 2661; Lightfoot, *Biblical Essays*, pp. 172-175). He thinks, however, that the mistake involved in the phrase 'high-priest in that year' outweighs all the

evidence of acquaintance with Palestine which may be found in these names. This point, however, has already been discussed, and a different conclusion reached.

Not only has the criticism of the writer's accuracy broken down, but the Gospel contains many positive indications of his acquaintance with Palestine. The author cannot with any plausibility be assumed to have derived his knowledge from the Old Testament, the other Gospels, or non-Biblical literature. He knows Cana of Galilee, which has not been mentioned before, also Ephraim near the wilderness, and Aenon near to Salim. His knowledge of distances and the relative position of places is accurate, but it comes to expression in a perfectly natural and spontaneous way. He knows Jerusalem well, the Pool of Bethesda by the sheep-gate with its five porches, the Pool of Siloam, Golgotha nigh to the city with its garden there, the Pavement with its Hebrew title. Some of these are not mentioned elsewhere. It must be borne in mind that the Gospel was written after the Jewish war, when Jerusalem had been razed to the ground and old landmarks had been effaced. It would not have been easy for one who had never been in Palestine to move so freely in the descriptions of a city which had been destroyed a good many years earlier.

An important question is raised in this connexion with reference to the doctrine of the Logos, found in the Fourth Gospel and the First Epistle. It is frequently asserted by opponents of the Johannine authorship, and by some of its defenders, that this doctrine was borrowed from Philo. Certainly the Logos has with Philo a very important place. He is represented as the medium between God and the universe, and as the agent through whom the world was created. Very lofty terms are used of him. He speaks of him as 'the Son of God,' 'God,' 'the first-born Son,' 'the head of the body,' 'image of God,' 'high-priest,' 'archetypal man.' It is doubtful whether he regarded the Logos as personal, his language being indecisive and perhaps inconsistent. The term with him means 'Reason' rather than 'Word,' and any idea of the Incarnation of the Logos would have been quite foreign to his thought. Nor has the Logos any relation to the Messianic hope or special connexion with Jewish history. The conception was mainly speculative and metaphysical rather than religious, and designed to secure the absolute separation of God from the world.

That Alexandrian philosophy influenced Christian theology at an early period is true. Apollos was an Alexandrian Jew, and the Epistle to the Hebrews bears clear marks of the profound impression made by the teaching of Philo. Yet it is significant that the term Logos is not applied to the Son in Hebrews, though substantially its doctrine coincides with that of the Prologue to the Fourth Gospel. This fact makes it possible that we should distinguish carefully between the contents of the doctrine and the term by which it was indicated. It lies on the surface that a deep gulf separates the Logos of Philo from the Logos of John, though it has to be recognised that Philo's conception must have been radically transformed if it was taken over into Christianity. Still, Harnack says with much reason, 'The conception of God's relation to the world as given in the Fourth Gospel is not Philonic. The Logos doctrine there is therefore essentially not that of Philo' (*History of Dogma*, E. Tr., vol. i. p. 114). He says elsewhere in speaking of the Johannine theology: 'even the Logos has little more in common with that of Philo than the name' (p. 97). Now the Johannine doctrine of the Logos has in common with that not only of Hebrews but of Paul essentially everything but the name. We are therefore more justified in looking to these authors than to Philo for the substance of the doctrine. Even if it be granted that the term went back to Philo, and behind him ultimately to Heraclitus and the Stoics, there is nothing in that which should make its use by the apostle John strange. He would find it in use in Asia, and partly, it may be, to rescue it from false associations, partly because it seemed a fit vehicle for his doctrine of the pre-existent Son, might adopt it as a fundamental term. This would involve no deep study of Philo, but simply the taking over of a term which he had introduced into theological phraseology.

Several scholars indeed argue that even the term is not borrowed from Philo but from Palestinian theology. In the Targums we have a doctrine of the Word or Memra. They constantly paraphrase the mention of an act of God in Scripture by saying that God did it through His Word. Thus 'God came to Balaam' is paraphrased 'The Word of Yahweh came to Balaam'; and the word of a man even is often used for the man himself. A third possible origin has been recently pointed out, that the term may have been derived from the Hermetic literature. There are several analogies between the *Poimandres* and the Fourth Gospel. The combination of Logos, Life, and Light occurs in both in a way not paralleled elsewhere. Pleroma ('fulness') is a common term in the Hermetic literature, and the Door, the Shepherd, and the Vine have also their analogies. The prevailing view has been that the literature belongs to a later time than the Gospel. Reitzenstein, the most recent editor of the *Poimandres* and probably the highest authority on the subject, dates it earlier, and thinks it has influenced Paul as well as John, though he rejects the idea that the Gospel can be explained out of the Hermetic literature. Grill seems inclined to admit the probability of influence; Clemen thinks it is really possible, but by no means certain, since it is not clear that the Gospel is the later. Mead in his *Thrice Greatest Hermes* strongly advocates the priority of the Poimandres and its influence on the Gospel. The latest discussion of the Hermetic literature, including an argument for early date, is to be found in Petrie's *Personal Religion in Egypt*.

The case stands then as follows. The doctrine of the Prologue was already formulated in Paul and Hebrews; the term Logos may have been a mere translation of Memra, and therefore requires no influence outside Palestine to explain it, and even if the term went back to Philo, there is no reason whatever why a Palestinian who had lived in Asia should not have used it, nor why he should have been unfamiliar with Hermetic speculations, if it can be granted that they had been formulated before his time. Wendt agrees that John actually used the term both in the Prologue to the Gospel, most of which he attributes to him, and in the First Epistle, though he adopts the dubious theory that the Logos is there regarded as impersonal. He thinks the origin of the usage is to be traced to Alexandria rather than Palestine.

(3) The author was an eye-witness. This is shown by the ease with which the writer moves among the circumstances that he describes, and by the way in which he constantly realises the situation. It has already been pointed out that the author exhibits a remarkable knowledge of the Messianic beliefs current in the Judaism of the time. Here the further point is to be observed that he describes how these beliefs affected the attitude of the people towards Jesus. In other words, it is not simply the enumeration of a series of beliefs, but the action of these beliefs in concrete situations that he describes. It would have been a matter of extraordinary difficulty for a writer even of great imaginative power to have delineated the play of these two forces on each other—the beliefs of the people on the one side, and the individuality of Jesus on the other. In Sanday's words, 'No genius, we contend, would have treated the collision between Judaism and nascent Christianity as the Evangelist has

dealt with it; and we securely rest upon that for proof that no middle link intervenes between the facts and their narrator' (*Contemporary Review*, Oct. 1891, p. 540).

The exact details as to time and place, persons and numbers, point to the recollections of an eye-witness. Special events are associated with definite localities; the nobleman's son was sick at Capernaum while Jesus was at Cana; Jesus finds the man, whom He had healed on the Sabbath, in the Temple; certain of His utterances are connected with the Treasury and with Solomon's porch. Persons are mentioned in a familiar and easy way; some of them do not occur elsewhere, *e.g.* Lazarus and Nicodemus. Various persons are connected with definite questions addressed to Christ. Points of time are exactly indicated: the sixth hour, the seventh hour, the tenth hour, in the early morning. The length of a period of time is indicated in several cases: the duration of Christ's stay in Samaria, of His delay before He went to Lazarus, of the interval that elapsed between the death and the raising of the latter. Definite numbers are freely given: the six water-pots, the four soldiers by the Cross, the twenty-five or thirty furlongs the disciples had gone before Jesus came to them walking on the sea, the thirty-eight years that the sick man had suffered, the two hundred cubits the boat was from land (xxi. 8), the number of the fish caught, one hundred and fifty-three (xxi. 11). To these may be added little touches such as that the loaves with which the multitude was fed were barley loaves, that the house was filled with the odour of the ointment, that the coat of Christ was woven without seam.

In a modern writer of fiction these details would not be surprising, since it is in this way that he makes on his readers the impression of reality. But it is very difficult to believe that the writer of a Gospel in the second century should have been so far in advance of his age in literary art as to trick his narrative out with details invented in order to make an impression of reality on his readers. And it must be remembered that the modern novelist intends his narrative to be taken as fiction, the details are introduced not to make his readers believe that his story is true, but to secure more powerful effects. In the case of the Gospel, however, the writer would deliberately invent precise details that he might mislead his readers into accepting as true what was simply the product of his own imagination. It is rather hard to believe that the moral sensitiveness of the author was so blunt as this. The case would be altered, however, if these details were invested with a symbolic significance. This view of them has been more or less taken by several scholars. Some of these, of course, consider that the narratives are purely allegorical, but some adherents of the traditional view who have asserted the historicity of the events narrated have nevertheless imposed upon them an allegorical significance. It is probably true that the writer has selected his material with this in view, as the connexion between narrative and teaching strongly suggests. For example, the feeding of the five thousand leads to the discourse on the Bread of Life, the healing of the blind man presents Jesus as the Light of the World, the raising of Lazarus teaches that Jesus is the Resurrection and the Life, the coming out of blood and water from His side is not only a positive refutation of Docetism, but symbolises that Jesus had come not with water only, but with water and blood.

But the attempt to carry through allegory everywhere leads to very strange results. When one reads the interpretation of the story of the woman of Samaria one is forcibly reminded of the Tübingen interpretation of Euodia and Syntyche, a striking example of the possibilities of theory divorced from common sense. The woman of Samaria is, of course, the half-heathen Samaritan community. She has had five husbands, that means the five heathen gods mentioned in 2 Kings xvii. 31, 32 as worshipped by the Samaritans. Her present irregular lover is Yahweh, whom she illegitimately worships. It is a pity for this interpretation, which may be found in numerous commentaries and discussions, that these gods were seven and not five; that they were worshipped simultaneously and not successively; and it is hardly likely that idolatry should be represented as marriage, when its usual symbol is adultery, or that the author should have represented Yahweh under so offensive a figure. Holtzmann, in fact, in view of this difficulty, supposes that by the irregular lover Simon Magus must be meant; but it would be very odd to place a man in line with deities, and was Samaria's connexion with him less legitimate than with them? Readers with any literary tact will feel that the story of the woman of Samaria is admirably told, full of life and movement, and even with touches of humour. The request for water, the woman's surprise, the attempt of Jesus to lead her to a sense of spiritual need, her crass misunderstanding, the probing of her conscience by the reminder of her past, the woman's ready-witted diverting of the conversation from the embarassingly personal channel to questions of theology, all follow simply and naturally. Yet of this scene, so admirably managed, Réville can say, and Pfleiderer can quote his words with approval, 'Taken literally, this scene is as absurd as that of the marriage of Cana.'

On the allegorical interpretation what are we to make of many features in the narrative—that Jesus was weary, that it was Jacob's well, that the place was Sychar, that the woman came at a certain hour, that Jesus had nothing to draw with, that the woman left her water-pot, that His disciples marvelled that He talked with the woman? The allegorist misses his mark if the allegory is not transparent, yet what symbolical meaning can be attached to these trivial details? If it is a real history that the author means to tell, whether truth or fiction they fall naturally into their places. If they are allegories it is hard to find a suitable meaning for them. Wrede does much more justice to the literary quality of the narrative; he says that the movement of the dialogue between Jesus and the Samaritan woman is incomparably finer than that with Nicodemus.

Similarly one might treat the story of the man born blind, or the incident of the feeding of the five thousand. And so we might accumulate a large number of points which speak against the allegorical interpretation. Think of the numerous trivialities in the Gospel, the reference to points of time to which significance cannot without violence be attached, or to distances. Why does the allegorist tell us that the boat was about twenty-five or thirty furlongs from the shore, which looks like the rough calculation of one who was actually there; or why that Bethany was about fifteen furlongs from Jerusalem? Why should he trouble to tell us that there were six water-pots of stone, and again give a rough estimate of their size, that they held two or three firkins apiece? What allegory lies concealed behind the lad at the miracle of the feeding, or the fact that his stock consisted of barley loaves? Why should the eyes of the blind man be anointed with clay? Why should we be told that Lazarus was buried in a cave? What is the object of saying at one time that Jesus spoke in the treasury, and on another occasion that it was in Solomon's porch, with the added touch that it was winter? What is the meaning of the fire of charcoal at the scene of Peter's denial? Why the curious new and insignificant names such as Cana and Ephraim and Malchus? Why the objectless visit to Capernaum mentioned in ii. 12, or the many other details that are not patient of a symbolical interpretation, which any reader of the Gospel may collect in abundance for himself? The cool stream of common sense which John

Spencer poured on those who found deep religious mysteries in the Levitical rites would not come amiss to those critics who in this matter also 'embrace a cloud instead of Juno.'

It may be granted that much which to us would seem absurd and fanciful might have come to seem quite natural to a writer saturated with Rabbinic and Alexandrian notions as to the significance of numbers and names. Yet when sufficient allowance for this has been made it can hardly be regarded as probable that a narrative written on these principles should be so spontaneous and give so slight an impression of artifice. Thus according to E. A. Abbott the sick man at Bethesda represents sinful Israel; he waits for the troubling of the water thirty-eight years, which corresponds to Israel's thirty-eight years of wandering; the intermittent pool symbolises the intermittent purification of the Law; the five porches represent the five senses of unredeemed humanity (though Schmiedel makes them represent the five books of Moses). The one hundred and fifty-three fish indicate the Church as evolved from the Law and the Spirit. Peter swims over two hundred cubits, a number that according to Philo represents repentance. (Numerous other examples may be seen in his article 'Gospels' in the *Ency. Bib.*) Schmiedel admits symbolical meanings to a certain extent, but says that 'the entire contents of the Gospel do not admit of being derived from ideas alone.' He thinks that mistaken statements in the Gospel have arisen in the course of oral tradition. It is open to very serious question whether this can be successfully made good in detailed application. Examples of this type of explanation may be found in his article 'John, Son of Zebedee' (*Ency. Bib.* 2539). And apart from this, it is a sound principle that the plain and literal sense should not be abandoned for a symbolical, and that lifelike touches must be held to prove accurate knowledge, either directly communicated by an eyewitness in writing, or preserved faithfully in a good oral tradition, unless there are cogent reasons to the contrary If the Johannine date for the Crucifixion is correct (see p. 215), this is important as showing that what looks like transparent allegory may nevertheless be historical fact.

Yet the argument from the presence of lifelike details does not carry us so far as its supporters often assert. More reserve should be shown in drawing the inference that the author of the document containing them must have been present when the events narrated take place. Vivid touches or a whole flood of accurate reminiscences do not prove apostolic authorship. This is perfectly clear from the Gospel of Mark. All that the graphic character of the narrative proves is that it embodies the tradition of an eye-witness, not that the eye-witness himself compiled the narrative. Now, if the Second Gospel cannot be proved by these features to be the work of Peter, we cannot prove the Fourth Gospel by similar argument to be the work of John. In fact, direct apostolic authorship is not the real point to be maintained; it is rather that the Gospel should be proved to incorporate a reliable historic tradition. And all the numerous arguments which are to be found in such copiousness in our commentaries and special discussions do not when pressed to the utmost really carry us further than that. The strongest argument for direct apostolic authorship is the claim in i. 14. This claim is corroborated by the internal evidence that has been held to prove authorship by an eye-witness, but of itself this does not suffice to establish it. Still it seems sounder to see in the details which have been enumerated genuine historical recollections rather than allegorical ideas or the outcome of a whole series of misunderstandings.

(4) The writer was an apostle. If he was an eye-witness he can hardly have been any one but an apostle,[1] for only

[1] On the attempt to show that the beloved disciple was not an apostle see pp. 147 ff.

an apostle is likely to have been present at so many different scenes, in such various places and at such various times. This is confirmed by the knowledge he exhibits of the feelings of the disciples, and what they said to each other. Thus after the cleansing of the Temple we read: 'And his disciples remembered that it was written, The zeal of thine house eateth me up' (ii. 17). Again when the disciples returned from the city they were surprised that Jesus should be talking with a woman, but did not venture to question Him; and when He replied to their offer of food 'I have food to eat of which you do not know,' they ask each other whether any one has brought Him food (iv. 27-33). The writer is aware that the garden in which Jesus was arrested was one which was known to Judas as a meeting-place for Jesus and His disciples (xviii. 1, 2). He also reveals an intimate acquaintance with the thoughts and feelings of Jesus. He mentions the reason for His leaving Judaea (iv. 1), and for withdrawing from the multitude after He had fed it (vi. 15). He explains that His question to Philip was for the purpose of trying him, since He knew Himself what He was going to do (vi. 6).

(5) The writer was the apostle John. If he was an apostle at all, only John can be thought of. Of the disciples most intimate with Jesus, Peter, James, and John, Peter is excluded by the way in which the Gospel speaks of him, James by his early death. This is confirmed by the fact that the name of John the apostle nowhere occurs, in spite of the fact that he was one of the three disciples nearest to Jesus, and that he occupies a prominent position in the Synoptists, in Acts, and in Paul. The sons of Zebedee are referred to, but placed in a position where no one else would have placed them, and the names are not given (xxi. 2). In view of the particularity with which the author specifies names, it is most significant that these names are not mentioned. And there is one minute

indication which is very striking. The author is careful about the exact identification of those to whom he refers, distinguishing them from others of the same name, thus Simon Peter, Judas Iscariot and Judas not Iscariot, Judas the son of Simon Iscariot, Nicodemus, the same who came to Jesus by night, Thomas who is called Didymus. But he never speaks of John the Baptist as the Synoptic Gospels do, but simply of John, apparently since he thinks that being himself the John from whom his namesake was to be distinguished, no note of distinction is required.

In looking back over these indirect arguments it may perhaps be granted that they are of different degrees of cogency. That the author was a Jew may be asserted without hesitation, and that he was a native of Palestine, or at any rate had lived long in Palestine, may be asserted with almost equal confidence, the phrase 'high priest in that year' being altogether insufficient to outweigh the minute acquaintance with Palestine exhibited by the author. Of the other points it must at present suffice to say that while taken in themselves they rather strongly suggest that the author was an eye-witness and the apostle John, yet they might perhaps be satisfied by a belief that he had access to an exceptionally good tradition, much in the same way as Mark had. It must be remembered that the main question is one of historical character rather than authorship, and this might be secured as in the case of Mark by faithful reproduction of a good tradition. No doubt first-hand evidence is better than evidence at second hand. But it would be premature to pronounce an opinion till the objections to the Johannine authorship have been stated and examined. It should be added, however, that these objections do, as a matter of fact, touch not only the question of authorship but that of historical trustworthiness.

Objections to the Apostolic Authorship.

Unfortunately the question of authorship is affected seriously by theological considerations. Those who take a purely humanitarian view of Christ's Person, or disbelieve in the possibility of miracles, naturally find a difficulty in admitting that such a work as the Fourth Gospel can have come from the hand of an apostle. Those for whom the Christology of the Fourth Gospel is untrue, and who consider that Paul started the Church down the fatal slope of mythology by his doctrine of the Divinity of Christ, will naturally find it difficult, if not impossible, to believe that one who had personally known Jesus should speak of Him as the author does in his prologue; still more, that he should represent Jesus as speaking of Himself as He does in the Gospel. On this point it must suffice to quote the words of one of the ablest and most moderate opponents of the traditional view. Weizsäcker says: 'It is even a greater puzzle that the apostle, the beloved disciple of the Gospel, he who reclined at table next Jesus, should have come to regard and represent his whole former experience as a life with the incarnate Logos of God.' After adding that no power of faith or philosophy can be imagined great enough to substitute this marvellous picture of a Divine Being for the recollection of the real life, and that in Paul's case such a thing would be possible since he had not known Jesus in His earthly life, he proceeds: 'For a primitive apostle it is inconceivable. The question is decided here, and finally here' (*Apostolic Age*, vol. ii. p. 211). Such a consideration can have no weight with those who believe that the Logos doctrine was true to fact. They will be much readier to admit that Jesus may have spoken of Himself in such language as the Fourth Gospel puts into His mouth. It is necessary to draw attention to this point, since an avowed or unavowed theological presupposition has in some cases not a little to do with the

Jesus died not when Lamb was (Passover) slain in temple but 24 hrs later

attitude adopted on critical problems in the strict sense of the term. A discussion of the point, however, would be improper here, since it would involve desertion of criticism for philosophy and theology.

Of purely critical objections by far the most important are those which rise out of a comparison with the Synoptists. The Johannine narrative is suspected to have been largely formed under the influence of definite theological preconceptions, or from the exigencies of theological controversy. This explains the transference of Christ's ministry from Galilee to Judaea, since it was fitting that the Messiah should do His work in the capital and not in the provinces. This also accounts for the transformation of the story of the baptism, since it was not fitting that the Incarnate Logos should be represented as receiving His baptism and the call to His work at the hands of John. Moreover, John loses the significance he possesses in the Synoptists, and is reduced merely to the position of a witness to Jesus. The date of the Crucifixion is altered so that the death of Jesus may coincide with the slaughter of the Paschal Lamb. The confession or self-revelation of Jesus as Messiah is made at the beginning of the ministry, rather than kept a secret till towards its close. The developed Christology of the author which originated with Paul has become the main theme of Christ's own speeches. The obstinate debates with the Jews of the author's own day have been carried back to His lifetime. Incidents which seemed to compromise the divine dignity of the Incarnate Logos have been removed, such as the agony at Gethsemane, or the cry of desertion on the Cross. The miracles here are not simply selected for their symbolism, but are presented on a more exaggerated scale than in the Synoptists; they are less the outcome of compassion than designed to exhibit the glory of Jesus. The author carefully guards Jesus against any yielding to the suggestions of others; hence if He does what has been suggested

Judea, Galilee, Perea.
Under obligation to go to lost sheep of Israel. No public ministry in Samaria

to Him, He first refuses and then acts on His own initiative. The homely and pithy discourses of the Synoptic Jesus, lit up by parable and packing the deepest meaning into lucid and pregnant aphorisms, have given place in John to mystical and monotonous harangues in which theme and style and manner are altogether different.

It must, of course, be recognised that there is a good deal of weight in this characterisation of the Gospel. Yet it is quite possible to suspect the writer of exaggeration, of conscious or unconscious transformation, when what we really have to do with is selection from a peculiar point of view. And in some of the more crucial points there is much to be said in favour of the Johannine report.

We may begin with the scene and duration of Christ's ministry. While the Synoptic Gospels limit the ministry to Galilee, and bring Jesus to Jerusalem only a few days before the Crucifixion, and, to take a related point, seem to allow a year only for its duration, the Fourth Gospel represents Jesus as several times visiting Jerusalem, and makes His ministry extend to two years and a half. There are, however, considerations which corroborate John's account. It is intrinsically unlikely that Jesus, conscious of His Messianic vocation, should be content to work simply in the provinces and make no appeal to the religious capital of Judaism, and the centre of its constituted authority, till the last week of His life. And this presumption is confirmed by the testimony of the Synoptists themselves. The lament of Jesus, 'How oft would I have gathered thee,' His words, 'I sat daily in the Temple,' the crowds that welcomed Him on His triumphal entry, the daughters of Jerusalem who wept as He was led to be crucified, the begging of His body by Joseph of Arimathaea, the lending of the ass on which He entered Jerusalem, the man with the pitcher of water who had made ready the guest-chamber for Jesus and His disciples, are all mentioned in the Synoptists, and they prove that Christ's connexion with

Jerusalem was far more intimate than a superficial reader would have been likely to suppose. It is in favour of John's representation that he connects Christ's visits with the feasts, since it was at the feasts that He would most naturally visit Jerusalem. As to the duration of the ministry nothing can really be urged against John's narrative. It is a mistake to make the Synoptists our standard here, for they have no chronology to speak of. Their account probably demands a longer period than their chronological statements might seem to suggest, otherwise the development of events would have to be unnaturally accelerated. Lastly, both for locality and chronology the Synoptists are not three authorities, but one only, Matthew and Luke simply deriving from Mark.

The question raised as to the date of the Last Supper and the Crucifixion is difficult. John seems to place them a day earlier than the Synoptists, and thus to make the death of Jesus coincide in time with the killing of the Paschal Lamb. The question is a very complicated one, and is to some extent associated with the Paschal controversy in the second century. The symbolism of John is thought to have controlled his narrative, and the change of date to have been due to the wish to represent Jesus as suffering as the true Paschal Lamb. This view is still taken by some, but by no means all of those who reject the Johannine authorship. Schürer, Wendt, Bousset, Harnack, and apparently Wellhausen think that the date in the Fourth Gospel is more likely to be correct. And this is the better view to take. Against what seem to be definite statements in the Synoptists that Jesus partook of the Passover on the proper date and was arrested that night, there are several indications in their own narrative that the supper was eaten a day before the proper date of the Passover, and that Jesus was already dead before Passover Day had begun. These are (*a*) the resolve of His enemies not to take Him on the feast day, (*b*) the illegality of a trial on that day, (*c*) the illegality of wearing arms, which would have been committed by the guards and one of the disciples, (*d*) the fact that Simon of Cyrene was impressed by the soldiers apparently as he was coming from work, (*e*) the purchase of linen by Joseph of Arimathaea and the preparation of spices by the women, (*f*) the words of Jesus in Luke xxii. 15, 16 which imply that His longing to eat the Passover was not fulfilled. And this victorious confirmation of the Johannine date by the Synoptists themselves is still further strengthened by the consideration that only in this way can we reasonably account for the abnormal haste with which the proceedings were carried through. It was in order that they might be all over before the Paschal feast actually began. It is also corroborated by Paul's reference to Christ as our Passover (1 Cor. v. 7).

A difficulty of the most serious character is raised by the representation of the teaching of Jesus, both as to its form and content. In form the Johannine speeches are abstruse and mystical, long and somewhat monotonous, and written in a peculiar type of phraseology, which recurs in the First Epistle, and, what is much more surprising, in the speeches of John the Baptist. Much may be said in modification of the sweeping judgment, which the facts at first sight seem to suggest, that the speeches are one and all the free composition of the author. As Matthew Arnold and others have pointed out, when we look more closely into the speeches in John they are seen to abound in just the same kind of pithy sayings that we find in the Synoptists. It has been calculated that nearly a hundred and fifty words are found in the discourses of Christ which are never used by the evangelist. Further, if Jesus spoke Aramaic, we should expect John to employ his habitual language in translating into Greek. It is often urged that the Fourth Gospel contains discourses to the cultivated residents of the capital or the disciples whom

He had trained, and naturally they differed much from the more popular discourses addressed to Galilaeans. This can hardly be admitted. On the one hand, Jesus talks in this way to the woman of Samaria and in the synagogue at Capernaum. On the other hand, the Synoptic discourses delivered in Jerusalem are like those spoken elsewhere. It is strange that in the Fourth Gospel parables have disappeared. Some allegories take their place, *e.g.* the vine and its branches. Some of the Synoptic parables might more fitly be called allegories, *e.g.* the leaven, or the mustard seed; and Luke has several stories of a type not found in Matthew and Mark, *e.g.* the Good Samaritan and the Prodigal Son.

When every explanation has been given, it remains true that the probability that Jesus spoke as the Fourth Gospel represents cannot be made good. In view of the marked similarity in style between the speeches of Jesus and the Baptist, the style of the author himself and that of the First Epistle, there should be no hesitation in recognising that the form in which the discourses are cast is due largely to the evangelist himself, who has stamped everything with his own idiosyncrasies; though here, too, it is easy to overstate the case. A Jewish writer would naturally adopt direct speech where a Greek would use indirect, yet one would not mean any more than the other to be taken as giving a verbatim report, but to be expressing largely in his own language the gist of what the speaker said. The subjective element in the report is probably larger than the average reader would imagine. That the author invented the discourses cannot be maintained, because they contain so much matter like that in the Synoptists, and because they were beyond his power, Jesus being, as Matthew Arnold well brings out, so much above the heads of His reporters. But it is probable that the speeches owe their peculiar form to the evangelist, genuine sayings of Christ being woven into a connected whole, which has passed through his own mind and received the impress of his form of speech.

As to the content of the speeches there is also a wide difference. As a general principle it may be said at the outset that the probability is altogether in favour of there having been a deeper element in the teaching of Jesus, which finding little response among many, would be welcomed by a finely sympathetic and receptive mind. It is no doubt surprising that so much more stress should be placed by Jesus on His own Person and the true relation to Himself than in the Synoptists, where the stress is rather on seeking the Kingdom of God and His righteousness. Yet we have to remember that the Synoptists themselves contain numerous sayings of Jesus which, while they do not bear the stamp of the Johannine vocabulary, express substantially the Johannine Christology.

The same instinct which rejects the sayings in the Fourth Gospel tends also to reject such sayings in the Synoptics. Yet the authenticity of some of these cannot be successfully challenged. The saying which places the Son above the angels is guaranteed as authentic by the confession of the Son's ignorance, which certainly could never have been invented. Elsewhere Jesus claims that a man should surrender everything and sunder the closest tie that he may follow Him. To help the suffering or to receive a little child in His name will be rewarded as if He had been helped or received. To receive Him is to receive God who sent Him. Those who confess Him before men will be confessed by Him before God. Prayer in His name is rewarded by His presence with those who pray, and the fulfilment of their desires by God. He who loses his life for Christ's sake shall find it. If He is David's son He is also David's Lord. And there is one passage in particular which has quite a Johannine ring: 'All things have been delivered unto me of my Father; neither doth any one know the Father save the Son, and he to whom the Son willeth to reveal him' (Matt. xi. 27, Luke x. 22). In this Jesus claims to stand in an altogether unique relation to God. He is the Son in a sense in which no other is; it is only the Father who truly knows Him, He alone truly knows the Father, nor can any know the Father unless He reveals Him to them. If Jesus was conscious of occupying this relation to God, perhaps we ought rather to be surprised that the Synoptists represent Him as speaking of it so rarely than that it is so frequent a theme in John. Moreover, in two highly important sayings the Synoptists bring the ground of salvation into the closest relation with Christ's Person and Death. 'The Son of man came not to be ministered unto but to minister, and to give his life a ransom for many'; and 'This is my blood of the covenant which is shed for many,' Matthew adds 'unto remission of sins.'

It is true that the Synoptists report no definite claim of Jesus to pre-existence, while such claims are prominent in the Fourth Gospel. But even if we do not base anything on the supposition that the pre-existence of the Messiah was already a doctrine in some Jewish schools it was certainly taught by Paul and the author of Hebrews, and since as Weizsäcker allows we find 'no trace of any opposition encountered by this doctrine in primitive apostolic circles,' a good case can be made out for the view that it was really taught by Christ Himself. Indeed, the dignity ascribed to His Person in the Synoptic sayings is so lofty that pre-existence might most naturally be postulated of such a Being. Lastly, it is difficult to overrate the significance of the fact that the Christology of Paul created no controversy such as raged fiercely about his doctrine of the Law.

Another difference between the Fourth Gospel and the Synoptists relates to the development of the revelation and recognition of Jesus as Messiah. Here it is said that in the earliest tradition Jesus, though certain of His Messiahship from the outset, did not for a long time advance the claim to be Messiah; that the disciples did not at first suspect Him to be the Messiah, as is shown by the question 'Who then is this that even the winds and sea obey Him?' and by Peter's confession at Caesarea Philippi; further that even when the disciples realised it they were forbidden to make it known, so that only at the end is it proclaimed to the multitude and to the Sanhedrin; and finally that John the Baptist first suspected Him to be the Messiah when he was in prison. As against this the Fourth Gospel represents Jesus in the narrative of the cleansing of the Temple as adopting the Messianic functions at the outset, the disciples as recognising His Messiahship, and John the Baptist as recognising it even before they do.

This sketch, which follows Schürer's discussion, is open to some criticism. The 'earliest tradition' is not that of the Synoptists as a whole, but the oldest stratum in them. This should be recognised, since there are elements in the Synoptists which look somewhat in the direction of John. In the next place it is not clear that the question in Mark iv. 41 necessarily implies that the disciples could not then have believed Him to be the Messiah, unless we assume that they expected the Messiah to be able to control the fury of the sea and storm. Moreover in Mark the demoniacs from the outset confess Him as the Holy One of God, the Son of God, or the Son of the Most High God. It cannot therefore have been a view which dawned on the disciples only later. Peter's confession, it is true, makes the impression that here we have his definitely formed conviction expressed for the first time. And according to the narrative in Matt. xi., Luke vii., John's question does seem to be one of expectation rather than despondency, since it is inspired by the news of Christ's mighty works, which he has heard in prison. This, however, involves a sceptical attitude to the narrative in Matt. iii. 14, 15, which, to be sure, is not found in Mark or Luke. Psychologically there is no serious difficulty in the usual view that John in prison had a more despondent outlook than when he was in full career, and the methods of Jesus may well have seemed too slow and gentle for one whose fan was in His hand. And the reply of Jesus, 'Blessed is he who findeth not occasion of stumbling in me,' gains much greater significance if John had sent to Him in a moment of despondency.

On the other side, the earliness of the Messianic development in the Fourth Gospel is perhaps overstated. The cleansing of the Temple need not involve anything more than might have been accomplished by an Old Testament Prophet; it does not necessarily assert a Messianic claim. It is true that a serious difficulty is created by the fact that the cleansing is placed by the Synoptists almost immediately before His death. It is not likely that there were two cleansings, and the Synoptic version has in its favour that it precipitates the crisis, and that it thus seems to be an integral part of the development as conceived by them. On the other hand, if we admit numerous visits to Jerusalem, there is much to be said in favour of John's account which at first sight appears to be particularly vulnerable. It is not probable that Jesus saw this desecration of the Temple again and again during His ministry and then acted only at the last. The action bears rather the impress of springing out of His first contact with the evil, after He had become conscious of His vocation. The Synoptic narrative suggests that matters moved with astonishing rapidity. Naturally, recognising only one visit to Jerusalem, the writers were compelled to place the cleansing there, if they narrated it at all. If the Johannine narrative implies that Jesus intimated His death and resurrection in the discussion that ensued, it would no doubt be natural to see in this the evidence for its original connexion with the Passion visit. This, however, is by no means necessary.

It is no doubt true that we find Andrew, Philip, and Nathanael confessing Jesus as Messiah or Son of God quite early, even before His first miracle. Yet we must beware of reading too much into this. We need to distinguish clearly between what Messiah meant to them and what it meant to Jesus. It by no means necessarily implied in their case a lofty view of His Person or Mission. There were numerous Messianic movements in this period. That Jesus revealed Himself to the Samaritan woman is not so surprising as it might seem, since the risks involved in a premature announcement were slight in Samaria. The Baptist's language about Jesus in John is certainly astonishing. It should be pointed out that the account given by Schürer of the presentation in the Fourth Gospel is not complete. Not so long before His death that Gospel represents the people as urging Jesus to keep them no longer in suspense, but to tell them plainly whether He is the Messiah or not. At an earlier period in chap. vii. the people are still disputing His real character. It is probably true that the evangelist read back to some extent the completed revelation into the earlier period, and imparted a certain precision to the utterances in it which they did not really possess. After the lapse of many years even an eye-witness might blur the lines of development and fail to recall the exact movement in all its sharp precision.

The silence of the Synoptists on the raising of Lazarus is a real difficulty which may be mitigated, but has never been satisfactorily explained. It is true that they give very little Judaean incident, yet Luke knows about Martha and Mary. It is also true that they relate narratives of the raising of the dead, and our modern grading of wonders must not be carried back to them. Yet the fact that the Jews regarded the spirit of the dead man as hovering about his body till the third day after death, and as then going to

Sheol, indicates that they would have seen in the resurrection of Lazarus when he had been dead four days something much more striking than in the raising of Jairus's daughter, or of the young man at Nain. On the other hand, the confidence with which the omission by the Synoptists is paraded as completely discrediting the historical character of the Fourth Gospel[1] is, in view of their one-sided character and their attitude to miracles in general, a violent exaggeration. The story of John bears such clear marks of historicity that Renan, who entirely rejected the miracle, but whose historic sense and literary tact compelled him to admit a genuine element of history, was driven to the conclusion that a fraud was palmed off on the people by Lazarus and his family, Jesus Himself being a party to it. This needs no discussion, but the theory is a striking testimony to the impression of truthfulness made by the narrative.

Good

Apart from the objections derived from a comparison with the Synoptists, there are others. One is that a Judaising apostle should have taken so free an attitude with reference to the Law. Really we know very little of John's Judaising tendencies. But the destruction of Jerusalem must have seemed to him a divine judgment on Judaism, and residence in Asia would conduce to a more liberal view. It is thought further that a Galilaean fisherman cannot have written a work at once so artistic and profound. But the accident of a man's calling in life may prove nothing as to natural gifts (it was a tinker who wrote *The Pilgrim's Progress*), and John had been trained by Jesus Himself. If he is to be identified with the beloved disciple and the testimony of the Fourth Gospel be received that Jesus entertained for him a special affection, this points to a nature which He felt to be in

OK

[1] See, for example, Wernle's sweeping statement: 'That the three Synoptists mention not a syllable of this greatest of all the miracles of Jesus, is enough, quite by itself, to destroy all faith in the Johannine tradition' (*Die Quellen des Lebens Jesu* (1904), p. 24).

sympathetic harmony with His own to a degree surpassing that of the others. And the style is not artistic, or that of a practised writer, nor does the author write as one who had received a scholastic training. These and similar objections rest on assumptions rather than facts.

Results.

In looking back on the various lines of evidence discussed, the present writer feels it difficult to share the confidence of the extremists on one side or the other. The external evidence favours though it does not demand Johannine authorship. The internal evidence seems to prove conclusively that the author had access to an exceptionally rich treasure of genuine historical reminiscences, whether stored in his own memory of scenes at which he had been present, or derived from an eye-witness. Accordingly we may reconstruct the circumstances and situation which gave rise to the Gospel somewhat in the following way. The apostle John came to Ephesus late in the sixties, living there till towards the close of the first century, and gathering about him a band of disciples to whom he was in the habit of imparting his reminiscences of the life of Jesus. He lived in an intellectual atmosphere wholly different from that familiar to him in Palestine, and, if not for himself, at least for his disciples, was forced to take up a definite attitude towards it. Within the Church the Docetic heresy was working havoc, and without it there was an unfriendly empire and a bitterly hostile Judaism. Possibly too he may have had to do with followers of John the Baptist, who pitted their prophet against the prophet of Nazareth.[1] There was

[1] This has been argued with great originality and acuteness, but also with much violent exegesis, by Baldensperger in his *Der Prolog des vierten Evangeliens*, 1898. His views have met with little acceptance, though the brilliance and suggestiveness of his discussion have been amply recognised. Pfleiderer and E. F. Scott think he has made out his point for the first three chapters of the Gospel. On the other hand, see Jülicher and Loisy, also an article in the *Journal of Biblical Literature*, vol. xx., 1901, part i., by Professor C. W. Rishell.

also the Alexandrian philosophy, and penetrating everything the subtle influence of Greek thought.

Over against this world which lay in the evil one the apostle stood firm in the consciousness that he was in possession of the absolute truth. For this truth he fought directly in his Epistle, indirectly in his Gospel. The latter work had primarily an apologetic interest; it was not so much, as he himself tells us, to give information about Jesus, as to create the belief that Jesus was the Son of God, thus bringing his readers to eternal life. The Synoptic Gospels, in part or wholly, were already known to him; it was not necessary to go over their ground again, unless it served his purpose specially to do so. At the same time he was able to rectify their limitations. The selection of his material, however, was dominated in the main by the situation with which he was confronted. He seeks to set Christianity in a favourable light before the empire; the kingdom of Jesus is not of this world, and Pilate would gladly have acquitted Him. Against the Docetists he insists on the reality of the Incarnation. His Logos becomes flesh, eats and drinks, sits weary by the well, groans in spirit, falters at the prospect of the Passion. From His pierced side comes forth blood and water, His risen body bears the print of the nails and the wound in the side. The Greeks come to Jesus, and the prologue strikes with the doctrine of the Logos the key for the whole Gospel. The author's sharpest polemic is directed against the Jews, who are shown as persistently opposing Jesus, and from quite early in His ministry planning His death. He plies them with the argument from the Old Testament, from the witness of John the Baptist, from the miracles of Jesus. If they do not receive this accumulated testimony it is because they are children of the devil and have no true knowledge of God. If he had to meet the claims made for the Baptist by his followers, he did so by putting the

Baptist in his right place, as not the Light Himself, but witnessing to the Light. There is, however, no trace of any tendency to disparage the Baptist; upon his testimony to Jesus the evangelist lays the greatest stress.

The apologetic and largely polemical purpose of the Gospel accounts for much that strikes one as peculiar. That the conditions reacted on the evangelist's representation of the life and teaching of Jesus, that subsequent meditation may have mingled with the report, that the stages of historical movement have not been distinguished in all their original sharpness, is no cause for wonder. But we should make a great mistake if we imagined that the Gospel was merely a romance of the Logos, freely invented as a vehicle of ideas. It embodies a large number of most precious reminiscences, though the interest which has dictated their preservation was largely theological and apologetic rather than historical.

In the preceding discussion no account has been taken of the problem whether the Gospel is a unity. That it is so has been and still remains the prevalent opinion of critics of all classes. In spite of this there have been several protests of which the most noteworthy must receive a brief mention. One of the best worked out partition theories is that of Wendt. This scholar considers that the apostle John compiled a collection of discourses of Jesus. The materials are substantially authentic, but the form and language are largely due to the apostle himself. This work was subsequently incorporated in our present Gospel by a writer who added the narrative sections for which he had some good traditions, but which is on the whole of secondary historical value. Unfortunately an examination of this theory would demand a detailed discussion such as it is not possible to give in our space. On the general distinction between narrative and discourse it may be said that the latter frequently creates the greater difficulty for defenders of the authenticity.

Moreover, it is questionable if this line of demarcation is the most natural one for an analytic theory to take.

In a work entitled *Expansions and Alterations in the Fourth Gospel* Wellhausen argued both for transpositions and later insertions. The view that chap. v. should be placed after chap. vi. is an old one, and in the present writer's judgment almost certainly correct, and there are some minor transpositions of which the same may be said. The most important question touches chaps. xv.-xvii. It had been suggested by Pfleiderer that these chapters were a later addition by the evangelist himself. Wellhausen considered that they were added by a later writer who reinstated the idea of the Second Coming which had been set aside by the author in the original text of chap. xiv. It is certainly difficult to suppose that they could stand in their present position, but unless we take with undue seriousness the divergence from the rest of the Gospel which Wellhausen detects in them, the difficulty may readily be solved by transposition of chapters xv. and xvi. Two long chapters are certainly not in place after the signal for departure has been given in xiv. 31. It is therefore likely that chap. xiv. should connect immediately with chap. xvii., and xv. and xvi. be inserted at an earlier point, perhaps after xiii. 31*a*. In his later work on the Gospel of John Wellhausen has advanced to a much more complicated theory. He finds in our present Gospel the result of a long literary process, the stages of which can at present be only imperfectly recovered. In the development of this theory he has had the advantage of frequent consultation with E. Schwartz, who has worked out his own theory of discontinuities in the Fourth Gospel in a series of articles in the *Göttingische Gelehrte Nachrichten*. A discussion of these theories is also impossible, and it must suffice to have called attention to the fact that very eminent scholars have definitely broken with the traditional view both of critics and apologists that the

Fourth Gospel is a unity. The fundamental objection to partition theories is the homogeneousness of the Gospel in style and standpoint.

O.K.

Whether, however, we should attribute the twenty-first chapter to the author of the Gospel is a question on which defenders of the unity are divided. Apparently it forms no part of the original plan, and the Gospel comes to its natural close with chapter xx. We have, however, no trace of the circulation of the Gospel without this chapter, and although there are difficulties in the way of attributing it to the author of the Gospel, these are perhaps sufficiently met if we assume that some interval lay between its composition and that of the preceding chapters.

BIBLIOGRAPHY

Note.—The abbreviations indicating the series to which a commentary belongs are appended to the full titles of the series in the opening list, so that each may be readily identified. It may be added that important discussions are often contained in periodicals, both British and foreign.

Introductions to the New Testament by S. Davidson (3rd ed.), Bleek (last German edition polemically edited by Mangold), B. Weiss (E. Tr., 3rd German ed. 1897), Salmon, Dods, M'Clymont, Holtzmann (3rd ed.), Bacon, Jülicher (E. Tr. 1904, 6th German ed. 1906), Zahn (3rd ed., translation announced). Pullan, *The Books of the N.T.*; Adeney in *A Biblical Introduction*, by Bennett and Adeney; von Soden, *History of Early Christian Literature*; G. Currie Martin, *The Books of the N.T.*; Wrede, *The Origin of the N.T.*; Reuss, *History of the Sacred Scriptures of the N.T.*; Clemen, *Entstehung des N.T.*; Sanday, *Inspiration*; Lightfoot, *Essays on Supernatural Religion*, *Biblical Essays*; Harnack, *Chronologie der altchristlichen Literatur*; Dictionaries of the Bible by Smith and Hastings, *Encyclopaedia Biblica*, *Standard Bible Dictionary*, Hastings' one vol. Bible Dictionary, Murray's one vol. Bible Dictionary, Hastings' *Dictionary of Christ and the Gospels*; Histories of the Apostolic Age by Weizsäcker, M'Giffert, Bartlet, Ropes; also Pfleiderer, *Urchristentum* (2nd ed.), E. Tr. *Primitive Christianity* (in progress), and Wernle's *Beginnings of Christianity*. Among commentaries on the whole of the New Testament, the following may be mentioned: Meyer, *Kommentar über das N.T.* (E. Tr. contains work of Meyer and his colleagues; the later German editions have been completely re-written by other editors); *Hand-commentar zum N.T.* (*H.C.*);

International Critical Commentary (*I.C.C.*); *Cambridge Bible* (*C.B.*); *Cambridge Greek Testament* (*C.G.T.*); *Expositor's Greek Testament* (*E.G.T.*); *Century Bible* (*Cent. B.*); *Westminster Commentaries* (*West. Com.*); *International Handbooks to the N.T.* (*I.H.*); Zahn, *Kommentar zum N.T.*; J. Weiss, *Die Scriften des N.T.* (*S.N.T.*); Lietzmann, *Handbuch zum N.T.* (*H.N.T.*); Moffatt's *Historical New Testament* (a new translation of the New Testament with books arranged in presumed chronological order, contains much valuable critical matter).

Of the above the most useful Introductions at present for the English reader are those by Jülicher and Adeney. Zahn's Introduction is a work of immense erudition, and a very important statement of the conservative case. The leading statement of the more advanced critical view in German is Holtzmann's Introduction. A new edition is badly needed, but its place is to some extent supplied by the author's commentaries, articles, and his *Neutestamentliche Theologie*, a second edition of which has been long announced.

CHAPTER II

ON THE PAULINE EPISTLES.—Godet, *Introduction to the N.T.: The Pauline Epistles*; Knowling, *The Witness of the Epistles* and *The Testimony of St. Paul to Christ*; Clemen, *Die Chronologie der paulinischen Briefe* and *Die Einheitlichkeit der paulinischen Briefe*; Findlay, *The Epistles of Paul the Apostle*; Shaw, *The Pauline Epistles*; R. Scott, *The Pauline Epistles.* The Lives of Paul also contain as a rule critical discussions on the Epistles: Bacon's *Story of St. Paul*, Clemen's *Paulus*, and Weinel's *St. Paul* are the most noteworthy of recent works; of the rest it may suffice to mention those by Conybeare and Howson, Lewin, Farrar, Sabatier, Ramsay.

ON THE EPISTLES TO THE THESSALONIANS.—Commentaries by Bornemann (in Meyer), P. Schmidt, Schmiedel (*H.C.*), Findlay (*C.G.T.*), Drummond (*I.H.*), Wohlenberg (in Zahn), Lightfoot (in *Notes on Epistles of St. Paul*), Adeney (*Cent. B.*), G. Milligan, Lueken (*S.N.T.*); Askwith, *An Introduction to the Thessalonian Epistles*; Wrede, *Die Echtheit des zweiten Thessalonicher-briefs.*

CHAPTER III

Commentaries by Lightfoot, Sieffert (in Meyer), Lipsius (*H.C.*), Beet, Perowne (*C.B.*), Ramsay, Adeney (*Cent. B.*), Zahn, Drummond (*I.H.*), Rendall (*E.G.T.*), Bousset (*S.N.T.*); Holsten, *Das Evangelium des Paulus I.* On the locality of the Galatian Churches, in addition to the commentaries, Ramsay, *Church in the Roman Empire*, *Studia Biblica*, vol. iv., *St. Paul the Traveller*, *Cities of St. Paul*; Askwith, *The Epistle to the Galatians*; Steinmann, *Die Abfassungszeit des Galaterbriefes*, *Der Leserkreis des Galaterbriefes*.

CHAPTER IV

Commentaries on both Epistles: Heinrici (in Meyer), Schmiedel (*H.C.*), Godet, Beet, Drummond (*I.H.*), Massie (*Cent. B.*), Bachmann (in Zahn), Bousset (*S.N.T.*), Lietzmann (*H.N.T.*), Heinrici (distinct from comm. in Meyer); Commentaries on 1 Cor. by Evans (*Speaker*), Edwards, Findlay (*E.G.T.*), Lias (*C.B.*), Goudge (*West. Com.*), Lightfoot (in *Notes on Epistles of St. Paul*); on 2 Cor. by Waite (*Speaker*), Bernard (*E.G.T.*), Plummer (*C.G.T.*). Hausrath, *Der Vier-Capitel-brief des Paulus an die Korinther*; J. H. Kennedy, *The Second and Third Epistles to the Corinthians*.

CHAPTER V

Commentaries by B. Weiss (in Meyer), Lipsius (*H.C.*), Godet, Oltramare, Gifford (*Speaker*), Beet, Moule (*C.B.*), Lightfoot (in *Notes on Epistles of St. Paul*), Sanday and Headlam (*I.C.C.*), Denney (*E.G.T.*), Drummond (*I.H.*), Garvie (*Cent. B.*), Jülicher (*S.N.T.*), Lietzmann (*H.N.T.*). Hort, *Prolegomena to St. Paul's Epistles to the Romans and the Ephesians*; Lightfoot, *Biblical Essays*, pp. 287-384 (including an article by Hort).

CHAPTER VI

Commentaries on Ephesians, Philippians, Colossians, Philemon, by E. Haupt (in Meyer), Moule (*C.B.*), O. Cone (*I.H.*), G. C. Martin (*Cent. B.*), P. Ewald (in Zahn) Beet, Lueken, (*S.N.T.*). On Ephesians, Colossians, and Philemon, by von Soden (*H.C.*), Oltramare. On Ephesians and Colossians, T. K. Abbott (*I.C.C.*). On Colossians and Philemon, Lightfoot, Lukyn Williams (*C.G.T.*). On Philippians and Philemon, Vincent (*I.C.C.*). On Ephesians, Macpherson, Klöpper, Salmond (*E.G.T.*), J. A. Robinson, Westcott, Lightfoot (in *Notes on Epistles of St. Paul*, on Eph. i. 1-14). On Philippians, B. Weiss, Lightfoot, Lipsius (*H.C.*), Klöpper, Moule (*C.G.T.*), H. A. A. Kennedy (*E.G.T.*). On Colossians, Klöpper, Peake (*E.G.T.*).

Holtzmann, *Kritik der Epheser- und Kolosserbriefe* (examined by von Soden in *Jahrb. für prot. Theol.* for 1885); Hort, *Prolegomena to St. Paul's Epistles to the Romans and Ephesians.*

CHAPTER VII

Commentaries by Holtzmann, B. Weiss (in Meyer), von Soden (*H.C.*), Bernard (*C.G.T.*), Lilley, O. Cone (*I.H.*), Horton (*Cent. B.*), Köhler (*S.N.T.*).

CHAPTER VIII

Commentaries by Bleek, Delitzsch, B. Weiss (in Meyer), von Soden (*H.C.*), Westcott, A. B. Davidson, O. Cone (*I.H.*), Farrar (*C.G.T.*), Peake (*Cent. B.*), Hollmann (*S.N.T.*). Works on the Theology of the Epistle to the Hebrews by Riehm, Ménégoz, Bruce, G. Milligan, contain discussions of the critical problems. Wrede, *Das literarische Rätsel des Hebräerbriefs*; Harnack's theory in *Zeitschrift für Neutest. Wissenschaft* for 1900; cf. J. Rendel Harris, *Side-Lights on New Testament Research*, Lecture v.

CHAPTER IX

Commentaries by Beyschlag (in Meyer), von Soden (*H.C.*), Plumptre (*C.B.*), Carr (*C.G.T.*), J. B. Mayor, Knowling (*West. Com.*), Bennett (*Cent. B.*), Hollmann (*S.N.T.*).

Spitta, *Zur Geschichte und Litteratur des Urchristentums*, vol. ii.; Massebieau, *L'épitre de Jacques est-elle l'oeuvre d'un Chrétien?*

CHAPTER X

Commentaries by Kühl (in Meyer), von Soden (*H.C.*), Bigg (*I.C.C.*), O. Cone (*I.H.*), Plumptre (*C.B.*), Bennett (*Cent. B.*), Usteri, Gunkel (*S.N.T.*), Hort (on i. 1—ii. 17).

CHAPTER XI

Commentaries by Kühl (in Meyer), von Soden (*H.C.*), Bigg (*I.C.C.*), Plumptre (*C.B.*), Cone (*I.H.*), Bennett (*Cent. B.*), Hollmann (*S.N.T.*), Mayor.

Spitta, *Der zweite Brief des Petrus und der Brief des Judas.*

CHAPTER XII

On the Four Gospels.—Baur, *Die Evangelien*; Weizsäcker, *Untersuchungen über die evangelische Geschichte*; Westcott, *Introduction to the Study of the Gospels*; Sanday, *The Gospels in the Second Century*, *The Life of Christ in Recent Research*; Cone, *Gospel Criticism and Historical Christianity*; Wright, *The Composition of the Four Gospels*, *Some New Testament Problems*; Godet, *The Collection of the Four Gospels and the Gospel of St. Matthew*; Wernle, *Sources of our Knowledge of the Life of Christ*; J. A. Robinson, *The Study of the Gospels*; Stanton, *The Gospels as Historical Documents*; Burkitt, *The Gospel History and its Transmission*; Jülicher, *Neue Linien in der Kritik des evangelischen Überlieferung.* Discussions on the 'sources' in the various scientific Lives of Jesus.

On the Synoptic Gospels.—Commentaries by B. Weiss (in Meyer), Holtzmann (*H.C.*), Bruce (*E.G.T.*), Cary (*I.H.*), J. Weiss (*S.N.T.*), Loisy. B. Weiss, *Das Marcusevangelium und seine synoptischen Parallelen*, *Das Matthäusevangelium und seine Lucas-parallelen*, *Die Quellen des Lukas-Evangeliums*, *Die Quellen des synoptischen Überlieferung*; Holtzmann, *Die synoptischen Evangelien*; Carpenter, *The First Three Gospels*; Hawkins, *Horae Synopticae*; Wernle, *Die synoptische Frage*; E. A. Abbott, *Clue*, *The Corrections of Mark*; Salmon, *The Human Element in the Gospels*; Burton, *Principles of Literary Criticism and the Synoptic Problem*; Wellhausen, *Einleitung in die drei ersten Evangelien*; Sharman, *The Teaching of Jesus about the Future*; Nicolardot, *Les Procédés de Redaction des trois premiers Évangélistes*; Harnack, *The Sayings of Jesus* (on Q). For work at the Synoptic Problem a synopsis is required in which the parallel sections are printed in columns side by side. Tischendorf's *Synopsis Evangelica* embraces the four Gospels; Rushbrooke's *Synopticon*, Wright's *A Synopsis of the Gospels in Greek*, Campbell's *The First Three Gospels*, Huck's *Synopse der drei ersten Evangelien*, the first three. Of these Rushbrooke is most valuable for disclosing at a glance the parts common to all three of the Synoptists, or to two and which two, and what is peculiar to each, Huck is the more convenient for ordinary use.

On the Gospel of Matthew.—Commentaries by Morison, Allen (*I.C.C.*), Carr (*C.G.T.*), Slater (*Cent. B.*), Wellhausen, Zahn, Klostermann (*H.N.T.*).

On the Gospel of Mark.—Commentaries by Gould (*I.C.C.*), Maclear (*C.G.T.*), Salmond (*Cent. B.*), Menzies (*The Earliest Gospel*), Swete, Wellhausen, Klostermann (*H.N.T.*), Bacon (*The Beginnings of Gospel Story*). Wrede, *Das Messiasgeheimniss in den Evangelien*; J. Weiss, *Das Älteste Evangelium*; Hoffmann, *Das Marcusevangelium und seine Quellen*; Wendling, *Urmarcus*, *Die Entstehung des Marcusevangeliums*; B. Weiss, *Die Geschichtlichkeit des Markusevangeliums* (brief and convenient summary of Weiss's special theory).

On the Gospel of Luke.—Commentaries by Godet, Plummer (*I.C.C.*), Farrar (*C.G.T.*), Adeney (*Cent. B.*), Wellhausen, Krenkel, *Josephus und Lucas*; Harnack, *Luke the Physician*; Ramsay, *Luke the Physician*.

CHAPTER XIII

Commentaries by Zeller, De Wette-Overbeck, Wendt (in Meyer), Holtzmann (*H.C.*), Lumby (*C.G.T.*), Page, Blass, Knowling (*E.G.T.*), Rackham (*West. Com.*), Bartlet (*Cent. B.*), Knopf (*S.N.T.*), Forbes (*I.H.*).

Spitta, *Die Apostelgeschichte*; J. Weiss, *Ueber die Absicht und den literarischen Charakter der Apostelgeschichte*; Clemen, *Die Apostelgeschichte*; Chase, *The Historical Credibility of the Acts of the Apostles*; Harnack, *Luke the Physician*, *The Acts of the Apostles*; Ramsay, *St. Paul the Traveller and the Roman Citizen*, *Pauline and Other Studies*, *Luke the Physician*.

CHAPTER XIV

On the Johannine Writings as a whole.—Commentaries by Holtzmann-Bauer (*H.C.*), Forbes (*I.H.*). Gloag, *Introduction to the Johannine Writings*; Schmiedel, *The Johannine Writings*; Schwartz, *Der Tod der Söhne Zebedaei*.

CHAPTER XV

Commentaries by Bleek, Bousset (in Meyer), Milligan, Simcox (*C.G.T.*), Scott (*Cent. B.*), Swete, J. Weiss (*S.N.T.*), Hort (on i.-iii., with Introduction to whole Book). Vischer, *Die Offenbarung Johannis*; Spitta, *Die Offenbarung des Johannes untersucht*; Milligan, *Lectures on the Apocalypse*, *Discussions on the Apocalypse*; Gunkel, *Schöpfung und Chaos*; J. Weiss, *Die Offenbarung des Johannes*; Wellhausen, *Analyse der Offenbarung Johannis*; Porter, *The Messages of the Apocalyptic Writers*; Ramsay, *The Letters to the Seven Churches*.

CHAPTER XVI

Commentaries by Westcott, B. Weiss (in Meyer), Plummer (*C.G.T.*), Bennett (*Cent. B.*), Baumgarten (*S.N.T.*). Findlay, *Fellowship in the Life Eternal*; On 1 John, Rothe, E. Haupt; Law, *The Tests of Life*; On 3 John, Harnack in *Texte und Untersuchungen*, vol. xv.

CHAPTER XVII

Commentaries by B. Weiss (in Meyer), Godet, Westcott, Moulton and Milligan, Reynolds, Plummer (*C.G.T.*), Dods (*E.G.T.*), M'Clymont (*Cent. B.*), Heitmüller (*S.N.T.*), Loisy, Calmes, Zahn.

Sanday, *Authorship and Historical Character of the Fourth Gospel*, *The Criticism of the Fourth Gospel*; Lightfoot, *Biblical Essays*; Watkins, *Modern Criticism and the Fourth Gospel*; O. Holtzmann, *Das Johannesevangelium*; Delff, *Das vierte Evangelium*; Wendt, *St. John's Gospel*; Réville, *Le Quatrième Évangile*; Drummond, *The Character and Authorship of the Fourth Gospel*; E. A. Abbott, *Johannine Vocabulary*, *Johannine Grammar*; Baldensperger, *Der Prolog des vierten Evangeliums*; Jackson, *The Fourth Gospel*; Kreyenbühl, *Das Evangelium der Wahrheit*; Wellhausen, *Erweiterungen und Änderungen im vierten Evangelium*, *Das Evangelium Johannis*.

INDEX

Note.—References to the Bibliography are not included.